The Producer's Business Handbook

PRAISE FOR THE PRODUCER'S BUSINESS HANDBOOK, THIRD EDITION

This is the single best work on financing independent films. Mr. Lee presents an overall structure clearly and efficiently. This is not a "war stories" book. The landscape of the film business is changing rapidly and this is one of the only producing books about real producing. Mr. Lee and Ms. Gillen address one of the most difficult aspects of producing – financing—in a direct way that lays out the tasks and challenges an independent producer needs to know; they do not sugar-coat the business – it's all business; they explain the intricacies of financing while making it understandable. There is more to financing a film than developing a business plan and this book shows why.

While there are a few, very few, books that are no-nonsense for producers, this is the only producing book that addresses financing with practical, in-depth information geared toward working producers that is efficiently written and presented. You can count on me to continue to use it.

—Don Smith, Associate Chair & Associate Professor,
Film & Video Department, Columbia College

This is a timely book, detailing a proven method for success and providing relevant data for both investors and filmmakers, especially now that the Commodity Futures Trading Commission recently approved trading of film box office performance futures by Cantor Exchange and media derivatives by Trend Exchange.

—Jillian Alexander, MBA, CM&AA, CHRC, Managing Director, Corporate Development & Strategy,
Conduit Consulting LLC, Former VP-Corporate Development,
SONY Pictures Entertainment and member SONY US Ventures team

Converging digital media and powerful new monetization models are growing entertainment amidst an overall slipping global economy. In show business, everyone is in love with the show, but it's the business of making significant money that turns on the big boys and girls inside the tent. Learn what they already know by reading this new edition.

—Steve Ecclesine, Independent Producer
(12 motion pictures and more than 700 Television episodes)

It is so sharply focused and so easy to digest, I am going to make it the official textbook for my online course in independent film marketing and sales across all platforms.

Regarding internet marketing strategies, Chapter 4 clearly states insights we have all heard about but are often too overwhelmed to focus in on. While clearly stating such marketing is not easily done and requires a full-time person, the writers Lee and Gillen make it seem easy enough to use the "most effective social network sites … that specialize in unique communities. There are thousands of these. As of January, 2010, there were 37 global social network sites with 10 million or more members each, plus the following five global social network sites with 100 million or more members". There are also really useful case studies on District 9 and Paranormal Activity.

Finally, Chapter 6 makes financing into an almost scientific activity, with clearly written and easily understood descriptions of various financial models which previously seemed veiled in obscure terms.

—Sydney Levine, SydneysBuzz on IndieWIRE and IMDb,
Online Instructor: UCLA Extension

PRAISE FOR THE SECOND EDITION

If you've ever wondered how most films can "lose" money while the studios remain in business, you'll find the answers here. This is a comprehensive and revealing examination of how distribution works and how the money flows.

—Robert Goodman, *Videography*

The Producer's Business Handbook

The Roadmap for the Balanced Film Producer

THIRD EDITION

John J. Lee, Jr.

Anne Marie Gillen

AMSTERDAM • BOSTON • HEIDELBERG • LONDON
NEW YORK • OXFORD • PARIS • SAN DIEGO
SAN FRANCISCO • SINGAPORE • SYDNEY • TOKYO

Focal Press is an imprint of Elsevier

ELSEVIER

Focal Press is an imprint of Elsevier
30 Corporate Drive, Suite 400, Burlington, MA 01803, USA
The Boulevard, Langford Lane, Kidlington, Oxford, OX5 1GB, UK

Notices
Knowledge and best practice in this field are constantly changing. As new research and experience broaden our understanding, changes in research methods, professional practices, or medical treatment may become necessary.

Practitioners and researchers must always rely on their own experience and knowledge in evaluating and using any information, methods, compounds, or experiments described herein. In using such information or methods they should be mindful of their own safety and the safety of others, including parties for whom they have a professional responsibility.

To the fullest extent of the law, neither the Publisher nor the authors, contributors, or editors, assume any liability for any injury and/or damage to persons or property as a matter of products liability, negligence or otherwise, or from any use or operation of any methods, products, instructions, or ideas contained in the material herein.

Library of Congress Cataloging-in-Publication Data
Application submitted

British Library Cataloguing-in-Publication Data
A catalogue record for this book is available from the British Library.

ISBN: 978-0-240-81463-6

For information on all Focal Press publications
visit our website at www.elsevierdirect.com

10   11   12   13   14   5   4   3   2   1

Printed in the United States of America

Working together to grow
libraries in developing countries

www.elsevier.com | www.bookaid.org | www.sabre.org

ELSEVIER   BOOK AID International   Sabre Foundation

Contents

Introduction

Welcome to the third edition of *The Producer's Business Handbook: Roadmap for the Balanced Film Producer*.

In addition to anticipated updates and new valuable features, this edition also (1) is more global, (2) has low-budget filmmaking special annotations, (3) includes insights to new and coming alternative marketing and distribution technology, and (4) has a chapter on the Internet's current and likely immediate entertainment industry changes as they relate to new marketing and distribution models.

We enjoy doing what we are good at, and most independent producers are good at motion picture production. By the shear volume of motion pictures made around the world that are either not distributed at all, in any form, or receive limited release but no audience traction, it is readily apparent that most independent producers do not understand or know how to use the fundamental business processes and tools of the motion picture industry. This is especially true when it comes to (1) preparing and engaging global rights distribution as well as (2) receiving sufficient financing for motion picture development and production.

Yet there are also independent producers who operate solid, amply funded, all pictures distributed, and consistently profitable production companies. The success of these companies is not attained by accident but rather through the application of sound business principles and practices that drive their ever-advancing motion pictures and businesses.

The purpose of this book is to assist producers in attaining this unquestionably preferable operating position. Specifically, it discusses how the global motion picture industry works and focuses on the processes used by successful independent production companies, enabling them, for each project, to (1) use a variety of financing sources to provide collateral and guarantee instruments; (2) use banks to accept these instruments, plus a completion bond, to secure their production financing; (3) release each of their pictures theatrically through the most effective and able distributors; and (4) improve the opportunities for their pictures to be consistently profitable.

This book is a global orientation to the business relationships that the most successful motion picture producers have with the various participants in the

DOI: 10.1016/B978-0-240-81463-6.00020-6

motion picture industry. This includes how these producers direct their relationships with domestic and international distributors and sales agents, agencies, attorneys, talent, completion guarantors, banks, and private investors. These producers are all "balanced producers" giving equal weight to the creative, audience, investment/profits aspects of each of their motion pictures, starting in the development stage and beginning with the end in mind. What this edition does *not* cover is the on-set film production and postproduction processes. There are many excellent books that already address that aspect. We recommend Focal Press's *The Complete Film Production Handbook*.

As *there is no natural relationship between the production cost of a motion picture and its earnings capacity*; this book also presents a thorough orientation to each project's business evaluation. The center of this process is each picture's *internal greenlight analysis* and is the discovery of the proportional relationship of the producer's share of global profits as compared to the picture's all-in production cost: its earnings-to-cost ratio. Each picture's greenlight results indicate its business feasibility and point to its likely funding sources, global distribution processes and partners, optimal release time of year, distribution costs, target audiences, ancillary products, and marketing strategies.

This volume also contains the producer's thorough orientation to planning, organizing, and operating a motion picture production company. This necessarily looks at development, production, and distribution as overlapping but separate operations, almost always costed separately and sometimes operated by the production entity through its separate companies. The business aspects of these processes are articulated from solicitation of literary properties, through direct rights sales and the management of global distribution relationships. Also presented is an in-depth discussion of the team needed to accomplish these operations, as well as how to find and attach them.

Additionally, there are worksheets and instructions for the business processes of development, financing, and distribution, which are used by many of the industry's consistently profitable production companies.

To assist readers in a deeper understanding and for use within their own companies, a website has been created for your use. On it you will have access to downloadable copies of the following files:

1. Studio Relationship Cash Flow Comparisons
2. The Production Financing Worksheet: Finance Plan
3. The Production and Development Companies' Organization Charts
4. The Multiple Picture Development and Production Activity Projection
5. The Multiple Picture Development and Production Cash Flow Projection
6. The Production Company Model
7. The Development Company Model
8. Film Comparables Chart
9. Most Successful U.S. Motion Pictures of All Time

This book provides both instruction and worksheet support to independent motion picture producers at all levels of industry experience. Specifically, it is written to do the following:

1. Provide experienced producers (as well as directors, writers, and other entertainment professionals), the entertainment industry business understanding, structures, and tools that well match their already hard-won creative experience, abilities, and resources. Often the difference between success and failure hinges on a producer's ability to dynamically engage and balance the full spectrum of business resources and relationships within the producer's reach. This book opens for producers a full-aperture view of the entertainment business and provides the tools and instructions they need to engage all aspects of the film industry related to global financing and exploitation. It opens the way to improved industry understanding and, more important, to the capacity to operate predictably profitable production organizations.

2. Assist entry-level producers in understanding how the motion picture industry operates, plot their most promising path to achieve their independent producing objectives, and provide documentation as well as relationship and operational support they will need to succeed as a balanced producer.

INDEPENDENT PRODUCERS

This book focuses on *independent producers*. These are not to be confused with attached producers (who may be executive producers, financiers, line producers, executives with a studio deal, or a star's relative, boyfriend, or girlfriend). Independent producers, as they are referenced in this text, are those who are at the creative and business helm of each of their pictures from development inception.

Often studio-developed pictures have a director and one or more actors attached before a producer is attached. Producers are later attached to perform production services but are rarely these pictures' creative genesis. Although these producers are typically seasoned motion picture makers, they do not have the same relationship with their pictures as do the independent producers who are this book's focus. The producer definition used in this book refers to those independent producers who choose to retain their pictures' development and production authority and creative genesis.

Investors

This book is also a breakthrough point-of-reference guide for investors. Prior editions of this book were widely used by private and institutional investors, as well as banks and attorneys representing investors, as a business orientation to assist them in evaluating investment opportunities and assessing the business acumen of their related independent producers. Investors with real estate development experience will find their orientation uniquely beneficial, as there are many funding and business parallels between motion picture development and real estate development.

BASIS FOR THE PRINCIPLES

Like most principles worth learning, those set forth in this book are simple and proven by their use in many of the industry's most successful independent motion picture production companies. The core of these principles is discovered in the answers to three questions, beneficially applied to all projects considered for development and production:

- Is the story worth being told?
- Who are the story's primary target audiences?
- What is the ratio between the story's production costs and the producer's share of global income?

Producers who make their decisions predicated on the analysis of the answers to these questions consistently guide each of their pictures through successful development, production, and distribution.

Though motion picture producers are the reader focus of this book and theatrical release motion pictures the product focus, the application of this volume's principles will be as beneficial to seasoned feature producers' continuing pictures as well as to a student's first film school productions.

SUMMARY

This edition covers seven key principles and practices consistently employed by some of the most powerful independent motion picture producers.

1. Each Uses an Internal Greenlight Analysis

Understanding a distributor's greenlighting criteria allows production organizations to replicate this process in their own shops. Performing an internal greenlight for each project enables the producer to evaluate the strength of the picture before distributor meetings and even points producers to which distribution team in each territory that will most predictably extract its greatest earnings. The discoveries from this absolutely critical process become the center of each picture's financing and distribution plan and overall success.

2. Each Operates with Fully Funded Development

Most production companies fail because of undercapitalization. This is especially true in development. Development is sophisticated, time consuming, and expensive. It should be approached with the same type of planning and funding that producers use during the production process. Producers should have their own development funding independent of a studio and sufficient to develop a slate of pictures. This provides a solid foundation, allowing each picture to predictably, unshakably move through development.

3. Each Uses a Bank to Coordinate Its Production Financing

The primary importance of this practice is not the obvious advantages of lower money cost and optimized project ownership. Though each of these advantages is valuable, even more advantageous is that using a bank to coordinate each picture's production financing assures a completion guarantor's beneficial checks and balances and pushes the producer into rights sales planning, with the engagement of each picture's major distributor, production incentive, cobranding partners, talent, and vendor relationships. These relationships are critical to understanding and valuing each picture, optimizing funding architecture, and engaging electronic game, publisher, branding, and other relationships that need one year or more advance commitments.

4. Each Engages U.S. and International Territory Distribution Relationships for Each Picture during Its Development

Internal greenlights are confirmed first with an international sales agent or with a distributor (theatrical, home entertainment, television, or video-on-demand) in the picture's core release market and then with at least two more distributors within the eight major international territories. These confirmations are typically the second step in each picture's early development evolution and the beginning of essential creative and marketing collaboration.

5. Each Plans the Rights Sales and Either Sells Some Rights Directly or Participates in These Sales

This is beginning with the end in mind. Understanding the vast array of highly profitable ancillary sales areas, and planning these rights sales with the producer negotiating and closing some of these sales, can substantially increase the producer's profitability and advance each picture's distribution power. This is the key to protecting and maximizing each picture's profitability.

6. Each Participates in the Campaign Management Planning and Execution of Its Pictures in Its Core and Major International Territories

Campaign creative, media planning, and media buying each exist in highly sophisticated worlds of their own. New media as well as viral and social marketing have rendered it even more important for producers to embrace early stage marketing. Understanding each picture's target audiences—as well as their new methods of messaging and making decisions and the reach and frequency of media buys that drive these audiences—allows producers to anticipate each picture's potential returns.

7. Each Is a Balanced Producer, Giving Equal Weight to Creative, Audience, and Profit

Production of the vision of a picture only seems like the producer's primary objective. When the picture is completed, especially if it fulfills the producer's *creative* objective, is when it is inescapably clear that the picture's capacity to play to its *audiences* and its ability to return a *profit* to the investor(s) and producer are at least as important as its creation. Balanced producers sustain an *equal* check and balance between these three elements. This balance assures the stability of each picture as it passes through the processes of development, production, and distribution.

This edition draws on each of the authors' understandings, harvested primarily from serving as production and distribution business affairs executives for a combined 50 years, currently, respectively, as CEO and president of The Gillen Group, a producer's business, funding, and global sales entity, and dean of Whistling Woods International, the largest international film school in Asia. Together the authors have provided business, funding, and distribution services for scores of major studio-released motion pictures, television network series, and specials, with combined production costs of more than $500 million and global rights earnings exceeding $4 billion.

This volume also employs the knowledge and experience of several film industry mavens to whom we are grateful for their help and includes data from the most reliable industry sources, some of whom are referenced in this book's final chapter. We would graciously like to extend special thanks to Maury Rogow and Kelly Yee of RipMedia Group (www.RipMediaGroup.com and www.mediawildfire.com) who provided information on New Media and Internet Marketing, which can be found in Chapter 4; Tekla Morgan of AON; Marc Cordova and the team at Entertainment Partners; Douglas L. Lowell for his excellent analysis notes to Chapters 2 and 6; Susan Muir at Film Finances; Adam Korn at Comerica Bank; our excellent assistants Joseph Niederhauser and Felicia Lopes; Sydney Levine at www.Syndeysbuzz.com; and the wonderful reviewers from Focal Press with special mention to Jillian Alexander; and finally, but importantly, to our editor Elinor Actipis at Focal Press.

As industry seminar speakers, we assumed that attendance and aggressive participation at our presentations resulted from producers' ongoing panic about securing production funding. Though this is surely true, in researching this arena we also discovered that although most books are excellent in some regard, none presented a complete picture of how the industry functions from an independent producer's perspective or, even more important, discussed the specific operating practices of the most successful production companies.

This book delivers this critical missing material.

CHAPTER 1

How the Motion Picture Industry Functions

This chapter presents the motion picture business by looking at its 10 major participant categories. It also profiles the most successful independent production companies as development and production businesses with well-exercised global distribution relationships, some with their own distribution capacities. Finally and appropriately, it examines story as the challenging critical core of a producer's universe.

MAJOR PARTICIPANT CATEGORIES AND THEIR FUNCTIONS

There are 10 motion picture industry participant categories, each with its fundamentally crucial functions, with whom producers have interrelationships. The most prosperous companies in each category are successful, in large measure, because they sustain a perspective of how the whole industry operates and continually sharpen their individual participation in the entertainment spectrum within which they are related.

This perspective includes the views that (1) the motion picture industry is a consumer-product business, (2) each participant contributes to and relies on other participants, and (3) audiences, in their various target definitions, are each picture's most important participants.

In their order of importance, here are the 10 categories of participants:

1. Audiences
2. Distributors
3. Producers
4. Retailers and licensed media
5. International territories
6. Financing participants
7. Distributor subcontractors
8. Production talent and subcontractors
9. Ancillary media and licensees
10. Major consumer brands

DOI: 10.1016/B978-0-240-81463-6.00001-2

Participant Category 1: Audiences

A picture's target audiences are its sources of income. Audiences are the highest priority participant in the industry, because without them, there is no industry. Most fundamentally, producers must know the specific target audiences for each of their pictures, evaluate each picture according to its audience's consumption of other pictures with a similar target audience (referred to as the picture's comparables or antecedents), and, after committing to a story creatively, make decisions to proceed on the picture based on its target audience's consumption dynamics and its related products and rights, compared with the picture's cost.

After finding a story that interests them, producers should ask two questions regarding its audiences:

1. By order of dominance, who are this picture's target audiences? This answer prepares the producer to research the size, entertainment consumption, and media-use profile of each of the picture's target audiences—first in the picture's primary global release territory and subsequently in the picture's other major international release territories. For example, if the picture's primary release territory is the United States, the leading 64 metros in this territory are the focus of the more than 300 U.S. metros, because each of these 64 has a half-million television households or more, and together they spend over two thirds of total U.S. entertainment dollars.

2. How have these audiences responded to at least five and up to seven pictures released in the prior five years that are most similar to the picture being considered in terms of story and genre, anticipated above-the-line talent (director and lead cast), and anticipated advertising and marketing campaigns? The answer to this question enables the producer to project gross receipts, and the producer's share of those gross receipts, for the picture being considered. Pictures with similar audiences are identified by comparing the proposed picture's dominant campaign elements and above-the-line talent with the campaign elements and above-the-line talent of comparable previously released pictures.

INTERNAL GREENLIGHT ANALYSIS

The answers to these two questions, weighed against a picture's estimated production and distribution costs, allow producers to determine whether they will greenlight the picture. This is a picture's internal greenlight analysis.

If the audience profiles and picture comparables are positive and the income-to-cost ratio is at least two-to-one (in other words, the projected producer's gross income is at least twice the picture's projected production costs), the producer should proceed to the next step in the development process. If a picture's target audiences lack dynamic consumption profiles or are too small or difficult to reach in comparison to the picture's costs, the producer should pass rather than proceed.

The specific methods of obtaining and analyzing this information and a complete explanation of obtaining a picture's internal greenlight are presented in later chapters, especially Chapters 2 and 14. The following diagram demonstrates the fundamental economics of this process.

(Ratios are from recent historical comparisons)	
Global projected gross income	$94
Less theatrical participations, distributor's fees, and expenses	$65.5
Distributor's net	$28.5
Negative cost and production financing expenses (actual estimated budget)	$12
Ratio of distributor's net income to production costs	2.38:1
Feasibility	Recommend proceeding

FIGURE 1.1
The Picture's Internal Greenlight Analysis (in millions).

AUDIENCE ORIENTATION

Producers should understand and use the consumer terms employed by global advertising agencies and reporting entities such as Nielsen Media Research, as these terms make up the audience semantics of the entertainment industry. Utilizing this language is an especially effective tool in the producer's relationships with global distributors, product placement and premium tie-in brand representatives, advertising agencies, and public relations and promotion companies.

Audiences in most global territories are categorized demographically by age as follows: Adults are separated into several categories, by gender, most significantly in the motion picture business by ages 18 to 24, 18 to 34, 25 to 34, 25 to 44, 25 to 54, 45-plus, and 55-plus. Audiences also are identified and evaluated by lifestyles, such as active adults, affluent adults, educated adults, inner-city youth, working women, and so on.

Audience Terms	Age Demographic
Kids	5–11
Youth	12–17
Adults	18+
Youth and single adults	12–24
Older Youth and single adults	16–24

FIGURE 1.2
Primary Audience Age Demographic Categories.

Excellent, easy-to-use audience research analysis tools and databases in the largest global territories (such as Arbitron and Nielsen in the United States; see Chapter 16 for information sources) are available to producers at reasonable costs or are accessible through major advertising agencies and media planning and buying companies. These audience research tools allow target audiences to be identified by an extensive array of demographic and lifestyle search criteria. The lifestyle options are broad, the data are reliable, and the reports are exceptionally useful for audience quantifying and qualifying.

For example, you can sort the major metros by men 18 to 34 who are college graduates, watch a movie at a theater at least twice a month, are active on at least one social network, download music at least once a month, and own a mountain bike. The requested report can reveal how many are in this audience; where their population concentrations are; what their consumption profiles for the various media are; which TV programs they watch; if they watch more movies on a laptop, at the theater, or on TV; and so on.

Becoming conversant with this information and the sources from which it is derived is crucially important, as the application of this information is a powerful tool for producers who will be originating prospective release strategies, creating early stage marketing campaigns, reviewing media buys, and projecting the picture's earnings.

DISTRIBUTOR PITCH PREPARATION

Many producers are skilled in highlighting the creative aspects of their pictures to pitch to distributors. However, they are not ready to successfully pitch until they also have prepared and can present information about their pictures' audiences as it directly pertains to the distributors' interests.

Pitching pictures to distributors, after having first fulfilled their internal greenlights, empowers producers to present the fundamental core information essential for distribution executives to evaluate their interest. This information includes the picture's audiences, recently released comparable pictures, and estimated gross receipts in the distributor's territory. Producers armed with this information are in the strongest position possible to both present and negotiate from the distributors' perspectives. Each distributor relies on its own sophisticated sources of information, evaluation processes, and experience. However, the producer's ability to point to the target audiences and comparable pictures is especially helpful for the initial distributor meeting. Chapter 2 reviews ways to present this information appropriately in order to receive optimal positive distributor responses.

Participant Category 2: Distributors

The major distributors are the motion picture marketing and sales companies in the global territories that establish the brand presence of each picture to their respective target audiences and are wholesalers of motion pictures to various media to whom they distribute.

In the United States, the major distributors are 20th Century Fox, Universal, Buena Vista, Paramount, Sony, Warner Bros., and Lionsgate. Each of these is a full-service studio in the traditional definition, with the exception of Lionsgate, which lacks a studio lot. These seven majors are all-rights distributors, globally able to distribute every theatrical, nontheatrical, and ancillary right associated with their motion pictures. And they are the prominent U.S. theatrical and home entertainment distributors for major U.S. independent producers.

In addition to the major studios are the following distribution outlets:

1. *Minor theatrical distributors.* There are several strong minor theatrical distributors, three of which are owned by major distributors (Sony Pictures Classics, Fox Searchlight, and Focus Features). One of the largest and best-operated of the minors is Summit Entertainment. The largest of these minors are all-rights distributors. A group of new or repositioned veteran distributors hope to fill the shoes left by studio divisions now chiefly concentrating on wide releases. Roadside Attractions, IFC, Magnolia Pictures, the Samuel Goldwyn Company, Here Films, Regent Releasing, and New Films International are among the companies that release niche/special-handling titles.

2. *Direct international territory distributors.* The largest of these are studios within their respective international territories, which produce and direct-distribute to all the major media in their territories and who also sell their pictures' rights globally. These distributors are presented in Chapter 3.

3. *International sales companies.* The largest of these organizations produce and co-produce some of their own pictures, in addition to acquiring motion pictures and performing international market sales and distribution services for their independent producers' pictures. These include Hyde Park, Inferno, Lakeshore, and Icon Entertainment International.

4. *Producers representative organizations.* These organizations plan and execute sales to international sales agents or distributors in international territories, and they may also plan and engage all U.S. rights sales of their independent producer clients' pictures. Among these are the major agencies such as CAA, ICM, WME, and companies such as Cinetic Media and Gillen Group.

5. *Television syndication companies.* These companies plan and carry out sales to television stations, cable television networks, and the cable and satellite television systems.

6. *Product placement companies.* These companies plan, negotiate, and manage the use, borrowing, giving, or fee earned by their producer clients for products appearing in the producer's pictures.

7. *Promotional tie-in companies.* These companies originate, plan, negotiate, and manage relationships in advertising or promoting the release of producers' motion pictures with other consumer brands. The most prolific brand categories that participate in the motion picture industry are soft drinks and fast food.

8. *Publishers.* These entities are discussed in more detail in Chapter 5 and primarily include book publishers who are either republishing novels associated with pictures being released or publishing new novels based on original

screenplays; graphic novels, comic book, coloring book, and workbook publishers who create and release books coordinated with picture releases; and paper-based role-playing and other game publishers who create and distribute their respective products timed with picture releases.

9. *Ancillary rights sales companies.* These organizations, examined in Chapter 5, include companies specializing in merchandising, in-flight, scholastic, ships-at-sea, and other sales and marketing.

ESTABLISHING EACH PICTURE'S BRAND AND THE STUDIO OPERATING PERSPECTIVE

The operations and functions of U.S. theatrical distributors are presented in Chapter 2. The following section introduces both the distribution phenomenon of establishing a picture's brand as well as the distributor's operating perspective.

Brand Presence

In each global territory, every picture's value for every other rights area is primarily established during its theatrical release. Audiences in a given territory are introduced to each picture during this distribution window's theatrical premiere. This is where the brand, the audience perspective, and the picture's entertainment value are established.

As is thoroughly explored in Chapter 2, although this is the most important release window, media expenses for brand establishment in many global territories are so costly that most motion pictures do not earn sufficient income from their theatrical releases to fully recover their media expenses.

The physical aspects of theatrical distribution are highly sophisticated. These functions include theater circuit bidding, booking the multiplexes and the screens within them that are best matched with each picture, negotiating favorable film rental terms with the circuits, staging the physical release of the picture through film exchanges, and, finally, the actual settlements that are negotiated with each theater circuit after each picture's play. These operations substantially affect the success of each picture. For example, audiences expect the finest pictures to be on the largest screens at the best theaters. A good picture booked at a questionable multiplex or playing on a smaller screen sends a message to the target audiences that it may be a poor picture, potentially overturning other well-executed distribution moves.

As complex and crucial as physical distribution is, however, the peerless genius in the art of distribution lies in establishing the public's opinion of each picture through paid advertising, publicity, promotion, and increasingly through sophisticated, mostly online, viral, and social network marketing campaigns. These are the processes through which motion pictures become must-see major brands to their target audiences.

A brand is the name by which consumers identify a product or group of products. Coke, Levi Strauss, and Nike have the luxury of fighting for sustained brand dominance. Theirs is a continuing and absolutely rugged battle, but it pales in comparison with motion picture brand establishment.

Every Motion Picture Released Is a Separate Brand

Each picture must come from absolute obscurity (with the exception of franchises, films based on novels, and sequels) to become top-of-mind with each picture's target audiences. In most major global territories, strategic marketing planning begins 12 to 24 months before a picture opens but is substantially accomplished in a final major media blitz beginning three to six weeks before the picture opens, often in concert with other established brands catering to the same target audiences. In markets that substantially rely on a television campaign, such as the United States, the television buy may have a reach and frequency performance as high as 12 impressions (advertising viewings) by 80 percent of that picture's target audiences before the picture opens. In the United States, depending on the target audience and time of year, the cost of media alone for a studio-released picture is typically $25 million to $45 million *before* a picture's initial street date. Brand presence is so fundamental to a picture's earnings performance in every succeeding distribution category that distributors' projections of the picture's gross earnings are forecasted as a percentage of each picture's opening weekend theatrical receipts.

Typically the distributor originates and directs the entire campaign, and it is the campaign, its media buys, Internet strategies, brand tie-ins, and promotions that drive each picture's initial audiences. In fact, even with prescreenings, the picture itself usually has little effect on the theatrical opening weekend gross, and only limited effect on the first week's earnings. Though critical reviews have little opening weekend effect on pictures with kids, youth, and young adults as primary audiences, these audiences are highly affected by Internet reviews, blogs, Facebook, and other global social network comments and tweets posted by opinion leaders and especially friends. These posted reviews most significantly affect their attendance after opening weekend.

In some territories, outdoor advertising, print, or radio is used to drive audiences (in India it is a picture's heavily promoted music that primes and drives audiences); for most leading global territories, the two major campaign elements that determine each picture's opening two weeks' theatrical gross are (1) how motivating the television and Internet spots are to the picture's unique target audiences and (2) the reach and frequency of the campaign's Internet buy and television schedule for these target audiences. Internet and television are the hammer media for all audience categories, though radio, outdoor, and print advertising are important, especially during the summer.

Consequently, producers benefit most when they focus on heightening the impact of their pictures' Internet and television campaigns by supporting the theatrical release window and assuring that the aggregate media buys are significantly beyond critical mass response and are optimized for their targets, as these largely determine each picture's opening weekend performance.

A picture's brand presence established during its theatrical release predicates its earnings capacity in all subsequent distribution release windows. The other earnings windows—especially home entertainment (DVD/Blue-ray rental and sales, Internet streaming, and downloading to all platforms and devices), premium cable (HBO/Cinemax, Showtime/TMC, and Starz/Encore in the United States), broadcast network television (ABC, NBC, CBS, Fox, and CW in the United States), and cable television (ScyFy, Comedy Central, Lifetime, and so on in the United States)—are typically the producer's highest earnings sources. Often those distributors who have established a strong positive brand with their picture's target audiences during the theatrical release but have seen competing pictures, weather, or other factors keep theatrical audiences low, experience a substantial audience increase, especially during the home entertainment release but also in subsequent earnings windows.

DISTRIBUTORS OPERATING PERSPECTIVE

Each theatrical screen is a unique retail environment. It accommodates only one product at a time. Consequently, distributors and exhibitors closely examine the earnings performance of each picture on each screen. When gross receipts fall below a screen's house-nut (the exhibitor's attributed cost to provide and operate that screen), the picture is soon replaced with another. For example, if an exhibitor in the United States has a weekly house-nut of $3,200 and that week's gross was $2,800, the distributor knows the exhibitor will soon replace that picture with one that has a higher grossing potential.

As discussed earlier, the theatrical earnings that a picture brings in during its opening two weeks are largely predicated on the effectiveness of its campaign. After the opening two weeks, audience opinion largely determines a picture's ongoing theatrical life. This being the case, distributors re-create and redefine the after-opening campaigns to drive the peak attendance of target audiences.

Internet and TV commercials and trailers are currently the most convincing campaign elements, largely because they allow target audiences to sample the movie before buying a ticket. This sampling is sufficiently motivating to initially overpower negative reviews. When viewing the campaign, the audience sees and hears evidence that a picture is indeed funny, exciting, romantic, scary, or contains other emotional connections that motivate them to see the picture or not. When making their ticket-buying decisions, audiences lean on their own experience, even when that experience is limited to 30-second commercials and 2- to 3-minute trailers.

The Internet is disrupting this dynamic, with some tech-savvy constituents even producing mash-ups (re-edits) of campaigns to show their enthusiasm or disdain for pictures. These are especially powerful because they are also audience samplings. Distributor-prepared audience pre- and during-release Internet sampling has much more of an impact on audiences than does TV, as it is (1) better targeted, (2) more personal than TV delivery, and

(3) significantly less costly than television. With the power of social endorsement, Internet campaigns are more influential with all audience profiles. Twitter, Facebook, and other social networking sites establish the "buzz," the "have-to-see," and peer-to-peer word of mouth both before and after a film opens. These are increasingly the major driving factors, especially for kids, youth, and young adults, but they also are growing high-impact influencers for all audiences in most territories

Every distributor's first responsibility is to get its pictures' target audiences to theaters. Campaigns drive audiences; audiences drive box office receipts; distributors focus on the new, hybrid, high-impact campaigns.

It should be no surprise, then, that in deciding whether they will distribute a picture, distributors look first to a picture's campaign elements, then to its overall entertainment power. That is to say, the distribution decision will primarily be based on the audience sales dynamics of the picture's story and the emotional (drama, comedy, action/adventure, romance) intensity of the picture's elements, which will be used in its Internet and TV commercials and theatrical trailers (the picture's campaign), and then the decision will be based on how the viewers may feel as they leave the theater (the picture's entertainment power or word-of-month driver).

Therefore, even in predevelopment, when producers make picture presentations to distributors or sales agents, they should weight their presentations accordingly. The distributors or sales agents must first be convinced of the salability of the picture—the audience's response to the picture's various campaigns—before they will seriously measure a picture's overall entertainment power, or how audiences will feel after they have seen the actual motion picture.

Participant Category 3: Independent Producers

Independent producers are the creators and manufacturers of the motion picture products. The industry's leading producers also plan and manage all their pictures sales and distribution and directly conduct some sales.

The final five chapters of this book present independent production company operations. This section introduces the two main independent producer operating profiles: creative protectionist producers and *balanced producers*.

Considering the two prior participant categories (audiences and distributors), we can now confidently embrace a fresh independent producer orientation. Audiences pay for the producer's goods, and distributors (1) connect producers with their audiences and (2) create and motivate a market for each picture. Though naturally uncomfortable, these simple realities render audiences and distributors preeminent to producers. Producers make the most sound and profitable decisions for their pictures and their companies when they hold themselves accountable to these two categories. Audiences and distributors are the producer's most beneficial and crucial sources of business checks and balances.

CREATIVE PROTECTIONIST PRODUCERS

We enjoy doing what we do well. For most producers, developing a strong story worthy of being told, bringing a solid team together, and producing a great movie are their passions. Typically, the majority of producers are not skilled business-people, well exercised in business planning and execution. These conditions are exemplified by creative protectionist producers constituting the greatest number of independent producers in the film industry around the world. In the United States, there are hundreds of these production companies, operating chiefly from New York, Los Angeles, Chicago, Atlanta, and other major metropolitan hubs.

The characteristic unique to these producers is their arm's-length, creative protectionist attitude toward distributors. They are so intensely focused on the creative purity of the vision they have for each picture that other opinions—especially those of distributors who must focus on the commercial success of each picture—appear to represent a threat to the artistic integrity of their pictures and are commonly blamed if their pictures financially underperform. This attitude often creates a love-hate relationship between producers and distributors.

If you ask these producers about their experiences with distributors, some assume a crazed expression and say, "I could tell you stories!" And they can. But so can their distributors. No matter the stories, this separatist operating style (1) promotes strained production financing, which then must come largely or wholly from private sources; (2) results in their pictures underearning for lack of market preparation; and (3) causes some of their theatrical feature films to receive no theatrical release at all in their primary territory, which typically dooms all other territory prospects.

Many of these producers are highly skilled and have industry and audience reputations for creative wizardry. Often, their pictures are released through major studios, and some even win Academy or other awards. At the same time, this high-risk operating style yields significant attrition among these producers, and unfortunately it creates a substantial disparity between their numbers of produced pictures, distributed pictures, and profitable pictures.

The lure of fame engendered by the one success among the thousands of failed such attempts each year is sufficient to attract new and even experienced producers. To those producing their first picture, this path is sometimes referred to as the "festival" or "Sundance path." The prescription to follow the festival path reads something like this (the following is an actual encapsulation from a current private-film-school text):

> Once you have found or written a screenplay that you are passionate about, then employ all your filmmaking craft, engage production associates willing to be paid chiefly from the picture's profits, pool all the money you have, borrow from relatives and any other sources who are willing to lend, run up your credit cards for the balance of the budget, and make the film. When it is complete, enter it in as many festivals as you can, and see how you fare.

Following this counsel, thousands of motion pictures are completed each year by well-intending producers and submitted to one or more of the approximately 2,500 annual film festivals. In 2010, the highest profile of these festivals, the Sundance Festival, considered more than 3,724 motion picture submissions and selected just 113 (3 percent), which were screened during the festival. Of these entrants, the industry trade papers (as of February 2010) recorded 8 (7 percent of those screened and one fifth of 1 percent of those submitted) distributor pickups. These were huge wins for the 8 producers, their financier(s), and creative associates, but what of the 105 producers who didn't obtain a distribution offer for their pictures? Even more telling, consider the 3,611 producers who didn't even get the opportunity to screen their films.

Wracked by the conflict between the thrill of producing their first feature-length picture and the reality of severe debt and disappointment, many of these producers eventually approach distributors directly to screen their films, or they continue along the festival path until their hopes abate.

A vital question that can open the way to a more productive approach to future filmmaking is, "Before you poured your talent and resources into this film, why didn't you contact a distributor to find out if that source was interested in distributing your picture?" At this point in the process, it is tough for producers to come up with an answer. Those who do offer an explanation generally fall into the creative protectionist category and enthusiastically defend their position, asserting that distributor involvement would have threatened their picture's creative integrity.

Perhaps from a purely artistic point of view, this may be true. The question then is, "Are producers motivated only by their opportunity to express their vision of the story, or would they also like their vision to be shared with audiences and earn a profit?"

Fundamentally, most producers want their films to fulfill these three major objectives:

1. *Creation.* To powerfully reveal the producer's vision of the story.
2. *Audience.* To play the picture to as extensive an audience possible.
3. *Profits.* To recoup production costs and receive a fair participation in the picture's earnings.

BALANCED PRODUCERS

Balanced producers are simply that. They understand and sustain a balance between their pictures' creative visions, audience, and profits. As of this writing, there exists a small group of balanced producers, operating principally in major global markets, including Working Title Films and GK Films (Graham King) in the UK. In the United States, most are in New York or Los Angeles, including Imagine Entertainment, Spyglass, Lakeshore, Alcon, and Hyde Park. The pictures that come from these producers and their production companies consistently receive global distribution, are profitable, and attain their producers' creative visions.

Balanced producers understand the essential importance of both preparing their pictures for the global marketplace and preparing the global marketplace for their pictures. Consequently, their creation and production decisions are based on their initial global distribution responses. It is these relationships that vet their pictures' production financing and assure each picture's maximum earnings in each global territory.

As a result of this operating model, most of these producers are able to use banks to aggregate and provide their production financing, secured by a combination of production incentive (tax credit/rebate) programs, above-the-line or major vendor equity/profit sharing deferment deals, presales, gap funding, and private equity financing. They release their pictures through distributors who participate in their valuation and greenlighting analysis, and they extract the maximum possible media and rights earnings from the various global territories.

To become an Imagine or Lakeshore Entertainment, producers must employ a sound, balanced approach to project selection and distribution that will lead them to such success. Producers should do the work that engenders the broad global industry relationships that these companies enjoy. Such an operating model is the result of a consistent, balanced approach to the creative development, financing, and distribution of their motion pictures.

These companies' operating processes naturally mitigate risk, their pictures are principally released by major studios (more than 90 percent), their pictures are generally profitable (more than 80 percent), and accordingly their organizations build value, some of them becoming publicly traded.

Before committing to a picture's production, in most cases even before acquiring a literary property or idea (with the exception of bidding frenzies, which rarely serve even the winner well), balanced producers proceed only when their research verifies that the producer's potential gross profits are sufficiently high compared with the picture's approximate production and distribution costs. If these numbers do not proof out, balanced producers have the following decisions to choose from: (1) lower the production budget, (2) increase the picture's earnings power, (3) pass on the picture, or (4) know it will be a money-losing project and be sure all investors and production members realize they are doing it for other reasons. Sometimes referred to as "passion projects," even creative triumphs can be shallow victories if few people ever see them and they do not earn enough income to cover production and distribution costs.

BALANCED PRODUCER'S DEVELOPMENT AND PRODUCTION APPROACH

To receive the greatest creative freedom and highest earnings, producers should sustain a balance among each picture's story, audiences (as vetted by a combination of domestic and international territory distributors or agents, preferably at the development phase), and ratio between the cost of production and the producer's share of profits (presented in Chapter 2). This is the business model serious producers seek to sustain.

Just as balanced producers' production analyses for their pictures include script breakdowns, production boards, schedules, and budgets, so should they include financial projections, global rights sales analysis, distribution window and ancillary products and license schedules, potential premium tie-in lists, and marketing recommendations for and eventually from sales agents or directly from distributors in the major international territories. These processes are more fully presented in subsequent chapters.

Understanding the intricate business of motion picture rights sales, for example, allows producers to plan, oversee, and even perform some of the distribution of their pictures with the same predictability as they manage the production of these films. Just as there is only one opportunity to produce a picture, there is only one opportunity to sell its rights.

For instance, knowing that a picture lends itself to merchandising products, in-flight screenings, and novelization allows a producer, while still in development, the advantage of including product development and cover shots (necessary for some television, in-flight, as well as international versions) in the picture's production plans and budgets. At the same time, the novelization of the screenplay can be planned and a publishing relationship put in play. With sufficient lead time, in multiple territories, the paperback can feature the picture's one-sheet (poster art) on its covers at retail checkout stands weeks before the picture's theatrical premiere. The merchandisable goods can further cross-promote the picture and be released in their optimal timing to benefit the picture's release. Without the producer's involvement in these processes, the marketing and income benefits from them would be lost or seriously compromised.

Independent production is inherently intense. Embracing the practices of balanced producers not only assures producers the greatest possible success in marketing their pictures, but it also delivers all those who are committed to the producer's success the greatest possible infusion of stability and sanity.

The studios are masters at evaluating and extracting the greatest income from their pictures. However, producers should not expect a distributor to plan and prepare as early or as comprehensively as they will. If the producer is the picture's parent, consider the distributors as aunts and uncles. Although a crucial part of the family, they will never care for the picture like the producer will.

Before a producer commits to a project, he or she should process it through his or her own in-house tests, as presented in later chapters and summarily in Chapter 14. After a producer internally greenlights a picture, then it is time to bring in the rest of the family.

To sustain sanity and balance in their companies and careers, independent producers should establish and follow these basic creative and business processes to experience the artistic, operational, and compensatory benefits. When producers (the third-tier participants) develop, produce, and distribute their pictures, deeply meshed with their audiences and distributors (the first- and second-tier participants), all other industry participants (tiers 4 through 10), will respect and confidently participate with them.

Participant Category 4: Retailers and Licensed Media

These participants are (1) theater circuits (exhibitors), (2) home entertainment rental and sales, streaming and downloading on the Internet, through kiosks and retail stores, (3) television VOD (Video on Demand) and SVOD (Streaming Video on Demand), as well as the Internet's IPTV (Internet Protocol Television), (4) television premium cable networks and major free television networks, and (5) free television syndication participants, including cable networks and independent television stations and systems. The producer's relationships with each of these are presented in subsequent chapters. This section focuses on the larger view of how these motion picture retailers impact and contribute to the motion picture arena.

It is important to realize that each of these represents a massive, sophisticated, and separate industry. Each has separate associations and conventions, and each makes its own crucial and specialized contributions in selling to its specific and unique audiences. They are similar, however, in that they all rely on producers to deliver dynamically entertaining pictures and theatrical distributors to initially establish each picture's powerfully motivating brand.

DISTRIBUTION WINDOWS

Although each picture's sales schedule is singular to its audiences, marketing power, time of year and date of initial theatrical release, financing, and distribution agreements, the typical U.S. distribution windows for a film made for U.S. audiences are as follows:

Distribution window	Time from prior window	Cumulative months
Electronic Games	6–12 weeks prior to theatrical release	3 months before theatrical
Paperback	3–7 weeks prior to theatrical release	2 months before theatrical
Theatrical	Opening day	Theatrical
Home Entertainment rental/sell-through	Day & date to 3 months later	3 months after
VOD/SVOD/IPTV	1 to 3 months later	3–6 months
Premium cable	3–6 months later	6–12 months
Network television	6 months later	12–18 months
Syndicated television	12–24 months later	24–42 months

FIGURE 1.3
Traditional U.S. Distribution Windows.

In addition to the substantial and sophisticated campaigns mounted by theatrical distributors, each of these participants makes the following contributions:

1. Theatrical exhibitors (theater chains) plan and purchase print (newspaper) advertising in their theaters' markets. Most exhibitors have their own in-house ad agencies that manage this process. They also show trailers (movie previews) of upcoming releases on their websites and their theaters and display one-sheets (movie posters) and standees in their lobbies of current and upcoming pictures. The distributors provide both trailers and one-sheets. The most sophisticated chain websites provide picture posters, promotional clips, reviews, ticket sales, movie times, and maps. Unquestionably the most motivating contribution that exhibitors make to each picture's success is providing a high-profile exhibition environment with large screens, superior sound, comfortable seating, and friendly, picture-informed staff.

2. The hefty home entertainment sector relies primarily on audience demand established for each picture during its theatrical release. For the highest profile pictures, distributors also provide some television and other media advertising, but much less than for the theatrical release.

Except for kiosks, all other in-market Home Entertainment sales and rental participants in major global territories (like Hollywood Video and Blockbuster in the United States), continue to recede in income and physical retail space. Home entertainment's unrivaled growth areas will continue to be Internet streaming and Internet/mail servicing distributors (similar to Netflix and Blockbuster in the United States and Movie Mail in the UK). Kiosk rental and sales units (like Redbox in the United States) went through rapid growth in some global territories, eventually saturating their markets, but will likely enjoy rapid growth in territories in which they will yet premiere. Eventually, Internet streaming/physical delivery sales and rentals will dominate every major global territory.

Home entertainment retail outlet chains also promote their pictures by displaying one-sheets, may run their promos on in-store video screens, may place local newspaper advertising, and, in the case of the largest chains, may even use television campaigns. As with theatrical exhibitors, the home entertainment outlets with the highest sales provide customers with a high-tech film industry environment. Further, ordering an adequate copy depth (volume of copies) of each picture satisfies the early heavy audience demands and also crucially extends each picture' audiences and earnings.

Retail sales and rental income have dropped, primarily because of the Internet's pervasive market expansion. Sales pricing continues to drop, and extra features are found in sales versions that are not found in rental versions. In offset, rental revenues have rallied as (1) consumers are less interested in owning, (2) renting has become increasingly convenient via in-store kiosks and mail, and (3) renting is less expensive than buying. The most effective retail marketers place motion picture products in high-traffic areas, some screening the product on a television monitor. Many use print ads as part of their newspaper campaigns, and some use direct mail. For the stronger titles, many retailers actually sell copies at or below their cost as promotions to draw traffic into their stores. Major U.S. sales retailers (also referred to as big boxes) include WalMart, Target, and Costco.

In 2009, DVD and Blu-ray sales combined were down 13.5 percent when compared with the year before, according to the Digital Entertainment Group. And combined DVD/Blu-ray sales in 2008 had already fallen 12.7 percent from $16.6 billion in 2004, considered the industry's peak, according to Adams Media Research.

3. VOD/SVOD/IPTV are helping fill the gap from DVD declines. Online movies are on the rise – in the United States, transactional online movie consumption (digital rental and digital retail) grew by over 135 percent in 2007 and will more than quadruple between 2008 and 2012. Apple's iTunes, Netflix, and Amazon's Video on Demand, as well as video-on-demand through cable boxes, websites, and videogame consoles from Microsoft, Sony, and Nintendo, are also seeing steady and significant increases in sales and rentals. Two key players currently dominate the transactional online movie market: Apple's iTunes and Microsoft's Xbox Live Marketplace. In the United States, these two services currently account for around 80 percent of all digital transactions.

4. Premium cable networks, such as HBO, Showtime, and Starz in the United States, are uniquely important licensees because producers can more easily license directly with them. These licensees use the brand power of the most popular pictures to expand their subscriber base by advertising on the Internet, on cable systems, and in a variety of magazine, newspaper, and direct-mail media.

5. Free television networks are also easier for producers to license directly. Although premium cable in most major global territories continues to grow, only about half of TV households in the United States subscribe to a premium cable network. Consequently, the television network premiere often attracts the largest single viewing audience during a picture's life. Television networks are masters at drawing mass audiences by using their networks as the primary source to advertise their premieres of theatrically released motion pictures.

6. Free television syndication participants, including cable networks and independent stations, deliver long-term audiences and income. Licensing to these participants is sophisticated, complex, and typically sold and managed by a television syndication company. These stations and station groups, like the networks, primarily advertise motion pictures via their stations.

Participant Category 5: International Territories

These participants include the audiences, distributors, retail media, and other rights purchasers in territories outside each picture's core distribution territory. International territories yield from about 60 percent to 70 percent of the earnings of most motion pictures created by U.S.-based producers, depending on the genre and above-the-line talent. The leading international territories and producers' relationships with them are reviewed in Chapters 3 and 14.

Participant Category 6: Financing Participants

These participants include banks and venture capital funds. These entities provide debt financing guaranteed by collateral in the form of production incentive programs, cash flow distribution contracts, presale contracts, or sales estimates of the value of certain territories. Financing participants also include studios and distributors that act as co-financing/co-producing partners for many independent producers. Governments—including countries, provinces, states, and cities—increasingly provide single to almost mid-double-digit financing through production tax or cash rebate programs. Private and institutional investors provide development, distribution, and, in some cases, partial production equity funding, some motivated by tax-sheltered programs. Other participants in this category include service providers such as postproduction, CGI houses, law firms, private attorneys, and accounting firms and accountants, who advise, author, and assist in the management of securities. The roles of these participants are explained fully in Chapters 2, 6, 11, 12, and 14.

Participant Category 7: Distribution Subcontractors

This category includes sales and licensing specialists, media planning and buying companies, campaign creators and producers, as well as advertising agencies (some of which contribute to all three of the just-listed items). This category also includes manufacturers and duplicators of products including CD, DVD, Blu-ray, and new generations of consumer technology. Distribution subcontractors are discussed in Chapters 5, 14, and 15.

Participant Category 8: Production Talent and Subcontractors

These participants include a diverse array of above- and below-the-line performers and crew members, imaginers, producers, and suppliers. Especially included in this category are writers, directors, actors, and their agencies, agents, managers, and the attorneys who represent them. Producer relationships with participants in this category are reviewed in Chapters 10, 13, and 14.

Participant Category 9: Ancillary Media and Licensees

This category includes licensed rights, such as electronic games (occasionally out-earning traditional motion picture income), publishing, printing, merchandising, sound tracks/music publishing, and clothing. This category also includes additional media income from hotels and motels, in-flight and ships-at-sea screenings, and other licensed free audiences, including prison systems, Indian reservations, and schools. Though these are all growing in earnings and promotion importance and occasionally out-earn conventional income categories, these markets typically represent a modest portion of a picture's income. These participants are reviewed in Chapter 5.

Participant Category 10: Major Consumer Brands

These participants are brands that link their products or name to a motion picture and advance that picture and their own brand by the nature of the relationship. Consumer brand relationships may take a number of forms, but they generally fall into two categories. The first and most common is the brand exposure of products used in the picture. For this type, the brand either pays for the exposure or gives or lends its products to the producer. The second relationship is a brand's use of a picture to advertise or promote its name or products. Fast-food chains, beverages, packaged goods, fashion goods, delivery services, autos, computers, and mobile phones are the most active participants in these relationships. Sometimes these relationships substantially contribute to the success and increase the income of their pictures by escalating their advertising campaigns during theatrical release.

These complementary brand relationships lend authenticity to pictures by using brands that create a sense of reality for the film's audiences. These relationships often offset production costs and may even become a revenue source or powerful advertising alliance for the producer. Consumer brand relationships are reviewed in greater depth in Chapter 5.

PARTICIPANT CATEGORY SUMMARY

It can be beneficial to review these motion picture industry participants, reconsidering their value order:

1. Audiences
2. Distributors
3. Producers
4. Retailers and licensed media
5. International territories
6. Financing participants
7. Distribution subcontractors
8. Production talent and subcontractors
9. Ancillary media and licensees
10. Major consumer brands

Although traditionally viewed primarily as creatives, independent producers who operate their own development and production companies are also business owners. In large measure, their creative and financial success relies on their understanding of, empathy for, and relationships with the industry participants above them on this hierarchical scale (audiences and distributors), as well as with those below them.

STORY

If the creative categories were listed in priority, as the business categories have been, one creative category would clearly stand above the others. This is the ultimate art of creative genius. It is where the picture is first produced. It is the screenplay.

Story is the most essential and important, and therefore the most powerful creative, asset in the motion picture industry. It is more powerful than money. Too many people with deep pockets have entered this industry to establish a motion picture production empire, only to leave months or, in some insufferable cases, years later, with a monument of odd and underperforming pictures to show for their substantial investments.

Story is even more important than star power or a great director. Even A-list actors and directors, for money or career politics, occasionally allow themselves to be attached to pictures that should never have been made. Fine direction and acting may lift a picture somewhat but ultimately can never redeem a weak story.

An audience-pleasing, entertaining story is the most powerful and essential asset in the motion picture business. Talent with story sense always gravitate to these pictures and want to participate in their creation. Business operating technique, organization, planning, excellent relationships with studios and great artists, or the availability of any other assets will never offset the essential need for producers to discover, develop, and produce stories that deserve to be told. The greatest independent producers recognize great stories.

Excellence in all other producer characteristics will not compensate for failure in this one. Call it story sense, having a nose for the audience, or what you may, this is the single essential attribute, if all the other producer qualities are to even matter.

At the same time, to sustain the whole perspective, it's important to remember that a great story alone is not sufficient justification for a producer to greenlight its production. Great stories without sufficient audience power as compared to their production and distribution costs should not be made—unless they are produced for reasons other than profit and all the major finance and production participants are fully aware of the alternative purposes. Great stories are always the germ, the genesis, the foundation of every consummate picture. If the story isn't worth being told, then none of the producer's other considerations matter.

CHAPTER POSTSCRIPT

One of the oldest business adages is, "Nothing happens until somebody sells something." Audiences and sales/distribution are more preeminent than production. As in all industries, marketing and distribution is the single largest determinate of each motion picture's success or failure. Distribution is also where the greatest profits are earned. Consequently, the most successful producers do the following:

- Have strategic relationships with global distributors
- Set up each picture's distribution in advance of its production, confirming the picture's basic global earnings value and assuring its release
- Are very involved in the initial brand establishment strategy, as well as the release and marketing of their pictures
- Retain some sales and distribution rights in each picture
- Either make or participate in these sales

The motion picture industry is expansive, robust, and intense. Success largely relies on well-served strategic business relationships with leading entities in every major category. The most successful producers sustain a balance between creative areas, audience, and profits. This core focus dominates all relationships and decisions, guiding their pictures to ultimate and consistent successes.

CHAPTER 2

U.S. Theatrical Distributors

Theatergoers in the United States spend more money on motion picture entertainment than they do in any other global territory, and their behavior is leading to a steady increase in the distribution of pictures the world over. This chapter specifically reviews who the U.S. theatrical distributors are and how they function. It covers both the major studios (the "majors") and the independents. Though this chapter specifically highlights U.S. distributors and distribution, much of the relationship approaches and distribution methods set forth are readily applicable to most major international territory distributors.

There are three traditional relationship categories that U.S. majors engage in with independent producers:

- In-house studio production
- Negative pickup
- Distribution agreement

Motion picture distributors, especially the major studio distributors, are the greatest advocates of independent producers. The more producers understand how studios operate, the various relationships they may have with them, and why studios function the way they do, the more producers will be able to appreciate these studios and forge more productive relationships with them.

THE STUDIO DISTRIBUTORS: THE MAJORS

The studio distributors are 20th Century Fox, NBC Universal, the Walt Disney Company, Paramount Pictures, Sony (TriStar & Columbia), Warner Bros. (WB), and Lionsgate. Several studios still retain within their structures, active art house/classics/genre divisions: Focus Features (Universal), Sony Classics (Sony), and Fox Searchlight and Fox 2000 (Fox). Each of the major studios is a massive, sophisticated media conglomerate. Most earn billions of revenue dollars each year. These distributors rigorously compete with each other in all markets and every media worldwide.

DOI: 10.1016/B978-0-240-81463-6.00002-4

The majors are the ultimate motion picture entities. They have evolved as completely self-contained entities, operating as both distributor and producer, as well as facilitating multiple independent producer relationships. Each studio has the advantages of global theatrical and ancillary sales power; global media alliances; availability of sophisticated bank, commercial, public, and equity funds; and sophisticated creative and operational checks and balances. They each have their individual committee operating styles, which in the main benefit marketing and distribution. They typically look to outside producer partners to provide them a significant number of pictures and mainly focus their development and production resources on franchises, branded projects, and sequels of successful properties.

The ultimate definition of a motion picture studio is *a global distribution entity with in-house production that includes owning its own soundstages and back lots.* Within the studio, every department and all operations in their best form are geared toward stabilizing and optimizing motion picture marketing and distribution. Studios are distribution-focused primarily for the following reasons:

- Distribution yields higher profits per picture than production
- Distribution accommodates a greater volume of pictures
- Distribution connects directly with the marketplace and is consequently a more stable and predictable business model

With a distribution focus, and with all the studios in 2009/2010 reducing their motion picture output from 20-plus a year to the midteens, studios look to independent producer relationships to deliver more of the motion pictures they will distribute. Studio executives enter many more picture relationships than do producers, are excellent negotiators, and are consequently exceptionally well prepared to set up relationships with producers.

Knowing this, before meeting with a studio, producers should thoroughly prepare, understand what they want, have *in writing* the deal points of a fair relationship for both sides, and should have reviewed the deal points with their entertainment legal counsel. An excellent book on negotiating to review is *Fearless Negotiating: The Wish-Want-Walk Method to Reaching Agreements That Work* by attorney Michael C. Donaldson.

Producers are classically underprepared and underexperienced. They too often leave the negotiating table without obtaining the benefits and power they should have and with a substantially different understanding of their relationship than the documented deal points define. Contract language is precise—it is enforced in its ultimate interpretation by contract law, not by the dictionary, and though most of the language is stable, definitions can literally change daily. Producers should be prepared in every creative, business, and legal aspect relative to the production and distribution relationships they negotiate. They should expect and respect that studio executives will be excellent negotiators and impeccably well prepared.

STUDIO ACCOUNTING

Having entered into a U.S. studio distribution relationship, producers may be confident that the studio will deliver an accurate, complete and timely accounting for each picture. A review of the theatrical performance example presented later in this chapter reveals that producers and other profit participants who complain that their picture has a box office of $50 million but cost only $20 million and conclude that the studio must have a creative accounting method are unfamiliar with marketing costs and earnings distributions to exhibitors and others. Where producers and their attornies and accountants should be especially cautious in their review of the licenses and other arrangements with studio television units and other studio-owned entities that could be preferentially negotiated with the entity, to the studio's benefit. Producers should understand how the money flows and how the producer's net profits are calculated. Participation definitions are complex and subject to contractual definitions. Again we stress the need for expert legal advice. We recommend reading *The Biz* by renowned entertainment attorney Schuyler M. Moore.

THE THREE STUDIO ARENAS

Each studio has its own unique organizational structure. However, it is important that producers be familiar with the three basic operational arenas the studios have in common:

- The *executive arena*, which consists of the ultimate studio chiefs
- The *distribution arena*, which is a combination of each of the distribution organizations within the studio (the most powerful are theatrical and home entertainment)
- The *production arena*, which consists of each studio's production organizations

Each of these arenas has its individual presidents. Some studios have multiple presidents within each of their distribution and production arenas.

Studio Executives

Studio executives are the studio chiefs and corporate-level directors of each studio, and at the time of this writing, they include Jeff Zucker at NBC Universal; Barry Meyer and Alan F. Horn at Warner Bros.; Michael Lynton, Amy Pascal, and Jeff Blake at Sony; Rich Ross at Disney; and Rob Moore at Paramount Pictures, along with their teams.

Only the largest of the independent producers play in this arena. The studio chiefs make decisions relative to conglomerate studio direction, studio assets, media alliances, global market positioning, and the leaders, direction, and disposition of the various studio operating units. All presidents of studio units report to and are evaluated by the studio chiefs, including all financial, accounting, and legal departments.

This is the arena that ratifies and, if appropriate, negotiates contracts with premium cable organizations, networks, the larger video chains, international studios, and ancillary media, among other powerful earnings sources. These relationships typically deliver a predictable stability to each studio. Understanding these relationships substantially affects the deal and negotiating perception of independent producers in their dealings with the studios. These relationships are reviewed later in this chapter.

The Distribution Unit

Distribution units include the global distribution executives and their staffs as well as each of the sales organizations for theatrical and home entertainment, which are the heart of most major independent producer's studio relationships. They also include every other international and domestic sales organization and their advertising, promotion, and publicity units.

This arena relies on obtaining pictures to distribute. The majority of these pictures come from independent producers, the rest from the production units within the studio.

The Production Arena

In most studios these are multiple organizations (such as Fox, Fox 2000, and Fox Searchlight at 20th Century Fox). These organizations are directed by production executives and their teams. The production arena manages a large motion picture development pool, fulfills all the production processes for in-house pictures, and participates in the development and production of independent films that are wholly or partially financed by the studio.

STUDIO RELATIONSHIPS WITH INDEPENDENT PRODUCERS

The studios engage in three conventional relationships with independent producers: in-house studio production, negative pickup (the studio agrees to acquire certain rights, typically at least all U.S. rights, for a fixed amount payable upon delivery of the picture), and distribution only. Some independent producers progress in their studio relationships by evolving from studio pictures (producer is a work for hire), to negative pickup productions, and then to strictly distribution relationships. There is also a popular hybrid deal whereby the studio and producer will share both the production costs and the print and advertising costs (P&A) 50/50.

There are many crucial deal points in each of these relationships. The central deal point categories common to all these relationships are as follows:

- Creative control
- Film negative and copyright ownership
- The specifics of the theatrical distribution commitment (especially minimums for advertising and number of screens)

- The distribution fees, studio charges and overhead, studio participation, and, for in-house producer relationships, the producer's profit participation
- The profit participation definition (this is often a 15 to 30 page portion of the agreement that most crucially determines even if the producer will receive any profits) and the license or assignment of the film's distribution rights between the producer and the distributor

In-House Studio Production

This relationship is typically engaged through the studio's production operations. The producer provides an acceptable story, plus the capacity to complete development and deliver a finished picture on schedule and within the budget. The studio provides all the development and production support, financial and business (legal and accounting) resources to complete the picture, and all the distribution resources to sell its rights. This relationship is less common, as the studios have reduced in-house development and increasingly look to independent producers to bring them at least partially developed projects.

Though the producer has creative freedom, the ultimate creative control typically resides with the studio. Also, the studio owns the negative, copyright, and all distribution rights. The producer is paid a production fee, refunded his or her development costs, if any, and typically has a net, adjusted gross or gross-profits participation in the film, commonly called *points*.

Some producers make all their pictures throughout their careers in this category, are creatively satisfied, and achieve excellent earnings. A good example of this relationship is the early producing career experience of Andrew Davis, who brought Warner Bros., (WB) *Above the Law* and attached Steven Segal. He entered a studio production relationship with WB that allowed him to make the picture using the support of the production department, yet giving him the flexibility even to rough-cut the picture in his home. The picture received WB's formidable marketing muscle and was successful enough to inspire a sequel and launch Davis's subsequently prolific career.

Negative Pickup

This relationship is substantially more independent than studio production, and typically it is entered through a studio production unit. The producer provides an acceptable story and the capacity to complete development and deliver a finished picture and the picture's production financing. The studio provides production support, a bankable contract for all or a substantial portion of the needed production funds to be paid upon delivery of the film, and license rights for global, U.S., or international distribution, as negotiated. The bankable contract typically states the studio will pay an agreed-upon amount when the film is delivered, plus royalties (a percentage of the picture's profits, according to a "net profits" definition). Negative pickup relationships commonly allow the producer more creative freedom during the production process, though the studio may have the right to the picture's final cut. Negative pickups are easier to understand and process than they are to receive, as studio's have tight script, producer, and above-the-line criteria that can be challenging to satisfy.

Though it is a negotiable point, the producer typically owns the picture's copyright, and as part of the agreement, the studio receives the distribution rights (as negotiated, consisting of global, U.S., or international rights). From the gross receipts collected by the studio, the studio is paid its distribution fee for all rights it sells, recoups its direct distribution expenses (DDEs), and may also have points in the picture.

An entertainment bank lends the producer the production financing, which necessitates that the producer have bank and completion bond relationships. The collateral provided to the bank for the production loan is typically a combination of a studio negative pickup contract and may also include foreign presale contracts and unsold territories estimated value (gap) financing. This collateral equals or exceeds the picture's negative cost, after deducting loan interest and fees. Contingency elements in the negative pickup contract are primarily that the producer will deliver the studio access to the picture's negative or a color reverse internegative (CRI, created to make release prints) and campaign materials, on or before the contract delivery date, and that the picture contain preapproved above-the-line talent, including the director and principal cast. An insurance company provides the bank a guarantee (referred to as a completion guarantee or completion bond) that the picture will be delivered within budget and by the contracted delivery date with the specified creative elements intact. (Obtaining the production funding from the bank is discussed thoroughly in Chapter 6; completion guarantees are discussed in Chapter 8.)

Distribution-Only Relationship

This relationship typically is entered through the studio's distribution arena. This is the most sophisticated relationship for producers to engage and delivers them the greatest overall benefits. This relationship naturally motivates the creation of the consistently successful motion pictures, better prepares the various rights areas in the major markets, grants producers the greatest autonomy, earns the most revenues for each film, and delivers the highest profits to the producer. Typically this is the most beneficial relationship globally for audiences, studios, producers, and licensees. One of the most successful production companies in this arena is Alcon (*The Blind Side, My Dog Skip*).

The distribution-only relationship takes many forms. Generally, the producer engages a U.S. studio to distribute U.S. theatrical and home entertainment. In this relationship, the studio does not provide negative pickup, other financing collateral, or advance fees. The producer provides the finished picture, developed, produced, and financed, and in some relationships, part or all of the direct distribution expenses (the hybrid deal). The studio's distribution unit provides production and campaign consulting from the picture's earliest development, along with U.S. theatrical distribution and, most commonly, U.S. home entertainment distribution.

Although the producer consults with major market distributors throughout the development and production of the film and is license-bound to deliver the picture represented to presale participants, the producer has complete creative freedom during the production process.

The producer owns the project's copyright and distribution rights and licenses distribution rights to U.S. and international distributors and global media. From the gross receipts, collected by the U.S. studio, the studio is paid its distribution fee for all rights it sells, recoups its direct distribution expenses, and may also have points in the picture.

THE U.S. INDEPENDENT THEATRICAL DISTRIBUTORS

Although the majors generate approximately 90 percent of the U.S. box office, independents still generate a respectable amount of more than $1 billion per year of theatrical ticket sales. The studios leave a rich turf for independents to operate within, and there are several excellent, active independent distributors in the marketplace. These include Summit Entertainment, Magnolia Pictures, the Samuel Goldwyn Company, IFC, Roadside Attractions, Strand Releasing, and Music Box Films.

Independent distributors typically employ more cautious picture release strategies than the studios. These include single market campaign tests on one to a dozen screens, as well as platform releasing on limited screens in three to six strong target markets. If test openings indicate campaigns, media buys, or both require changes, this is done until results are sufficiently pulling in audiences. Many independents are too small to financially support a studio-level wide release. However, the largest and best-operated independents are able to release as expansively in the United States as the majors. For instance, Summit Entertainment employs studio-like wide releases, as evidenced by its *Twilight* picture with more than 3,600 screens and *New Moon* with more than 4,000. Both IFC and Magnolia have the added the ability to book their films into theaters owned by their parent companies—IFC as part of Rainbow Media's Cablevision (a sister company to the Clearview theatres) and Magnolia as part of the HDNet (which includes Landmark Theaters).

There are also myriad smaller distributors that specialize in certain niche markets. They include Regent Releasing (soon to be renamed Here! Releasing), National Geographic, Palm Pictures, Zeitgeist, and Indican, to name a few.

Finally, there are the DIY (Do It Yourself) or rent-a-system operations, whereby the producer provides the P&A and the distributor is paid only a distribution fee. Examples are Susan Jackson's Freestyle Releasing, MJ Pekos' Mitropoulos Films, and Richard Abramowitz' Abramorama. (See Chapter 4 for more detailed information.)

Most independent distributors employ lower-cost distribution strategies that rely more heavily on viral and social networking campaigns, less expensive Internet advertising, and that maintain minimalist distribution operations. Independents will also be more creative in their timing of release windows and simultaneous theatrical and video-on-demand (VOD) release schedules.

STUDIO RELATIONSHIP COMPARISONS

To understand more fundamentally the three primary studio relationships, let us examine the individual and comparative financial performance of each, as shown in Figure 2.1.

Description	Studio Producer	Negative Pick-up	Distribution Only
NORTH AMERICA			
Theatrical Gross Box Office	50,000,000	50,000,000	50,000,000
Film Rental (at 50%)	25,000,000	25,000,000	25,000,000
Studio Distribution Fee (at 35%/30%/25% of Film Rental)	8,750,000	7,500,000	6,250,000
Direct Distribution Expense (P&A expenses included)	28,000,000	28,000,000	28,000,000
Theatrical Distributor's Net	(11,750,000)	10,500,000	9,250,000
Home Entertainment Rental Gross Income	17,200,000	17,200,000	17,200,000
Video Dup & Dist Expenses	1,462,800	1,462,800	1,462,800
Home Entertainment Sales Gross Income	14,000,000	14,000,000	14,000,000
Video Dup & Dist Expenses	4,950,000	4,950,000	4,950,000
Home Entertainment Streaming Gross Income	3,800,000	3,800,000	3,800,000
Video Dup & Dist Expenses	900,000	900,000	900,000
Home Entertainment Download Gross Income	1,000,000	1,000,000	1,000,000
Video Dup & Dist Expenses	119,700	119,700	119,700
Total Home Entertainment Gross Income	36,000,000	36,000,000	36,000,000
Total Home Entertainment Advertising and Duplication Expenses	7,432,500	7,432,500	7,432,500
Total Home Entertainment Distribution Fees (at 35%/30%/25%)	9,998,625	8,570,250	7,141,875
Home Entertainment Distributor's Net	18,568,875	19,997,250	21,425,625
N. American Theatrical & Home Ent. Distributor's Net	6,818,875	9,497,250	12,175,625
Sales Agent Fee (at 5%)	–	–	608,781
N. American Theatrical & Home Ent. Dist.'s Net	6,818,875	9,497,250	11,566,844
Premium Cable Gross	5,500,000	5,500,000	5,500,000
Premium Cable Distribution Fee (at 35%/30%/0%)	1,925,000	1,650,000	–
Direct Distribution Expenses	150,000	150,000	150,000
Sales Agent Fee (at 15%)	–	–	802,500
Premium Cable Distributor's Net	3,425,000	3,700,000	4,547,500

FIGURE 2.1
Studio relationship cash flow comparisons.

Network Television Gross	7,000,000	7,000,000	7,000,000
Network Distribution Fee (at 35%/30%/0%)	2,450,000	2,100,000	–
Direct Distribution Expenses	200,000	200,000	200,000
Sales Agent Fee (at 15%)	–	–	1,020,000
Network Television Distributor's Net	4,350,000	4,700,000	5,780,000
Syndicated Television	12,500,000	12,500,000	12,500,000
Syndicated TV Distribution Fee (at 35%/35%/0%)	4,375,000	4,375,000	–
Direct Distribution Expenses	200,000	200,000	200,000
Sales Agent Fee (at 5%)	–	–	615,000
Syndicated Television Distributor's Net	7,925,000	7,925,000	11,685,000
TOTAL NET NORTH AMERICAN EARNINGS	22,518,875	25,822,250	33,579,344
INTERNATIONAL			
Gross International Sales- All Territories and Rights	24,000,000	24,000,000	24,000,000
Gross International Overages- All Territories and Rights	20,000,000	20,000,000	20,000,000
Gross International 2nd Cycle- All Territories and Rights	6,000,000	6,000,000	6,000,000
Gross International Revenues	50,000,000	50,000,000	50,000,000
Sales Agent Fee (at 35%/20%/20%)	17,500,000	10,000,000	10,000,000
TOTAL NET INTERNATIONAL EARNINGS	32,500,000	40,000,000	40,000,000
Global Consumer Product Royalties Gross	1,184,000	1,184,000	1,184,000
Merchandising Distribution Fee (at 45%/16.5%/0%)	532,800	195,360	–
Sales Agent Fee (at 9%/15%)	–	106,560	177,600
Global Consumer Products Distributor's Net	651,200	882,080	1,006,400
Total Distributor's Net	55,670,075	66,704,330	74,585,744
Production Financing Expense (at 12%/6%/6% for 18 Months)	4,500,000	2,250,000	2,250,000
Negative Cost	25,000,000	25,000,000	25,000,000

FIGURE 2.1—CONT'D

Studio Burden	687,500	–	–
Talent Residuals	2,265,099	2,479,376	2,884,903
Sales Agent Direct Sales Expenses	–	250,000	500,000
Producer's Gross	23,217,476	36,724,954	43,950,841
Talent Participation (at 7%)	–	2,570,747	3,076,599
Producer's Net	23,217,476	34,154,207	40,874,282
Studio's Share	20,895,728	17,077,103	–
Producer's Share	**2,321,748**	**17,077,103**	**40,874,282**
Distributor's Net Earnings to Cost Ratio	0.1:1	0.7:1	1.6:1

FIGURE 2.1—CONT'D

Please refer to *"Studio Relationship Comparisons"* on Focal's companion website for this book. The cells are formula driven, allowing the user to perform "what ifs" and to analyze specific pictures. As you move the cursor to each cell, the formula reveals its performance relationship to other cells. Each relationship example is for the same picture, earning the same from each distribution and rights area.

The following definitions will help those unfamiliar with the terminology used in this example.

Theatrical Distribution

Gross box office refers to the total box office receipts collected from theater attendees for a particular picture. This example uses $50 million for each picture. Just 62 pictures released in 2009 earned $50 million or more in the United States. Most films hitting this box office level generate the highest grosses in the major cities such as Los Angeles, New York, and Chicago. However, pictures with uniquely strong concentration of target audiences in nonmajor metros, break this mold, such as *The Blind Side*, which had its highest grossing cities in Sacramento, Dallas, Birmingham, and Nashville.

Film rental is the share of the gross box office due the distributor. The *film rental agreement* is the document setting forth the terms between the exhibitor and the distributor. Sample U.S. exhibitors are AMC Entertainment, Regal Entertainment Group, Cinemark USA, and Carmike Cinemas. The terms of these agreements commonly allow for higher earnings for the distributor early in the picture's run, when the box office is highest, and lower as exhibition continues and the receipts are lower. The example uses the commonly applied portion of 50 percent each for exhibitor and distributor. (Note that studios typically negotiate better film rental terms because they have a stronger and higher volume of pictures than do independent distributors. Further, studios' film rental collections, *settlements*, are usually fulfilled sooner and at a better percentage than that obtained by independent distributors for the same reason—stronger and higher volume pictures.)

The distributor earns a *theatrical distribution fee*, which is calculated as a percentage of the film rental. For studios this amount is typically 25 percent to 35 percent of film rental, unless the producer provides most or all of the direct distribution expenses and negotiates a lesser fee. Established producers with output relationships with the studios, regularly delivering pictures into their systems, negotiate significantly better distribution fee percentages.

Direct distribution expenses (DDE) are the expenses incurred by the distributor in the process of distributing a picture; the distributor can recoup these expenses from the picture's gross receipts remaining after deducting distribution fees. These expenses are principally advertising (often $25 million to $35 million) and prints (for example, $2 million for 2,000 prints at $1,000 each). Together these are commonly referred to as P&A (prints and advertising). However, direct distribution expenses also include campaign creation and production, promotion and publicity, film exchange costs and festival expenses, among many other out-of-pocket expenses.

The *distributor's theatrical net* is the film rental less the distribution fee and direct distribution expenses. The application of fees and expenses are the same for all three distributor relationships, yielding the same amounts each. Consider how difficult it is for pictures even to recoup their distribution expenses from just North American theatrical distribution. With a $50 million gross box office, the typical picture is eight figures away from even recouping its distribution expenses.

Home Entertainment Distribution

HOME ENTERTAINMENT GROSS INCOME

Though home entertainment income continues to shift to digital soft copies, Internet streamed or downloaded, and away from traditional hard-copy DVD and Blu-ray formats, together in all its many forms, home entertainment remains the single most profitable earnings category for most motion pictures. Each picture has its own earning dynamics in each category and changes substantially, depending on the success of the theatrical campaign and its target audiences. The example uses a formula of 0.72 times film rental. Home entertainment distribution is very sophisticated, but not nearly as much as theatrical distribution. This continually changing window is discussed more thoroughly in Chapter 5.

The home entertainment release window continues to be incrementally dissected and shared with the VOD and pay-per-view release window. Aspects of this area, including price point and every facet of marketing, continue their business model evolution. Recent examples include experimenting with staggering release dates and only having bonus features on purchased copies and not rental copies. The *home entertainment distribution fee* is negotiable, but in the example it is 35 percent (studio), 30 percent (negative pickup), and 25% (distribution only).

DVD AND BLU-RAY DUPLICATION AND DISTRIBUTION EXPENSES

DVD and Blu-ray duplication is very competitive. If the duplicator performs all aspects of printing the sleeve, duplicates the product, and manages the inventory and shipping, the typical 120-minute movie in DVD or Blu-ray is still not more than about $2 each. The additional advertising, promotion, publicity, and other expenses vary widely from picture to picture, with the ad budgets of some major sell-through titles rivaling their theatrical budgets. The projection in the example uses $3 per total units sold, a conservative estimate that will be higher than most actual expenses but lower than higher titles with larger theatrical grosses.

DISTRIBUTOR'S HOME ENTERTAINMENT NET

This is the home entertainment gross income less the distribution fee and duplication and distribution expenses. The application of fees and expenses is the same for all three distributor relationships, yielding the same amounts to each of these categories. Even with the drastic changes in the marketplace, the home entertainment gross income exceeds all other domestic earnings categories. Again, a picture's brand power is established in its theatrical release, but the greatest potential U.S. earnings and profits area is typically in the home entertainment release.

Premium Cable Gross

Premium cable companies are those television networks in each of the major global territories that are commercial-free and earn their income principally through monthly viewer subscriptions. The major U.S. premium cable networks are HBO/Cinemax, Showtime/The Movie Channel, and Starz/Encore.

This category's primary income follows the greatest audience tune-in, which occurs during the window that covers the picture's premium cable premiere. The license for the premiere of a picture with a $50 million gross should be about 11 percent.

The *premium cable distribution fee* should not exceed the 35 percent used in the projections. Because the market for these rights is limited and the licensing is comparatively unsophisticated, it is common for some balanced producers to sell these rights direct from their production companies.

The *premium cable direct distribution expenses* are primarily legal fees, travel, and trade-show representation. They should not exceed the $150,000 indicated in the projections.

The *distributor's premium cable net* is the premium cable gross income less the distribution fee and direct distribution expenses. The application of fees and expenses is the same for all three distributor relationships, except the distribution fee retention for the distribution-only category.

Network Television Gross

Network television refers to television networks that do not charge a separate subscription fee (i.e., free television) and are broadcast in every global territory where television programming is available. In the United States, these broadcast networks are principally NBC, CBS, ABC, and Fox, as well as major "netlets" including CW and major cable networks including CNN, TNT, USA, TBS, Lifetime, and Spike.

The *license income* for the free television network premiere of a picture with a $50 million gross should be approximately 14 percent of the picture's U.S. theatrical gross, or the $7 million used in the projections. All television networks attempt to own their programming. Though this is a programming mantra, a higher dictum is to win more of your target viewers than any competing network in a given time-slot. Consequently, major brand pictures are able to license to the major television networks. However, the license fees of these sales are adroitly weighed against a network's ability to create its own programming that may win similar audience shares. If pictures are not a major brand, they likely have no licensing chance with the major television networks but may fit well into the programming budgets of cable networks at license fees more proportional to those networks' audience shares.

The *free network television distribution fee* should not exceed the 35 percent used in the projections. Because of the limited number of broadcast networks in most major territories and because the licensing is comparatively simple, balanced producers frequently also sell these rights directly from their production companies.

The *free network television direct distribution expenses* are primarily legal fees, travel, and trade-show representation. They should not exceed the $200,000 indicated in the projections.

Distributors free television network net is the network gross income less the distribution fee and direct distribution expenses. The application of fees and expenses is the same for all three distributor relationships, except the distribution fee retention for the distribution-only category.

Sales Agent Fees

For producers who directly manage their pictures' distribution rights, the use of either a sales agent or an in-house sales division will be utilized to liquidate sales rights. Typically, the negative pickup producer performs all or some of the international sales independent of the primary release territory distributor, and the distribution-only producer performs all sales directly, even those within the primary release territory that do not become a part of that territory's distribution agreement.

International Territory Gross

Chapter 3 reviews international territories in depth. These projections are for a U.S. core-territory picture. The calculation is based on two primary factors: a percentage of the budget for the base value or minimum guarantee for each territory (i.e., all rights for Germany is valued at 8 percent of the budget) and the distributor's projected earnings in its territory for all rights. The gross international sales are the total of those two primary factors, and the gross international overages are the profits revenue earned after the distributor earns back its distributor fees, direct distribution costs, and the minimum guarantee. The application of earnings is the same for all three distributor relationships.

SHARE ANALYSIS REVIEW

Total Distributors Net

This is an accumulation of the net income from all major earnings categories.

Production Financing Expense

This is the producer's cost of interest and fees for production funding. Because the studio is a commercial lender rather than a bank, the financing is more expensive, typically 3 to 5 percent over LIBOR (London Inter-Bank Offer Rate). Further, because the distributor allocates all the funding at the time the motion picture documentation is engaged, it is common for interest to be charged on the entire amount from the first day of this relationship. Depending on the producer's credit history with the bank, the ratio between the collateral pledged and the loan amount, among other factors, the bank may charge an interest fee of one half to 3 percent. It's important to note that most of these bank financings are lines of credit, drawn down by the producer in increments as needed and accumulating interest only on the total amount drawn rather than the whole loan. The example is for a motion picture costing $25 million.

In this example, the advantage of bank interest and charges on only the amount actually in use will save the negative pickup and distribution-only relationships' half of this expense.

Negative Cost

The negative cost refers to the actual total costs of creating the picture including contingency, delivery items, and completion bond, but excluding financing costs as we calculate that separately per the preceding paragraph for this exercise. This picture's cost is $25 million. Though such expenses are not reflected here, studio relationships sometimes make it mandatory for producers to use their costlier studio facilities, equipment, and departments.

Studio Burden

This is a common expense for studio pictures. This expense is a portion of the studio's total distribution arena overhead (this does include direct distribution expenses). Each picture's expense formula is set forth in the agreement. It may be a picture's percentage of the studio's total earnings for the year. (Considering theatrical earnings only, if a studio earned $750 million during the year and your picture earned $25 million, your studio burden expense would be 3.3 percent of the total.).

Producer's Gross

This is typically the distributor's net less the production financing expense and the picture's negative cost.

Talent Participations

These are the points in the film's profits that are owed to key participants, typically the director and one or more key cast members. This projection applies 7 percent of the producer's gross to talent participations.

Producer's Net

This is the producer's gross less any other distribution, production, or profit participant expenses.

Studio Share

This is the amount of the producer's net in which the studio participates for its share as a partner of the producer in making the production and distribution of the picture a reality. For the in-house producer, this is the whole remaining amount except for the producer's points—in this example 90 percent. For the negative pickup producer, this is 50 percent for the studio. For the distribution-only producer, the studio is not a further participant.

Producer's Share

This is the amount remaining for the producer after all production, distribution, and financing expenses and participants have received their portions.

The in-house producer's shares are 0.1:1, the negative pickup producer's shares are 0.7:1 net earnings-to-production cost ratio, and the distribution-only producer's share is 1.6:1. This substantially greater profit share for the distribution-only producer is chiefly why balanced producers have the capacity to establish businesses with greater creative and financial freedom than many of their creative contemporaries.

CHAPTER POSTSCRIPT
The Critical Effect of U.S. Distribution

For the U.S. producer, the theatrical commitment is the central element that affects the picture's preproduction sales, financing, and international earnings power.

For international licensees and major brand tie-in partners, their first query is, "Who is distributing the film in the United States?" In every major international territory, U.S. studios have powerful reputations for releasing pictures with substantial earnings power and related marketplace brand impact. Though every licensee internally assesses each picture, licensees are substantially attracted to or wary of each picture, depending on the picture's U.S. distributor commitment.

For prospective equity financers, a strong U.S. distributor or international sales relationship should be mandatory, as most independent pictures that are produced are never distributed theatrically and consequently receive little or no income. Production is a shallow accomplishment without distribution and its associated income. Producers should ally each of their pictures, early in their development, with the distribution entity(ies) they believe will be optimal for that picture.

CHAPTER 3
International Territories

This chapter examines the eight dominant international territories and the top-tier international sales agents. It also explores how to initiate and sustain the relationships with international sales agents or directly with distributors in each of the lead territories that are necessary for pictures to perform at their peak distribution and earnings levels. Finally, the chapter discusses the process of negotiating and licensing these territories.

THE "FLAT WORLD" OF INTERNATIONAL DISTRIBUTION

Nowhere is it more obvious the world is flat than in motion pictures. Perhaps music led the way, but as digital content conversion combined with the pervasive Internet's cultural blending, motion pictures increased this blending and feeding to all territories and platforms. These are pushed almost faster than the major international territories' keen-edged marketing and distribution teams can control (1) audiences growing appetite for the strongest content from around the globe, (2) the ease of viral marketing/runaway social reviews/blogs/postings, and (3) the Internet's distribution via streaming and downloading.

Further, the "bottom of the pyramid" (the 5 billion in population climbing to the top) is increasing its speed to be Internet enabled, even faster than this group is becoming television connected, which accurately reflects the growing international middle class. By their sheer numbers (40 percent of the world's population), China and India also have the highest numbers of daily new Internet users and new middle class entrants, and they hold the number one and number two slots for most annual motion pictures released. But these Internet adoption and globalization trends are worldwide, not an Asia phenomenon.

The big eight markets—the United States, Japan, UK, France, Germany, Spain, Australia, and Italy, whose audiences spend more on motion picture entertainment than any others—now more than ever demand the attention of producers.

DOI: 10.1016/B978-0-240-81463-6.00003-6

The best balanced producers already prepare their pictures for the expanding audiences around the world, especially in the major territories, delivering these producers the greatest income. Their distribution to these audiences has not only become a rich income area, but it has also seeded their market's unique stories and production styles with new international audiences that now look forward to their releases.

Recognizing the dominance of the English language internationally, some territories have become successful by producing English-language pictures, either dually with their own language or exclusively in English. France is perhaps the most seasoned and successful in this process with a string of global English language hits, including the *Transporter* franchise.

Regardless a producer's approach to production, embracing the income benefits of territories outside one's primary release market should encourage a producer to seriously evaluate and determine the most earnings-beneficial territories for each of the producer's pictures. It should be noted that many pictures are too culturally specific to warrant general audience release outside the core market. However, even these will likely merit a specialized release in territories with sufficiently dispersed audience populations.

Producers should learn to recognize pictures that justify releases outside of their core territory and should identify these additional markets and the distributors who have released the pictures most similar to the greenlit picture. Contact with these distributors should occur soon after greenlighting. Just as producers identify each picture's core territory distribution windows and sales breakdowns, they should also prepare each picture's unique major international territory marketing and releases with the support of their international sales agent or, if warranted, directly with their prospective international territory distributors.

THE GLOBAL POPULARITY OF AMERICAN MOTION PICTURES

U.S. gross box office earnings exceed $10 billion annually, chiefly from U.S. producers. Though the United States is the single highest earnings territory for pictures created by U.S. producers, approximately 60 percent to 70 percent of the theatrical earnings for the most popular U.S.-produced motion pictures are earned outside the United States. Consequently, U.S. producers who have not done their international territory research may not appreciate the pervasive popularity of U.S. pictures in the major international territories.

Though U.S.-produced picture dominance gradually increased until 2006, this growth has curtailed over the past few years. This appears to be due to a combination of international production of more audience-competitive pictures and U.S. pictures reaching their international saturation peak. Speaking to this point, Stuart Ford, founder and CEO of IM Global, said that international earnings for many independent U.S. pictures is now just 10 percent of their box office "on all but the most slam dunk commercial movies." Whether 10 percent or much more, each picture deserves its analysis and preparation for earnings, potential financing participation, and global brand tie-ins.

Still, U.S. motion pictures continue to dominate consumption. It is not the quantity of motion pictures coming from the United States that appeals to international audiences; producers in some international territories produce more feature films per year than those produced in the United States. The international popularity of U.S. productions occurs for one or a combination of the following reasons:

- The entertaining presentation of great stories uniquely prepared for each major market
- The ever-increasing spectacle
- A broad fascination with American culture

Global and International Box Office Statistics

Because the international box office reports best demonstrate the dominance of U.S. pictures in international markets, we will review the performance of the top 10 box office hits for 2009 in each of the largest entertainment-consuming international territories and also review the international-territory box office earnings of the top 30 motion pictures ever released globally.

The chart in Figure 3.1 reveals there is an average of eight U.S. pictures of the top 10 grossing pictures in these seven dominant international territories, and U.S. pictures earned an average 81 percent of the theatrical gross revenues in these territories in 2009. The dominance of U.S.-produced motion pictures in international territories has been a consistent trend for many years and has continued into 2010.

Figure 3.2 reveals a broader view of American films in the global market. These statistics clearly indicate the broad spectrum of motion pictures that capture audiences globally, the picture preference similarities between U.S. and international audiences, and the earnings dominance of U.S. films in international territories.

This analysis is prepared by Gillen Group LLC for *The Producer's Business Handbook.*

The top 30 pictures earned $29.1 billion in global box office receipts, with $17.9 billion of this income earned from international audiences. Typically the split between the distributor and exhibitors/theater owners is 50/50 domestically and 45 percent/55 percent (distributor/exhibitor) overseas. Although the single largest earnings territory for U.S. pictures is the United States, it is crucial for U.S. producers to understand that approximately 60-plus percent of a picture's major earnings income is derived from international audiences and that well over half the international audience income comes from the seven territories shown in Figure 3.1, which are the United Kingdom, Japan, Australia, Germany, France, Italy, and Spain. Producers should include the leading distributors within these territories in their motion picture development and production marketing and major creative planning decisions.

Territory	Picture	$ Gross	% U.S.
Australia	Avatar	95.5	
In U.S. Dollars	The Twilight Saga: New Moon	35.2	
In Millions	Harry Potter and the Half Blood Prince	35.0	
	Transformers: Revenge of the Fallen	33.6	
	Up	25.3	
	Ice Age: Dawn of the Dinosaurs	24.7	
	Sherlock Holmes	22.8	
	Alvin and the Chipmunks: The Squeakquel	19.8	
	2012	18.1	
	The Hangover	17.9	
Total Gross		$327.8	100%
Territory	**Picture**	**$ Gross**	**% U.S.**
France*	Avatar	158.3	
In U.S. Dollars	Ice Age: Dawn of the Dinosaurs	69.2	
In Millions	Harry Potter and the Half Blood Prince	54.2	
	Le Petit Nicolas	48.4	
	2012	44.0	
	The Twilight Saga: New Moon	39.2	
	Up	38.7	
	Arthur et la vengeance de Maltazard	35.9	
	Laughing Out Loud	28.9	
	Gran Torino	27.9	
Total Gross		$544.7	79%
Territory	**Picture**	**$ Gross**	**% U.S.**
Germany	Avatar	142.2	
In U.S. Dollars	Ice Age: Dawn of the Dinosaurs	82.2	
In Millions	Harry Potter and the Half Blood Prince	64.7	
	Angels & Demons	47.1	
	Wickie und die starken Männer	41.3	
	Zweiohrküken	41.0	
	2012	37.7	
	The Twilight Saga: New Moon	34.6	
	Up	29.4	
	Pope Joan	25.0	
Total Gross		$545.2	88%

FIGURE 3.1
Leading international territory motion picture theatrical grosses, 2009.

Territory	Picture	$ Gross	% U.S.
Italy** In U.S. Dollars In Millions	Natale a Rio	36.1	
	Madagascar: Escape 2 Africa	34.9	
	Kung Fu Panda	22.0	
	Grande, grosso e Verdone	21.9	
	I Am Legend	21.0	
	Scusa ma ti chiamo amore	20.9	
	Il Cosmo sul comò	19.3	
	Indiana Jones and the Kingdom of the Crystal Skull	19.0	
	Hancock	17.8	
	Gomorra	17.7	
Total Gross		$230.6	50%
Territory	**Picture**	**$ Gross**	**% U.S.**
Japan In U.S. Dollars In Millions	Avatar	163.9	
	Rookies: Sotsugyô	88.0	
	Harry Potter and the Half Blood Prince	83.8	
	Michael Jackson's This Is It	58.4	
	Red Cliff: Part II	56.4	
	Up	51.9	
	Pokémon 12	48.7	
	One Piece Film: Strong World	48.2	
	20th Century Boys: The Last Chapter - Our Flag	48.1	
	Zenpen	42.7	
Total Gross		$690.1	52%
Territory	**Picture**	**$ Gross**	**% U.S.**
Spain In U.S. Dollars In Millions	Avatar	93.9	
	Up	37.1	
	Ice Age: Dawn of the Dinosaurs	32.1	
	Agora (Mists of Time)	29.6	
	The Twilight Saga: New Moon	28.6	
	2012	22.6	
	Angels & Demons	21.9	
	Harry Potter and the Half Blood Prince	20.8	
	Gran Torino	19.0	
	The Curious Case of Benjamin Button	16.2	
Total Gross		$321.9	100%

FIGURE 3.1—CONT'D

Territory	Picture	$ Gross	% U.S.
UK	Avatar	144.4	
In U.S. Dollars	Harry Potter and the Half Blood Prince	84.1	
In Millions	Ice Age: Dawn of the Dinosaurs	56.9	
	Up	55.4	
	Slumdog Millionaire	52.2	
	Transformers: Revenge of the Fallen	44.4	
	The Twilight Saga: New Moon	43.4	
	Sherlock Holmes	39.8	
	The Hangover	36.0	
	Alvin and the Chipmunks: The Squeakquel	35.8	
Total Gross		$592.4	91%

Average Number of U.S. Pictures of the Top 10:	**80%**
Average Gross Box Office of U.S. Pictures of the Top 10:	**81%**

**Italy 2009 figures not available, 2008 figures and films listed
*France grosses include: France and Algeria, Monaco, Morocco and Tunisia
Source: Box Office Mojo, International Yearly Box office

FIGURE 3.1—CONT'D

All amounts in USD Millions
Leading 30 Motion Pictures Globally
and the International Share of Global Box Office

Global Earnings	Motion Picture	Released	Gross Box Office		International Share
			International	Global	
1	Avatar	2009	$1,775.0	$2,481.9	72%
2	Titanic	1997	$1,242.4	$1,843.2	67%
3	The Lord of the Rings: The Return of the King	2003	$742.1	$1,119.1	66%
4	Pirates of the Caribbean: Dead Man's Chest	2006	$642.9	$1,066.2	60%
5	The Dark Knight	2008	$468.6	$1,001.9	47%
6	Harry Potter and the Sorcerer's Stone	2001	$657.2	$974.7	67%
7	Pirates of the Caribbean: At World's End	2007	$651.6	$961.0	68%
8	Harry Potter and the Order of the Phoenix	2007	$646.2	$938.2	69%
9	Harry Potter and the Half-Blood Prince	2009	$632.0	$934.0	68%

FIGURE 3.2
Leading 30 motion pictures globally.

10	The Lord of the Rings: The Two Towers	2002	$583.5	$925.3	63%
11	Star Wars: Episode I - The Phantom Menace	1999	$493.2	$924.3	53%
12	Shrek 2	2004	$478.6	$919.8	52%
13	Jurassic Park	1993	$557.6	$914.7	61%
14	Harry Potter and the Goblet of Fire	2005	$605.9	$895.9	68%
15	Spider-Man 3	2007	$554.3	$890.9	62%
16	Ice Age: Dawn of the Dinosaurs	2009	$687.9	$884.5	78%
17	Harry Potter and the Chamber of Secrets	2002	$616.7	$878.6	70%
18	The Lord of the Rings: The Fellowship of the Ring	2001	$556.0	$870.8	64%
19	Finding Nemo	2003	$524.9	$864.6	61%
20	Star Wars: Episode III - Revenge of the Sith	2005	$468.5	$848.8	55%
21	Transformers: Revenge of the Fallen	2009	$433.2	$835.3	52%
22	Spider-Man	2002	$418.0	$821.7	51%
23	Independence Day	1996	$511.2	$817.4	63%
24	Shrek the Third	2007	$476.2	$799.0	60%
25	Harry Potter and the Prisoner of Azkaban	2004	$546.1	$795.6	69%
26	E.T. The Extra-Terrestrial	1982	$357.8	$792.9	45%
27	Indiana Jones and the Kingdom of the Crystal Skull	2008	$469.5	$786.6	60%
28	The Lion King	1994	$455.3	$783.8	58%
29	Spider-Man 2	2004	$410.2	$783.8	52%
30	Star Wars	1977	$314.4	$775.4	41%
	Totals		**$17,977.00**	**$29,129.90**	**61%**

FIGURE 3.2—CONT'D

PRODUCER RELATIONSHIPS WITH INTERNATIONAL DISTRIBUTORS

Producers should begin their major international territory relationships for each of their pictures early in the picture's development. License relationships in these major territories should occur naturally as part of development for some key territories, and after completion, for other territories. Producers should attend the major motion picture annual international sales markets to expedite international territory relationships:

- The American Film Market, held in Santa Monica, California, in November, for one very focused week of picture rights sales that also accommodates the full spectrum of international studio relationship activities.
- The Cannes Film Festival and market, held in Cannes, France, in May, the most relaxed of the festivals, focusing more on production packaging and promotion than rights sales. With international media gathered from around the world, Cannes is arguably the world's largest press junket. Especially if the film will be opening soon after the festival, one can get a lot of significant press without having to travel to all those territories.
- EFM (European Film Market) runs for nine days in conjunction with one of the most important film festivals in the world, the Berlinale, in Berlin, Germany. It is the first major film event of the year and is viewed as a barometer for the upcoming year in film.

Balanced producers most often use these markets for the following reasons:

- To centralize their meetings with major international territory distributors, studio heads, and distribution chiefs. The distribution top executives may attend meetings in London before Cannes, or may stay in Cannes for a few days, attending meetings, and leave actual market attendance to their staffs. This is also true of the American Film Market (AFM). International distributor chiefs often travel to Los Angeles just prior to AFM's opening and stay perhaps into its first week or longer. But they often exclusively conduct their business outside the market.
- To pursue and consummate all non-major international territory sales. The major territories should be sold in the manner introduced in the preceding chapters, which is reviewed in Chapter 14.

For pictures to flourish in international territories, producers should do the following:

1. Manage relationships with international distributors much as they manage and value their core-territory distribution relationships, applying the relationship principles presented in Chapter 2.
2. Recognize that the best international distributors focus on target audiences and the power of each picture's campaign, and they do everything reasonable to optimize each picture's exploitation and profits within their territory.
3. Recognize that international distributors have their various marketing strengths, just as U.S. distributors do. One distributor may have greater capacities and successful experiences distributing romantic comedies; another may be stronger in releasing action-adventure pictures. These relative strengths in marketing and releasing different types of pictures is a reflection of each distributor's familiarity with preparing campaigns, buying media, and creating promotion for these unique target audiences. It is important that producers develop an understanding of, and eventually relationships with, all the leading distributors in the major markets, so that each picture will have the benefit of the greatest earnings power, matched with its particular audience dynamics.

4. Consider that though each of the largest territories has the four major distribution windows, the window timings vary in each territory, and all of them may be different from those in the core-release territory.

5. Anticipate that territories entering license agreements before production on a picture is complete, commonly purchase all of that picture's distribution rights within their territory. Territories that purchase distribution rights after a picture's completion, however, may license theatrical, home entertainment, premium cable/satellite television, free television, and the other rights separately or in combination with other rights.

Each major territory distributor allied with a picture should participate in the production of that picture from its earliest development. The producer's mantra to the major international distributors is the same as it is to those in the core market: "We will neither develop nor produce a motion picture that you are not committed to distribute." This commitment and performance on a global basis allows producers to evaluate clearly the whole global dynamic of each picture before financially significant development begins. It also allows the producer to sustain global marketplace integrity throughout development and production.

When a producer is passionate for a picture, there is a natural reluctance to accept negative comments about it. However, with potentially over half the audience and income coming from outside of a picture's core territory, producers receive crucially important creative and business insights about their global audiences if they seek and receive counsel from their international distributor partners. Producers should at least understand each major territory's response to every picture's creative, audience, and earnings performance profile. Only when producers approach and receive responses from these major territory distributors can they make accurate and informed judgments on "go" or "pass," talent, and other creative decisions for their pictures.

Rarely will a producer gain unanimous consensus from all their international territory distributors relative to a picture's creative, audience, or earnings ability. However, knowing each distributor's position informs producers as to which distributors are potential presale licensees and allows them to adjust their license forecasts for those distributors who will be licensing after the picture has commenced production.

Each international territory has language and cultural peculiarities. However, it is thrilling, if not a little unsettling, to see how global cultures are beginning to blend. Entertainment is "a" if not "the" dominant content driving this impact. Its influence escalates not only with the Internet's wildfire adoption, but also as governments relax import and programming restrictions, allowing people to decide what they will watch. New, especially handheld, wireless Internet-connected devices and other new technologies will continue to deliver a more direct entertainment-based link between the content provider and the audience. Producers demonstrate integrity and receive significant business benefits when they are sensitive to the major cultures and peoples who are their largest combined audiences.

Through dubbing or subtitling, producers and distributors can substantially mold and shape each picture to better mesh with international audience cultures. In addition, creative suggestions should also be sought from each territory's distributor. If they do not compromise the creative integrity of the picture, these suggestions ought to be used to prepare cover shots, captured during principal photography, that will be used in the pictures released in these markets. The end game is to amp each picture's creative, audience, and revenue performance.

ESTABLISHING NEW INTERNATIONAL DISTRIBUTION RELATIONSHIPS

Engaging new relationships with each of the major international distributors is a natural part of the balanced producer's operations. Chapter 14 discusses in detail a producer's earliest development plan, which most often precedes the project's final greenlight determination and includes distributor meetings in at least some of the leading international territories. This may be a producer's first meeting with these distributors, but the producer and distributor may have already met during film industry events. Meetings with international distributors should be set four to six weeks in advance, as these executives typically have tight schedules.

In the first meeting, distributors expect the customary producer presentation. This presentation is usually focused on the creative aspect, leaving the distributor to perform most of the picture's audience and comparable picture research and analysis work. Knowing this, producers should not be offended by distributors' first-contact skepticism or lack of enthusiasm.

Being prepared and confident by doing the work discussed in Chapters 1, 2, and 14 will be very advantageous. When distribution executives receive the information they most need to measure if a relationship for a given picture is of interest for them, they will be more receptive to the creative presentation and potential relationship.

As distributors realize you understand and value their position, they will become earnest meeting participants. Discuss your picture's target audiences, campaign elements, and projected grosses in the distributor's territory. The distributor's reaction to this presentation determines if the pitch continues. The distributor who responds positively to the review and your discussion will be more interested in the story and other creative elements.

If the international distributor is enthusiastic about the picture, demonstrate that you have a finance plan in place (see Chapter 6 and Figure 6.1) to proceed with the development of the picture. If the distributors are preliminarily interested in distributing this picture in their territory, assure them you will immediately begin the picture's development, following a schedule that will allow you to deliver it to them during a specific predisclosed release time, typically 18 to 24 months in the future (after development and production).

The objective of this meeting is not to have the distributor sign an agreement or even provide an unbinding letter of intent. You simply are establishing the parameters of the relationship. These basic parameters are as follows:

1. We (the producer) are convinced that you (the international distributor) are the ultimate distributor to release our picture in your territory.
2. We are going to perform as your fully funded development and production unit for this picture.
3. If you are not interested in distributing this picture, we are not inclined to proceed with its development. (In fact, if this distributor is not interested in releasing the picture because it has a similar one already scheduled during that period, or for any other reason, you might approach a competing distributor in that territory. However, this distributor is your first choice because of its abilities as demonstrated by successful releases of other pictures that have similar target audiences, campaigns, and above-the-line talent.)
4. We are proposing a best efforts, good faith, no obligation relationship.
5. We will include you, and you will assist us, in validating our continuing audience and marketing research for this picture in your territory.
6. We will continue to request your creative consultation throughout the major steps of this film's development and production.
7. We will exclusively communicate with you for all matters relating to this picture in your territory.
8. We will exclusively coordinate with you the press and advertising for this picture in your territory.
9. We will provide you with copies of all this picture's promotion and advertising material for your use in promoting this picture during the various trade events in your territory.

These parameters may seem simple and under-committal, but this is early in the relationship. The parameters allow prospective major market distributors, some of whom may eventually provide advances, to consider their potential interest in releasing the picture in their territory, before serious relationship pressure. This is more beneficial for producer and distributor. This early approach allows producers to make distributor discoveries before decisions are made that may miss opportunities or even close doors in important markets—such as talent, budget level, and script dynamics that cripple the picture in their territory. After the producer leaves, the distributor still has to research similar pictures, identify and evaluate the target audiences, break down the script for the strongest campaign elements, and so forth. Following this analysis, the distributor who is still interested in the picture is faced with the formidable relationship deterrent of premature deal engagement. From the distributor's perspective, this is the difficult phenomenon that occurs when a distributor begins to invest in a picture both before development and preproduction are complete and before the producer has demonstrated that he or she will closely correlate the picture's creative and marketing aspects with the distributor as the producer prepares for and proceeds with production. Considering the most common prior-to-production relationship offered to distributors, producers should expect distributors to be wary when they approach them for the first time.

NURTURING THE RELATIONSHIP

This process is wonderfully straightforward, though to the uninitiated, it may seem sophisticated. Each time producers meet with their international distribution partners, they fulfill a mutual objective and begin an agreed-upon next-step target. These objectives and targets weave integrity into the deepening relationship.

The objective following the first meeting is to commit to the project and commence its development. Each of the participating international territory distributors and the core-territory distributor are immediately and confidentially notified of the dates and methods for the producer's trade press release and advertising, if any are to be utilized at this stage.

In the next meeting with each distributor, the producer reviews the list of proposed directors. Again, the producer leads this meeting with an overview of how the proposed directors' pictures have performed in the distributor's particular territory. A producer rarely chooses a director who is the unanimous first choice of all the territories. The producer's target after the second meeting is to successfully negotiate the director. The next objective is to prepare, with the director, the ultimate leading cast.

After the producer successfully attaches the director, each of the distributors is immediately notified and given promotion and advertising plans. Within a week the announcement and possible advertising appear in global trade papers.

As this process continues throughout development and initial preproduction, the distributor becomes increasingly confident in the producer's competence and delivery. In addition to development and production meetings and other communication, the producer is meeting with this picture's distributors at one or more of the three annual international markets.

INTERNATIONAL TERRITORY LICENSES

As is discussed more thoroughly in Chapter 6, balanced producers principally use bank financing to cash-flow the production of their pictures. Of the several collateral elements that enable each picture's funding, presale licenses from one or more international territories should be considered. Only pictures that are likely to succeed in a given territory will typically receive a presale commitment. Only the strongest genre films will engage substantial presales with "A" list talent or auteur directors. Therefore, it has become critically important to work closely with international distributors to assure that the story and talent are at the level likely to secure these presales.

As part of the final preproduction process, the producer performs a final participating distributor analysis and updates the financing plan with actuals that include presales, equity, tax/rebate credits, and other soft money sources.

Presale contracts typically are closed about six months before the picture is scheduled to commence preproduction. By this time potential presale participants have been closely associated with the picture for several months during its development and are comfortable with the producer and their own territory's advance response to the picture. Participants for whom presale relationships may be beneficial can be offered two substantial incentives to participate. First, the picture becomes officially theirs and is no longer subject to competitive bidding. Second, the producer might offer the distributor to discount the advance by as much as 20 percent. The producer should know, before approaching the proposed prebuy licensees, if the discount will be necessary and sufficient to engage the licensees in the picture.

The presale licensees typically advance producers 10 percent to 20 percent of the license fee upon signing the agreement and guarantee to remit the balance when they are delivered access to the completed picture's elements

LICENSE DOCUMENTATION

The Independent Film & Television Alliance (IFTA or "the alliance") operates the American Film Market (AFM). The alliance has developed and continues to refine effective and high-demand international license resources for international producers and distributors. The alliance has standardized international rights sales deal memos, licensing agreements, and delivery documentation.

The alliance is a singularly responsible resource for independent producers. Most of the forms and instructions essential for carrying out the operational aspects of documenting and fulfilling international territory rights sales and delivery are available through this universally recognized organization.

Licenses' terms are most often agreed to during a meeting of the parties representing the picture (licensor) and the distributor (licensee), and they are confirmed in the form of a deal memo soon thereafter. Deal memos are generally letters that set forth the basic agreed terms and typically provide for the other party's confirming signature. Though there are license relationships that are bound without additional documentation, most sales are further documented by an actual license agreement that fully addresses all the terms and conditions relative to the license relationship.

The alliance has created widely used licensing deal memos and fulfillments that are broadly used by producers and distributors. These documents are available for purchase from the alliance by mail at 10850 Wilshire Blvd., 9th Floor, Los Angeles, California, 90024, United States; by phone at (310) 446-1000; or through its website at www.ifta-online.org.

The deal memo identifies the parties, the project or series being licensed, the territory or territories the license covers, the particular rights covered by the license, and the window length for each.

License Income

Earnings may come to the licensor from two sources: an advance/minimum guarantee or profit participation (overages). One direct distribution expense difference unique to international territories is the often substantial postproduction expense related to talent and dubbing or subtitling. One unique income category from international territories is that of payments from the distributor for elements provided by the producer. These elements include mechanicals or color separations for printed promotion and advertising materials along with tangible film and DVD elements of the picture and its related DVD and film advertising, promotion, and publicity products.

Minimum Guarantee

The minimum guarantee amount initially performs as payment "binder" to the agreement. The guarantee amount is usually paid in installments as indicated on the deal memo and is most often 10 percent to 20 percent of the total paid upon execution of the deal memo.

The minimum guarantee balance payment is most often triggered by delivery of the picture or by access to specific elements of the picture by the licensee. To delay payment, the licensee may not accept immediate delivery of the elements, though they have been delivered to a freight forwarder within the territory, on the licensee's behalf. To regulate this, there may be language in the deal memo stating that the licensee will take delivery within a certain period, for instance two months from notification that the materials have been received. Also, for the bank to discount (i.e., cash flow) the presale contract, the bank will require that the contract be assigned to the bank and that the distributor sign the notice of assignment and distributor's acceptance document, which confirms that the distributor will pay all amounts owed directly and waive all defenses the distributor may have to avoid payment.

Letters of credit (LCs) are occasionally required from smaller, more remote, newer, or less stable licensees. LCs are reviewed in Chapter 6. An example of a new release picture payment language and terms is "10 percent on agreement execution, via wire transfer, 90 percent within 14 calendar days from agreement execution, by letter of credit."

Allocation of Gross Receipts

In a "costs off the top deal," income accounting with international distributors is similar to the accounting with U.S. distributors. Distribution fees are paid on first receipts, direct distribution expenses are recouped next, the minimum guarantee is recouped, and then, typically, the producer participates in the picture's remaining profits. "Distribution deal" accounting is most commonly used in licenses with little or no advance guarantee.

Using the alliance's deal memo has many advantages. Because it is widely used, it is widely understood, accepted, and litigation interpreted. Further, its menu form allows easy selection, and it compels the parties to consider all the major points of the license.

Regardless of what you use, the alliance deal memo remains an excellent guide for those less accustomed to the international licensing process.

Territory Differences

Each territory's earnings value is not defined so much by its size and population as by the territory's media sophistication, which is principally gauged by the presence and availability of all four major distribution windows, as well as by the concentration of television households, Internet penetration, and mobile phone users among its total population. This value is also defined by the strength of the economy, measured substantially by the audience sizes per capita for each medium and by ticket cost, home entertainment rental and sales costs, and premium cable service subscription cost, along with average consumer discretionary spending and currency exchange value.

Strengths vary greatly between territories. For instance, Mexico has a land mass about five times that of Japan, but it has only a fraction of Japan's population. Further, Mexico has comparatively underdeveloped media and, though a high percentage of the population attends theaters, the admission price in Mexico is several times lower than in Japan. The most effective territory financial comparisons are drawn by examining each territory's box office and four major media category earnings records.

MANAGING INTERNATIONAL RELATIONSHIPS

Though the balanced producer will engage and sustain first-person relationships with the leading territories, this will not be possible for the remaining international territories. A small, busy, in-house international sales staff or a foreign sales agent typically manages these other valuable relationships. This is a powerful and increasingly important area, worthy of each producer's focus, accountability, and generous investment. The international sales department deserves the placement of a highly skilled, focused, and professional team. A closely correlated relationship with a strong, compatible international sales agent can be a solid alternative to an in-house international sales department. There are many small, midsize, and large companies that can effectively handle all other international distribution relationships and manage delivery and collections for all territories.

Distributors hope their independent producers will become regular suppliers of significant films. It is important for these distributors to understand their producers' five-year plans and the scope of pictures they intend to produce. Whether it is three pictures a year or two every three years, distributors need to know. Knowledge of production plans significantly affects the value distributors attribute to each production company relationship.

As a producer's inventory of motion pictures increases, it is good business for producers to consider the library they are building, not just picture by picture but by the effect each new film has on those in their libraries.

GLOBAL TRENDS

International territories are a rich resource and continually changing landscape that deserves producers' attentive relationship development and study. Consider the following two trends.

Crossborder Productions

Searching around the globe to find appropriate partnerships or financing models is becoming increasingly important in producers' planning and execution. Films, as well as TV series, are now being developed to be international blockbusters with global reach on multiple platforms. Crossborder productions are a powerful new financing model.

3D Pictures

History has shown us that studios and producers must tread carefully in their aggressive push of 3D. Once the novelty wears off, the film itself must be good. The goal for producers is to be sure the picture quality and story strengths are there and not just the gimmickry. Among the $100 million to $250 million budgeted blockbusters that audiences have made their top 10 pictures globally are the comparatively low-budget (under $50 million) wonders *The Blind Side*, *New Moon*, and *High School Musical*. It is good for producers to remember that global audiences will always have their heads turned by the latest motion picture industry wonders, but it is great stories, well told, that span across audiences in all markets and become evergreen classics.

CHAPTER POSTSCRIPT

It can be significantly advantageous for producers to understand the play and earnings dynamics of their pictures internationally and to develop and produce them to maximize their performance in at least the leading international territories. Motion pictures created by these producers are better received by international audiences and consistently turn in substantially higher earnings.

As a group, U.S. consumers outspend every other international audience in every distribution window. However, the international dynamic is radically shifting. The international middle class is growing exponentially. Technology is enabling the Internet as a broader interactive delivery platform, and all screens, from portable mobile phones to big screens, are saturating viewers around the world. Producers sensitive to the current and rapidly evolving international marketplace will optimize their pictures for international audiences and deepen their alliances with international distributors and co-producing partners.

CHAPTER 4

Internet Marketing and DIY Distribution

This chapter provides insight into how the Internet is hyper-enabling the marketing, distribution, and consumption of media and entertainment. It presents what producers are doing and can do to reap the advantages of and even accelerate the beneficial conversion of these and other technologies. This chapter also reviews self-distribution strategies and resources available for producers wanting to become their projects' marketer and distributor.

DIGITIZED CONTENT

Content digitization provides audiences with instant availability to stream or download to any of their Internet connected devices. Streaming and downloading (1) removes at least some distribution participants between content owners and audience and (2) radically reduces content delivery and marketing costs.

This is exhilarating news for independent producers. For instance, uploading to YouTube removes everyone from distribution but the producer and the audience. Even more exciting, according to neowin.net and the BBC, as of mid-May 2010, YouTube surpassed 2 billion daily downloads and is hardly slowing in audience growth.

However, brand establishment is still the primary determiner between a picture's success or failure. Most of YouTube's billions of daily viewers are watching the strongest productions that attained their position via some form of social media, email, or combination of conventional and unconventional marketing. Consider the 20-plus hours of new content uploaded to YouTube per minute. This is more than 1,200 hours per hour and 28,800 hours per day of new content. Clearly, audiences and content creators are escalating their possible Internet connections with one another. It is easy for audiences to decide what to watch, as they follow their often tightly targeted social recommendations. But the issue for producers is not distribution. It is simple to upload to YouTube, as well as other sites. The challenge is marketing—how to attract their target audiences, rise above the clutter, and become a viral-driven recommendation.

Motion picture marketing has always been an extreme-strategy exercise. We examine two new-technology examples later in this chapter. Being your own marketer

DOI: 10.1016/B978-0-240-81463-6.00004-8

and distributor takes an immense amount of time and intelligent, dedicated effort. The most able producers have at least one additional full-time person on each film, a Chief Marketing Producer (CMP) to manage these efforts. Producers are faced with the same problem as the studios and other distributors: How do you establish each picture's brand and get its target audiences to buy or view it?

SOCIAL MEDIA MARKETING

Small indie film and niche distribution companies were first to embrace social media marketing strategies out of budget restriction necessity. Artisan's release of *The Blair Witch Project* is a good early example. Even studios, which still rely on millions of dollars in ad campaigns to open a mainstream movie in the United States, have a keen-edged Internet social marketing campaign for every picture. This was accented in early 2010 with Disney's hire of M. T. Carney as head of marketing. Carney is the founder of Naked Communication, a communications strategy and planning firm known for promoting brands with social media marketing and minor traditional ad spending.

Based on extensive research by RipMedia Group and Forrester Research since 2007, advertising, viewers, and revenue are changing to become primarily viral word of mouth, which tends to drive audiences stronger than traditional paid advertising. Audiences are keen to see pictures their opinion-leading peers recommend more than just those advertised. Filmmakers are beginning to realize that access to the superfan is suddenly both necessary and economically available.

Some of the most effective social network sites are those that specialize in unique communities. There are thousands of these. As of January 2010, there were 37 global social network sites with 10 million or more members each, plus the following five global social network sites with 100 million or more members:

Site	Members in Millions, as of 2010
Facebook	500
Myspace	130
Orkut	100
Qzone	200
LinkedIn	75

Here are some leading Internet communities that are especially able in creating motion picture viral social networking. (Source: Maury Rogow and Kelly Yee of www.ripmediagroup.com.)

Twitter

Twitter is a microblogging service and one of the fastest-growing social media websites today. The 140-character limit for updates was originally put into place in order to be compatible with the same limit on text messages (for most phones). It has proven to be successful for launching low-cost marketing campaigns. It is said that Twitter contributed to the rise of *District 9 (D-9)*, when

Twitter was flooded with positive feedback during the movie's opening weekend. During the same weekend, it is speculated that Twitter contributed to the demise of *Bruno*.

Facebook

With more than 500 million users, Facebook is used for more than just social networking. It functions as a pseudo-blog for many, hosting pictures and other media. Fan pages work well for building communities with similar interests. There could be a community for every interest on Facebook.

YouTube

YouTube is the largest provider of online video hosting in the world. The number of daily views is in the billions. In addition, it offers basic social media features, such as user profiles and commenting.

TV.com

TV.com is an online video aggregator that has more social media features than its more popular competitor, Hulu. Similar sites may be overshadowing TV.com, but its focus on building a social community demonstrates the trends occurring on online video sites.

IMDb

This site doesn't fit perfectly into the social media category, but IMDb depends on a community of people to provide important information. The site's message boards are where the real interaction occurs.

FilmNet

FilmNet is primarily based around sharing video content. It links filmmakers and viewers with its social networking tools. The site offers an "in-depth industry database" as well.

Eventful

Fans can vote for a particular band, artist, film, and the like to come to their town. This site played a major role for the success of *Paranormal Activity*, allowing the film's distributors to see where it was in demand.

Bit.ly

For blogs, Twitter, and website updates, sometimes a shortened URL (internet address) is needed, and sites like this one are the place to go. If you create a username/password, the site will also store how many clicks your links gets so you can measure your conversion rate.

The following two case studies show the power of social networking and each producer's critical participation in bringing these pictures from obscurity to successful global release.

Case Study 4.1

District 9: Media Strategy and Results Just the Facts

- Star power: None
- Budget: $30 million estimated
- Studio support: None during the initial phase
- Distribution in place: None initially (QED International fully financed the production of the independent film, underwriting the negative cost before American Film Market (AFM) 2007. At AFM 2007, QED entered into a distribution deal with Sony Pictures under TriStar Pictures for North America and other English-language territories, Korea, Italy, Russia, and Portugal.)[wiki]
- Rating from Rotten Tomatoes: 89
- Obstacles: Low initial funding, no name stars, did not have distribution in place

Social Media Strategy

- Many say that the success of *D-9* is contributed to social media. Online marketing that included viral video campaigns contributed to the success of the hype before the movie was released. Before the movie was released at the box office, its trailer already had more than 25 million views on YouTube, 325,000 Facebook fans, and 47,500 Twitter conversations a day (starting the week of the premiere).
- During the first week, massive Twitter updates raved about *D-9*. The movie had a surge of positive tweets and kept the activity and box office numbers up. The movie made $14 million on opening night and $12.6 million the second night
- During the same week of the *D-9* release, another movie, *Bruno*, was also released. Massive Twitter feeds panned the comedy and convinced many moviegoers to skip it. The movie made $14 million on the opening night and dropped to $8.7 million the second night.

Results and Down the Road

- Revenue to date: Worldwide over $200 million, widest release 3,180 theaters, 12 weeks total.
- The film was nominated for a Best Picture Academy Award, quite unusual considering its category.
- Director/writer Neill Blomkamp won the Austin Film Critics Award Best First Film for *District 9* (2009). Blomkamp has another deal with QED and started filming in 2010.
- The lead and first-time actor Sharlto Copley was cast based on previous work and because he is a friend of Blomkamp. He next starred in the studio film *The A Team*.

Source: Courtesy of Maury Rogow and Kelly Yee of www.ripmediagroup.com.

Case Study 4.2

Paranormal Activity: Media Strategy and Results Just the Facts

- Star power: None
- Budget: 15,000 initially
- Studio support: None initially
- Distribution in place: None initially
- Rating form Rotten Tomatoes: 82
- An ultra-low-budget horror film with a twist

Getting Release Traction

- October 2007 screened at Screamfest Film Festival
- CAA signs representation of writer/director/editor Peli
- Jason Blum engages relationship and picture rework
- Rejected for screening at Sundance (So, do not fear rejection.)
- January 2008 screened at Slamdance
- Picked up by DreamWorks at Paramount
- September 2009: U.S. theatrical test release
- October 2009: U.S. theatrical wide release

Release Traction Narrative

Paranormal Activity's 2007 Screamfest Festival screening led to Creative Artists Agency signing representation of Oren Peli. Working this relationship, the agency sent the

Case Study 4.2

picture's DVDs to industry sources, catching the attention of Miramax Films senior executive Jason Blum. Blum worked with Peli on the picture's re-edit. DreamWorks executives Adam Goodman, Stacey Snider, and eventually Steven Spielberg also screened the DVD and struck a deal with Blum and Peli.

Blum said DreamWorks was uncertain what to do with the original picture and intended to remake it with Peli directing and to include the original film as a DVD special feature. Blum and Peli supported this approach, only if the theatrical audience test screening of the original failed.

The test screening was very strong, leading to Paramount's acquisition of the picture's domestic rights and international rights to any sequels for $300,000 U.S.

On September 25, 2009, the movie opened in 13 college towns across the United States. On his website, director Oren Peli invited Internet users to "demand" where the film went next by voting on eventful.com. This was the first time a major motion picture studio used the service to virally market a film. Twelve of the 13 venues sold out. On September 28, Paramount issued a press release on Peli's website announcing openings in 20 other markets on Friday, October 2, including large-market cities such as New York and Chicago.

Wikipedia records that on October 3, it was reported that a total of 33 screenings in all 20 markets sold out and that the movie had made $500,000 domestically. A day later, Paramount announced that the film would have a full limited release in 40 markets, playing at all hours (including after-midnight showings). On October 6, Paramount announced that the movie would be released nationwide if the movie got 1 million "demands" on eventful.com. The full limited release started on Friday, October 9. On October 10, the eventful.com counter hit more than 1 million requests. Paramount announced soon after that the film would get a wide domestic release on Friday, October 16, and then expand to more theaters on the 23. By November it was showing in locales worldwide. The picture has played in 52 international territories in addition to the United States.

Social Media Strategy

- Paramount tested the waters by opening with midnight screenings in just 13 small college towns in the end of September. From the small showing, immediate chatter about the movie sprouted on sites like Twitter and Facebook.
- Paramount then hired Eventful, a viral marketing campaign company that specializes in event scheduling. Eventful started a campaign for each city and stated that if there were enough of a demand for the movie, Paramount would release the movie in that particular city. It was through this campaign that they determined that more than a million people wanted to see the movie.
- In addition, Paramount took to its audience, launching other online grassroots campaigns. For example, on Twitter, the campaign "Tweet Your Scream" stuffed the Twitter feeds for weeks, generating additional buzz about the movie. Some people who originally had no interest now needed to see the film just to see what the hype was all about.
- Social media enabled Paramount to capitalize the movie's success. *Paranormal Activity* is the most profitable movie to date with the highest earnings-to-cost ratio of approximately $194 million in U.S. gross box office to initial production cost $15,000 and marketing costs $1 million.

Results

- During the screening, people began walking out. Originally, Paramount thought the film was bombing, until they learned that the viewers were actually leaving because they were so scared.
- The global theatrical box office earnings to date total approximately $194 million, the largest ROI (return on investment) in Paramount's long history.
- Producers, directors, and stars now have multiple projects lined up.
- The film was nominated for "best first feature" in the Independent Spirit Awards, 2009.
- As a result of the movie's success, Paramount has opened an entire Indie Film division to acquire or shoot films costing less than $100,000 each. The target is 20 per year.
- The writer/director has two pictures signed up. One is the sequel to *Paranormal* and the other is titled *Insidious,* scheduled for release in 2011.
- The lead actress has been signed by a large agency and is in another film scheduled for release in 2011.

Courtesy of Maury Rogow and Kelly Yee of www.ripmediagroup.com.

MULTIPLATFORM MARKETING

The audience is not just watching TV, they are also screening content on their computers, on and offline, accessing shows on iPhones, Blackberrys, iPads, and media/gaming consoles. Producers should develop and execute marketing strategies that provide their target audiences with social media impressions on several fronts simultaneously. The objective is to reach each target demo multiple times during the campaign drive. The new media environment allows us to connect with our pictures' core audiences on multiple platforms every day leading to and supporting the picture after its launch.

DIY DISTRIBUTION MODELS

Theater conversion to digital is a global phenom. U.S. digital screen current and future growth, plus transactional online movie consumption (digital rental and digital retail), grew by over 135 percent from 2008 to 2009 and will more than triple by 2012. According to the MPAA (Motion Picture Association of America), by the end of 2009 worldwide digital screens reached more than 16,000, up a staggering 86 percent in just one year. What this offers the smaller indie producers is in essence a new world of do-it-yourself (DIY) distribution models:

- Ability to focus on niche and crossover global audiences
- Direct to consumer and retail sales
- Flexible release strategies
- Release alternatives to the expensive theatrical model
- Hybrid distribution by splitting rights, which is when producers enter distribution deals with multiple companies to uncross and maximize revenue.

DIY: Theatrical Distribution

Theatrical distribution is potentially the single most beneficial release window, as it can extend a picture's brand to all other distribution windows. It is also by far the most time consuming, expensive, and risky of all the DIY windows for the indie producer to undertake. The following are the primary producer options:

- *Four wall*. In this model, the producer literally rents each screen from each exhibitor for a flat fee, typically for one week, with an option for additional weeks depending on the picture's success. In the United States, exhibitors require the producer to cover the "house nut" (the exhibitor's overhead cost to run that screen for one week, of approximately $3,000 to $10,000 per screen for a seven-day run). The exhibitor's prime incentive is concession earnings, so those booking the theaters must approach the circuit with a convincing marketing strategy likely to fill seats and sell concessions. The producer receives 100 percent of all ticket sales. If the film performs, the exhibitor will most likely agree to extend the run to successive weeks until ticket sales drop below alternative pictures.
- *DIY or subsistributor*. In this model, the producer either (1) hires a subsistributor to book one or more markets or (2) does this work with his or her

in-house team. This is sophisticated work. It requires (1) knowing each venue including its screens, (2) selling a theater circuit on the picture's marketing campaign (designed, carried out, and financed by the producer), sufficient to convince the circuit of its likely box office profitability, (3) negotiate acceptable terms, (4) service the relationship through the play dates, (5) reach a settlement with exhibitors, and (6) collect. The producer or subdistributor's booker negotiates a percentage-of-box-office-receipts deal. In the United States, this might start out at sharing the box office gross 50/50, then steadily adjusting the percentage each week based on the picture's box office performance, typically deescalating—that is, the second week run would see a split of 60/40 (exhibitor/producer), and the third week and thereafter would see a split of 65/35. These percentages are most often subject to offset, to meet each screen's house nut.

- *Service deal.* In this model, the producer hires a distribution team to book and administrate all the exhibitor negotiations and collections. This can also include the producer using the distribution team's services for media planning and buying. In the United States, the service company typically takes a flat fee retainer and a percentage of collections. The stronger the campaign and picture, the better the terms of these deals. Solid campaigns and pictures typically negotiate for close to the distributor's costs plus 10 percent to 20 percent of film rental, and the producer retains 80 percent to 90 percent of film rental and has all creative and business control. The producer advances all the costs of advertising, as well as prints or digital formats. Some companies managing U.S. service deals are Freestyle Releasing, Truly Indie, and Rocky Mountain (which is faith based). Although a more costly option among DIYs, this can be extremely beneficial as the service provider has years of experience in setting smart release patterns, has seasoned relationships with theater circuits and individual exhibitors, can negotiate optimal percentage deals, and, because the provider is distributing other picture's through these exhibitors, has leverage for final settlement amounts and exhibitor collections.

In any of these models, even if a producer's picture is performing well, a major supplier distributor could push the picture to a lesser screen or out altogether to make room for their new incoming picture.

DIY: Direct to Consumer DVD Distribution

This DIY model has the potential to be the most financially rewarding of all the models. It is much less expensive and time consuming than the theatrical DIY models. However, producers should not undertake this distribution window until they have either completed their picture's theatrical release or determined that the picture will never have a theatrical release. It is highly unlikely that the exhibitors or third-party theatrical distributors will consider the theatrical release of a picture already available on DVD.

The significant hurdle beginning in this release window is establishing the picture's brand. If this picture has one or more highly unique target audiences, say private pilots, scuba divers, quilters, or long distance runners, and the producer's marketing plan has inspired these audiences to track the picture's creation and they are awaiting its availability, then there is reason to believe that when the film is released into the market, it will get traction. If it is merely a great picture, but no marketing plan has been created or carried out, then creating DVDs, websites, or making it available on Amazon will likely receive little or no success. Further, retailers will not buy copies without audience traction. The challenging reality is that there is no escape from marketing. The fabulous news is that producers have the ability to accomplish sophisticated, high-impact marketing for very little cost. Still, it must be done.

The producer has two primary distribution options in this market.

DIY

In this model, the producer outsources the manufacturing of the DVDs (there are several excellent duplicators accessible online to send a "request for quote") and fulfills the orders individually or outsources the fulfillment to a third party (again, send a "request for quote" to fulfillment shops you find online, although one of the best and most cost effective in the United States is Amazon) and sells from the producer's website/eStore. Again, the challenge is getting audiences to visit and purchase from the website.

ON DEMAND

Under this model, you handover the manufacturing and fulfillment to an Internet site such as Create Space in the United States, which is owned by Amazon.com. You can sell your film via DVD on Amazon.com and your own personal eStore. Create Space ensures your DVD is in stock and shipped out per order. The company charges producers $4.98 per unit for manufacturing and takes an additional fee of 15 percent if it is sold from the producer's eStore or 45 percent if it is sold on Amazon.com. Producers using Create Space have the option to later pull it off the virtual shelves and secure an exclusive relationship with a traditional distributor.

VOD/VOD AGGREGATORS

Video-on-demand (VOD) allows consumers to download your film to view for a limited amount of times or to own. Services in the United States like Apple's iTunes, Amazon's Video on Demand, CinemaNow, Hulu, and YouTube are just some of the players in this field. Not all services are available to indie producers, but there are enough to enable this DIY model.

These companies usually license your film on a nonexclusive basis, charge the consumer a per-download fee, and (in the United States) split the fee between 65 percent/35 percent to 40 percent/60 percent (distributor/producer). Higher producer participation comes with the producer's ability to create brand presence/audience demand before the negotiation.

To get on the larger sales services, producers need to go through an aggregator company. The aggregator acts as a middleman and has the time and human resources to deal with all the indie submissions and put together film packages that the company then takes to the larger platforms for distribution. Aggregators bridge the gap between cable, satellite, and Telco operators, and the content owners (you, the producer). They handle all logistics to acquire content rights, secure errors and omissions insurance, and supply marketing materials, screeners, and content masters. Most have direct deals with the major systems, such as (in the United States) Comcast, Time Warner, Cox, and AT&T.

MEDIA CONVERGENCE

Considering how technologies have reshaped media since the late 1990s allows the producer to gauge what is coming. The new changes will include *deep media convergence*, which is assured by (1) the steadily increasing mass migration of viewers to Internet-connected devices, (2) the Internet's growing ability to keep ahead of viewer adoption and enable a motion picture's heavy bandwidth demands at the viewer's last mile (to the viewer's home/phone/computer), (3) the Internet connectivity of a growing variety of user devices, (4) the digitization of traditional content, and (5) the creation of new content for unique user devices.

These five items provide the crucial inescapable staging for convergence of all media into what could be termed supermedia: user access to all new and existing motion pictures, television, radio, music, print, and user-generated content (UGC) on all devices, all the time.

This convergence will continue to reshape every culture that allows its populous open Internet access. It will deepen global person-to-person proximity and perspective and further merge global communication, art, information, music, politics, currency, and commerce. Import and export duties between countries will continue to be relaxed or deregulated. Global commerce stimulus legislation will advance. Global trading by most every legitimate means will be enabled. Consumers will continue to support open-source enterprises and initiatives. There will be a natural global redistribution of resources. Growth of the global middle class will continue to exponentially increase. Almost everyone's voice will have connectivity and traction to the entire global voice. Language barriers will continue to drop, through automated text and voice interpreters.

This near-term transition will bring several important shifts and valuable new opportunities for producers. It will be easier and less expensive for producers to reach their audiences, as well as to complete marketing and promotions tasks. Distribution costs will be negligible for digital delivery. Much as cable and satellite systems enabled niche cable networks, enthusiasts from surfers to scrapbookers will eagerly receive even finer audience-defined niche programming.

Digitized viewing will allow audiences the ability to watch movies, series, documentaries, and so on, much like they presently read novels. For example, a viewer can begin watching a program on a home television, then continue watching on a mobile device or computer while commuting to work, then he or she can finish watching on the mobile during lunch. This will naturally bring the deregulation of program length. Theatrically released pictures needed to be no longer than audiences were willing to sit in a theater—typically, three hours max. Television programs were mostly 30 to 60 minutes, with features filling two hours. Content now will be as long as it needs to be to continue to entertain its target audiences.

There will be a massive new production surge of interactive content for all media. Television's almost exclusive delivery, in history-making mass conversion, will be via the Internet. Audiences will be able to pause, rewind, and fast-forward their programs at will, much like they do now with current DVR remotes. A new feature will provide viewers the ability to use a remote control to move a curser over paused content and look for highlights that will give them information about actors, music, cars, and the like, as well as provide hyperlinks to sites and return them to the program, all with the ease of a click. This interactive production discipline will build audience commitment to programming, as well as provide a new commerce spectrum.

OPEN SOURCE MEDIA CULTURE

The Internet is spreading a user-centric sensibility to almost everything. This has increased the common person's desire to have access to all information. Transparency is expected from companies, institutions, governments, and their chiefs and politicians. There is a new expectation for user understanding, provision, and protection, as well as a desire to make products and goods—especially digitized ones—available to everyone at mass-consumer cost. This culture has taken on the name *open source*, which was provided by early cooperative Internet software development.

Craigslist, Firefox, and Wikipedia are excellent examples of open source culture entities. However, so are Google, Amazon, and Apple. The more open the source, the greater the consumer loyalty and support. When these users are abused, their virally expressed disfavor can be lethal. There are many examples of entities that refused the open source culture and later either demised or became severely crippled. The music industry still wavers to find its way, users preferring to support its conversion but using the dysfunctional relationship until the music industry revises it. Almost everything transacted over the Internet that not only succeeds, but thrives, will be open source culture.

Producers are sampling with open source distribution. In early 2010, a UK producer launched her direct-to-DVD site, posted the download price of her picture, and provided two alternate purchase points: one for those who could not afford the retail price (who could pay whatever they could afford, including nothing) and another for those desiring to pay more, simply to express their satisfaction for the production. Fewer than half paid the retail price, even fewer elected to pay nothing, and, to the producer's delight, some paid extra. She posted her production cost and regularly showed her income and the balance needed to break even. In less than a month, this producer recovered all her costs and was turning a profit. This is not the suggested model, but it demonstrates an open source approach to monetization.

The open source culture advances each audience member's freedom, combined with power of the multitude to act. Given this culture, what can producers, distributors, and global audiences accomplish that they have never done before? With Wikipedia, Firefox, and Craigslist as examples, the answer is "almost anything."

CHAPTER POSTSCRIPT

Technologies are providing producers with new marketing and distribution flexibilities and economies never before available. Further, both media convergence and open source operating and monetization structures will continue to open new audience demand for content, delivered in more diverse and satisfying methods. Understanding, anticipating, and acting on these opportunities will give producers striking advantages.

The consortium of the studios and the major international distributors that largely controls motion picture marketing and distribution is quickly adopting and consequently enabling new social-networking marketing methods, utilizing if not primarily driving the establishment of each motion picture's brand. The Internet and digital screening devices are rapidly dissolving current space, time, culture, currency, and language borders. Motion pictures will continue to be seen by more people, worldwide, with formidable use and economic advantages to producers, distributors, and audiences.

We have entered a new era in which we are able to watch anything, anywhere, at any time, on any device, and the audience has developed a sense of entitlement to that freedom. To succeed, producers must embrace and use the enabling tools that these new technologies provide. Traditional storytelling (i.e., scripts) will continue to be the cornerstone content success enabler and will be opened to new levels of interactivity, multi-platform marketing, and decentralization of creation and distribution.

CHAPTER 5
Ancillary Windows, Rights, and Products

This chapter presents the ancillary release windows, rights, and products for theatrically released motion pictures and pictures released directly into these ancillary windows; reviews their audiences, income, and license relationships; and details how producers may strategically plan, engage, and manage them.

THE EFFECT OF THEATRICALLY RELEASED MOTION PICTURES ON OTHER WINDOWS, RIGHTS, AND PRODUCTS

For a motion picture to warrant beginning its distribution in theaters, it must appear to meet its theatrical target audiences' expectations. Audiences expect these pictures to be substantive entertainment. Theatrical feature films should create an emotional fire in their audiences. This quality ought to be the "event" even in event motion pictures. Special effects–driven films may generate a respectable gross in the first or second film in which a new effect is used, but effects quickly lose an audience's respect if they are a picture's centerpiece.

Motion picture industry living legend Peter Guber made one of the finest expressions of this effect when he addressed independent producers during a session of the American Film Market:

> So is there a specific ingredient that's essential for [a picture's] success? My instinct, my curiosity, and my experience tell me that the key component is emotion. The story must have resonance and emotion. It must reside in the story…Watch your audience come out of a movie and see their state. Ask them to tell you about the film…When they tell you, or better yet show you, the impact it has on them, the emotion generated, then you better buckle your seat belt because you have a hit, even if the reviews aren't good. That doesn't mean a film can't be thoughtful, it means the emotion must carry the information, not the other way around. What you have to move are not boxes of popcorn, or subs on a cable system, but people's hearts and spirits.

DOI: 10.1016/B978-0-240-81463-6.00005-X

Audience reactions are the ultimate measure of a picture's entertainment power. Audiences look to theatrically released pictures to entertain and move them more than any other pictures made.

Theatrically released motion picture campaigns create an event aura that continues with these pictures through all distribution windows. If they deliver the emotion-packed entertainment they promise, audiences will view them again as these pictures pass through subsequent release windows.

AUDIENCE SIZES IN MAJOR WINDOWS

In Chapter 2, we reviewed how improbable it is in most major global territories for pictures to become profitable from their theatrical distribution alone. Each motion picture's brand-establishment media costs are simply way too high in most major territories for the picture to financially break even from only theatrical earnings. However, use of the Internet's social media platforms are already radically reducing media costs for some independent and even major pictures. For most pictures, the larger the theatrical audience and earnings, the greater the ancillary audiences and earnings.

Though the following audience statistics are for the United States, most leading international territories perform similarly, and many others are moving closer to U.S. ratios.

In the United States, there are approximately 115 million television households and a potential audience of 2.5 per household (anyone between the ages of 5 and 80 is considered a potential ticket buyer). This creates a total potential audience of approximately 300 million people for each picture's several distribution windows. Each picture's audience varies depending on the target audiences the picture appeals to; the dynamics of the film's campaign; and the heat of its media buy, promotion, and Internet viral and social media campaigns.

According to the National Association of Theater Owners (NATO), the average U.S. theatrical gross box office revenue among all pictures released in 2009 was approximately $18 million; the average gross box office per picture for major studio releases alone was closer to $31 million. Most pictures are considered successful if they attain a U.S. box office gross of $50 million, although each picture's box office success can only be measured in relation to its production and release costs. At the 2009 approximate average ticket price of $7.50, a picture with a U.S. theatrical gross of $50 million (almost three times greater than the average picture) will have played to a theatrical audience of only approximately 7 million people. Picture titles attaining such success become household names to most consumers, but only about 2 percent of the total potential U.S. audiences will have seen them during their theatrical play. As most pictures that theatrically gross $50 million or more (U.S.) will be seen by at least 50 percent of all U.S. audiences by the time they have completed their initial U.S. television syndication, their theatrical audiences may represent only 4 percent of their total audience reach. Whether measuring each picture by its audience or income, though the theatrical window is crucially important and substantially determines the audiences and incomes in subsequent ancillary release windows, the theatrical audiences and income are the lowest of all release windows.

During its home entertainment release, a picture that earned $50 million during its U.S. theatrical box office release should earn an additional $54 million (110 percent of gross box office) in DVD/Blu-ray sales, rental, streaming, and download income. This varies substantially depending on each picture's target audiences and genre. For instance, a picture with an audience dominated by kids ages 5 to 11 may have a U.S. DVD/Blu-ray gross closer to $125 million and reach a DVD/Bly-ray audience of about 20 million viewers, which is more than double the U.S. theatrical audience.

Per Adams Media Research, U.S. consumer spending on motion picture tickets in 2009 exceeded the retail *sales* of motion pictures on "packaged video" (buying physical copies of DVD and Blu-ray at retailers) for the first time since the mid-1990s, as the recession drove consumers to what they perceived as the best value for their dollar: going to the theater rather than renting the movie later.

In the U.S., approximately six months after its theatrical premiere, the picture is released on premium cable, and this picture that has become a household name still has not been seen by 85 percent of its potential audience. U.S. premium cable audience penetration in 2009 was 52 million homes. An ample premium cable allowance for a picture with a U.S. theatrical gross of $50 million will deliver another 30 million viewers. This increases the total U.S. audience reach to 58 million, still just over half its eventual total U.S. audience, leaving about 42 million new viewers who will see the picture during its network television premiere—an income window now realized by less than 10 percent of studio released pictures—which traditionally occurs about 30 months after the theatrical release. This is followed by cable television network and television syndication release. Though theatrically released motion pictures often win the dominant network audience share, the networks typically broadcast a picture only once, leaving a substantial audience for cable television network and television syndication.

In every distribution window there are also repeat viewers, which are not included in the previous total audience figures. These are especially important revenue-building audiences for network, cable, and syndicated television.

Many theatrically released motion pictures become important social references that are a must-see-early for their target audiences and a free television curiosity tune-in for their distant fringe audiences. Whether it is *Robin Hood, Toy Story 3, Grown Ups,* or *Avatar,* most of the 300 million potential U.S. audience members will eventually experience theatrically released motion pictures, even if they have this experience at home on their surround-sound, big-screen television where they must sit through ads or channel-surf during a few commercials. Theatrically released motion pictures are often powerful, culture-shifting audience attractions that uniquely sustain their value, substantially because of their entertainment power and their status as a major theatrical event.

ANCILLARY AUDIENCE CHARACTERISTICS

Each of the major four ancillary windows (home entertainment, premium cable, network television, and cable/syndicated television) has unique audience characteristics, which are defined more by their audiences' lifestyles and preferences than by their economics. Although audiences spend more of their entertainment time in their particular favorite distribution window, most consumers have purchased the equipment, are prepared, and want to experience each motion picture in the distribution windows they determine the motion picture warrants.

Consumers are passionate about making merchandise decisions, and motion pictures carry unique social importance. Pictures are exotic merchandise, universally known and talked about, and our opinions about them and their impact on us make them one of the most high-profile and socially significant consumer product categories.

Consuming motion pictures is all about emotions, and most people make up their minds about how they will view a picture by the time they have seen a picture's third commercial. Typically, emotions rule over financial and even review considerations. Choosing among a theater ticket ($8 in the United States), a DVD/Blu-ray purchase ($10 to $15 in the United States), a DVD/Blu-ray rental or stream ($2 to $3 in the United States), a monthly premium cable subscription ($5 in the United States), or free network/cable/syndicated television is rarely as important as wanting to see it now, or with a friend, or on a theater screen, or in its full uninterrupted length.

Some pictures are so compelling they override our viewing preferences and habits. Many people who never see a movie at a theater, or never buy/rent/stream/download a DVD/Blu-ray, or who never see a movie twice will do so with certain pictures. This is demonstrated by audience-motivating entertainment like *Titanic*, *The Lord of the Rings, Harry Potter,* any of the *Twilight* series, and *Finding Nemo*, all of which drew uncommonly high audiences in all distribution windows.

In addition to our emotional connections with pictures, capriciousness often sways a person's viewing choice. A consumer may just *feel* like seeing a picture at a theater, buying, renting, or streaming one, so the consumer goes online, goes to the local multiplex, or visits a retailer and seeks a title. If the movie the viewer wanted to see is not available, then he or she will most often buy a ticket, a copy, or stream/download/rent a picture anyway. It may even be a picture he or she has already relegated to a later ancillary window, but the viewer takes a chance.

Because they are aware of this phenomenon, producers and distributors often stage their release windows when school is out of session (the summer) or during holidays (especially Christmas and New Year for much of the world). These are the dominant seasons during which consumers seek more movie experiences, often making their picture selection while they are in the marketplace. This tendency is largely the motivation behind the industries' five- to six-month window structure, the holidays and summer being five to six months apart. Many of the strongest pictures are released in their two most critical distribution windows (theatrical and home entertainment) during the seasons when audiences are most aggressively seeking entertainment. U.S. audiences consume more entertainment, in more windows, than any other territory's audiences; but Western European and Asian audiences are quickly closing the gap.

Despite the increasing availability and audience acquisition of sophisticated home entertainment equipment, theater audiences have sustained a solid market position in most global markets. Theater ticket purchases are gradually declining; although the MPAA reported the 2009 total U.S. box office to be $10.6 billion, up from $9.6 billion in 2008, this increase is due to increase in ticket prices, especially for higher-priced 3D films. Actual attendance is about the same as the prior year. Theatrical audiences are strong, willing to spend extra for the big screen, big sound, and social experience motion picture theaters provide. During this same period, the entertainment consumption rate has increased proportionally higher in every major ancillary window, with audiences averaging over an annual 1 percent increase since the late 1990s.

Youth are the greatest consumers of motion pictures in all media. As a group, they attend the theater more often, stream/download/rent more videos, and watch more premium cable, network, and syndicated television. They are also easier to sell to because they view and listen to more advertisements and are less influenced by critical reviews—though they are highly influenced by peer/social network reviews—than older audiences as to what they will stream/rent/buy and watch.

Although in the late 1990s there was significantly male attendance dominance, MPAA statistics reveal that women now attend theaters more than men, with women accounting for 55 percent of ticket sales. Statistics are important indicators that are worthy of analysis by those who produce, distribute, and license motion pictures. However, statistics are easily misinterpreted. For instance, has the gap between men and women motion picture viewers closed because women have become more aggressive entertainment consumers or because more pictures are being produced and distributed that interest them? The consensus of the best industry analyzers supports the latter conclusion. Responding to the demand of women to view theatrically released motion pictures in all media, producers and studios are increasing their delivery to this powerful audience.

Regarding family movie viewing, there is a fairly even split among industry mavens, between those who believe families don't attend theaters more regularly because they spend less discretionary money than other audience categories and those who believe that there are simply fewer motion pictures that are targeted to couples with children at home.

Motion pictures such as *The Nightmare on Elm Street* and *The Sisterhood of the Traveling Pants* have almost exclusive single audience skews, whereas films like *Pirates of the Caribbean, Avatar,* and *Spider-Man* are made for multiple target audiences. All of these pictures were successful, and targeting for a specific audience often ensures a solid response; however, pictures with a strong appeal to multiple target audiences have higher potential income in all distribution windows and rights sales.

PRODUCERS RELY ON ANCILLARY EARNINGS

For U.S. and all major international territories, the theatrical release is unquestionably the most important distribution window through which each motion picture passes. This is almost exclusively so, because this is where audience perception of each picture's entertainment value is established. As discussed in previous chapters, producers rarely forecast any producer profits from the theatrical distribution of their pictures; however, producers should be keenly aware that though their largest audiences and substantially all their income will come from their pictures' ancillary windows, the size of these audiences and earnings will be determined by the pictures' performances during the theatrical release.

If the theatrical window is analyzed alone, neither the producer nor the distributor would release the picture. But when the ancillary windows are also considered, pictures often become sound business. For instance, if the $24 million in advertising and associated promotion and publicity for the picture sufficiently motivates the picture's audiences, then its first ancillary audience—the home entertainment audience—may even be larger than traditional ratios by drawing in theatrical audiences who did not get a chance to see the picture during its theatrical run.

You might wonder why more movies don't begin distribution with home entertainment, spending the $20 million in advertising there. This would be the logical choice, save for the "theatrical dimension" it would never be able to gain, no matter how much home entertainment release advertising is done. If the project is made for the small screen first, it will never shake its small-screen stigma. The only motion picture exceptions are children's audience animation sequels, which perform in a uniquely "toylike" manner for this particular audience.

THE FIRST ANCILLARY WINDOW: HOME ENTERTAINMENT DISTRIBUTION

Home entertainment includes DVD/Blu-ray, streaming, and download motion picture delivery for sale, rent, and single viewing. This window traditionally opens three to four months after a picture's theatrical premiere. Video-on-demand (VOD) is received via cable, satellite, Telco, and online operators. As DVD copy sales and rentals continue to decline, digital sales and Internet streaming/VOD have and are expected to continue to increase and grow by double digits annually.

When these pictures open in their home entertainment window, they still carry their theatrical marketing power and sometimes are still playing in theatrical situations (usually second-run theaters). Some smaller independent distributors (Magnolia, IFC Films) are releasing films day-and-date with theatrical and VOD. IFC Films now operates two VOD channels, one for films in limited theatrical release and one for films that have appeared only at film festivals and will never make it to a theater. Warner Bros.' Home Entertainment strategy is releasing nearly all of its films simultaneously on DVD and VOD. Warner has said the simultaneous release strategy boosts VOD sales without hurting disc sales. Other studios are keeping the window between DVD and VOD open. We are likely to continue technology transitions through which distribution windows and business models will shift, seeking to stabilize as distributors experiment with fresh models.

As indicated previously, most members of the potential audience (98 percent for an average picture) still have not seen this picture; having missed seeing the picture while it was in theaters, they are either waiting for its home entertainment release or for a later ancillary window.

Pictures are currently released into home entertainment simultaneously, in all their various forms. To differentiate and promote sell-through income, rental DVD/Blu-ray versions typically do not include the extra features available in their sell-through versions. Theatrically released pictures, three to six months after premiering in home entertainment, if justified, are released again at 40 percent to 60 percent less than their original sales/streaming/rental price.

For breakout pictures in the U.S. with box office earnings of at least $120 million, the home entertainment strategy is especially well crafted. The strongest of these titles have the capacity to earn five times or more than their film rental and typically are released at lower sell-through prices to optimize volume and overall profits.

Because home entertainment earnings in the U.S. represent the highest single income category for most pictures, every studio's home entertainment distribution department concisely configures a separate release strategy, including price variance for each picture, which keeps the studios, as well as those in their distribution chain, on their toes. The changes that will continue to be apparent to consumers is that venues and platforms will eventually saturate all viewing devices and transaction prices will continue to drop.

The producer's home entertainment distribution agreement with the studio is typically and appropriately linked with the picture's theatrical distribution agreement. Terms vary, but the traditional relationship pays the studio a 25 to 35 percent distribution fee and recoups the studio's direct distribution expenses, then the studio's loss-carry-forward from theatrical distribution, if there is any. A returns reserve is usually also held, and, finally, the balance goes to the producer.

THE SECOND ANCILLARY WINDOW: PREMIUM CABLE TELEVISION

Consumers eagerly embraced this release window, and it experienced aggressive growth in the United States during the early 1980s with HBO's bold advent. The premium cable window provides theatrical release and original motion pictures and series, through a television network, without commercials. Subscriber growth in mostly single-digit annual percentages in the United States is a significant earnings window in the major international markets and continues to be introduced in other territories.

Premium cable networks provide an important audience and earnings window, delivering a far less complicated arena for producers to work in. There is a short list of potential licensees in each major global territory. In the United States, these include HBO/Cinemax and their sister channels, Showtime/The Movie Channel and their sister networks, and Starz/Encore and their sister networks.

These networks are very competitive for pictures because of the stability and growth of their subscriber bases, which are determined by the popularity and quantity of the pictures they broadcast. These networks gain subscribers by delivering major theatrically released motion pictures and original series they develop in-house. There is no revenue sharing on this playing field. The license fees paid are the total income from this release category.

In this window, the exclusive premiere license is the greatest single income tier. The premiere license provides for a limited number of airings for a limited period of time. The fee is determined by each picture's theatrical release success. For pictures with unimpressive theatrical tickets sold, they may receive a license fee in the United States of five or six figures, if at all. For moderately and better performing pictures, they may engage U.S. license fees of seven or low eight figures. For licenses engaged before a picture's theatrical release, they should include a license fee escalator clause. This clause calls for the license fee to increase if the picture's gross box office earnings exceed a certain minimum (for instance, $40 million) and then increases it again for every additional gross box office increment attained (for instance, each $10 million), but not to exceed a total license amount (for instance, $20 million).

The nonexclusive premium cable license tier allows for a greater number of airings for a substantially reduced license fee and is most often included in the premiere license agreement. This tier continues until the free television network premiere occurs. Following the network premiere, the picture may still be licensed by premium cable networks, but for lesser amounts.

Consumer marketing in this window is accomplished by the licensee network, primarily through network promotional spots, crossover network advertising through cable systems, and print ads.

Larger producers who consistently deliver multiple pictures yearly engage and manage these licenses directly. The producer must know each picture's value to the network. Producers discover this as they research each picture during the preparation of the picture's first draft global sales breakdown. This is discussed in Chapter 1 and is reviewed in Chapter 14. Basically, this is the process of identifying recently released pictures with similar target audiences, campaign emotion signatures, and media buys. Then producers identify these pictures' audience and financial performance in the United States and other leading international territories. This information allows the producer to more accurately forecast earnings as well as confidently prepare and negotiate these and other rights.

To assist them in securing and managing these licenses, producers often use an independent producer sales representative, hire an employee experienced in ancillary sales management, or use an industry attorney well exercised in this process.

THE THIRD ANCILLARY WINDOW: NETWORK OR CABLE TELEVISION PREMIERE

Licensing network television is similar in most respects to licensing premium cable networks, although the marketplace is quite different. The economy, the networks' broadcast time allotment and content constraints, and their average 30-month window from theatrical premiere to network premiere make for very different chemistry.

The network premiere of motion pictures is one of the most important distribution windows for two reasons: The network premiere is the first opportunity for audiences to view the picture without cost, and, more important, it is the first opportunity for almost every person in that particular territory to watch the picture at the same time.

At a time when network executives are challenged more than ever to capture high audience shares for their respective network, theatrically released motion pictures consistently deliver dominant audience shares. In some respects, the time from a picture's theatrical release to its network premiere works to build its audience. Many viewers who have seen the picture before and enjoyed it will tune in again. Pictures that have been aired so heavily through the three prior windows pull especially massive audiences, both new and repeat, to their network premieres.

Though the approach to this license sale is similar to premium cable, there are a greater number of potential licensees in the market for television premieres. These primarily include NBC, ABC, CBS, Fox, and the CW broadcast networks, and the major cable television networks, including TNT, TBS, USA, Discovery, A&E, and Lifetime, in this expanding license arena. Unlike premium cable, this license typically calls for a single broadcast and a window length of 12 to 24 months.

Because each picture's forecasted audience share determines its value to the network, there is a broad range of potential license fees. Most pictures forecasted licenses uses 7.5 percent of gross box office. As with premium cable, larger producers license broadcast television directly. The preparation for this license is a natural part of the development and production process. Before earnest development, producers should have identified the most likely network license candidate and the value of the picture to this network, if it meets its box office forecast. By preparing thoroughly, producers can explore entering pretheatrical release licenses with a network that can accommodate a tie-in "film-about-the-film," which could provide programming to the network and additional marketing heat for the picture during its theatrical release. The network provides promotion and advertising for the picture principally via tune-in promotional spots over its own network.

Most producers use either in-house ancillary sales talent or a producer's representative to fulfill and maintain these relationships, and the producer's attorney typically is essential in this process. Occasionally producers license directly to network television, collapsing the premium cable window altogether, which substantially washes out earnings for premium cable premieres. Producers electing to do this are motivated by an aggressive network willing to pay license fees equal to the combined fees for traditional premium and free television premieres.

THE FOURTH ANCILLARY WINDOW: FREE TELEVISION SYNDICATION

Television syndication is the evergreen audience and earnings television window. Syndication opens 12 to 24 months following the network premiere and continues to license-renew as long as the picture has audience draw. For most pictures, this is several decades.

This window is sophisticated in every global territory because it deals with many television station groups and independent stations. It requires continual sales, license management, and physical delivery maintenance. This window usually is managed by a television syndication organization in each territory, which is compensated through distribution fees and expense recoupment. License fees vary widely in this window, depending substantially on the global territory, how long the picture has been in syndication, the number of airings allowed, the audience reach, the number of stations, and the length of the license.

OTHER ANCILLARY RIGHTS

Producers should examine, identify, plan, and exploit every rights area that may be applicable to each of their pictures. Some nontraditional ancillary rights actually may exceed the producer's share of the picture's traditional earnings areas. In the case of electronic games, this category alone can generate, in U.S. dollars, nine-figure incomes for some pictures. Their closely correlated marketing campaigns can also substantially increase income from traditional primary release windows.

Novelization

There are profits for producers from novelizing the picture's screenplay or re-releasing an existing novel on which the picture is based. Typically, the greatest benefits to these licenses are realized by having the novel released four to twelve weeks prior to a picture's theatrical premiere, with the picture's one-sheet (poster) on its front cover. Producers are best served if they negotiate first with publishers for the quantity of the run and retail placement, then for profit participation. Having the novel for sale at most mass merchandise, supermarket, drugstore, bookstore, and airport checkout lines just prior to a picture's theatrical premiere is valuable advertising.

The management of novelization rights begins during the motion picture literary rights negotiations. Some producers manage the whole universe of their pictures, including novelization rights, as part of their negotiations for their picture's story. No matter how strong the novel has been previously, the motion picture likely will become a household name and drive novel sales as no other influence can.

If producers fail to acquire their picture's novelization rights, then they should at least participate in the novelization (or re-release) publishing profits and should receive publisher commitments relative to the novel's distribution tie-in to the picture's theatrical marketing.

Each picture's novelization should be scheduled with the publisher before principal photography commences, allowing at least five months for the publishing process after the novel has been completed.

Product Placements

An effective unit production manager (UPM) will make notes of proprietary items needed for principal photography. These are critical, and depending on a picture's target audiences and how these products or locations may appear in the picture to the audiences, they typically are provided to the production company at no cost.

Motion pictures are the most powerful merchandise vehicles with which other branded merchandise can be associated. More than the typical reach and frequency methods used by advertising agencies to gauge audience exposure, motion pictures can elevate a brand by putting it in the highest sphere of consumer consideration. Even negative use of a product in a motion picture may have substantial positive marketing effects. For this reason, sophisticated brands increasingly participate within and in conjunction with motion picture marketing, which helps propel their products with greater power than they can achieve from alternative promotion and advertising processes.

There is no income amount that should motivate producers to infringe on the creative integrity of their pictures; however, the best brand relationships have deepened pictures' creativity, increased their profits, and pumped up their marketing campaigns. There are well over a hundred excellent examples of this effect, such as *Wall Street*. Motorola was one of the only players in the then sluggish cell phone business. It just was not launching at dynamic proportions. When audiences around the world watched Michael Douglas using his cell phone as an indispensable lifestyle device, an entire industry was dramatically launched. Delivery services, clothes, food products and services, cosmetics, hotels, destinations, automobiles, motorcycles, computers, cameras, and mobile devices are all major categorical players in this arena, and it is growing.

Producers should carefully review their pictures, even period productions, for opportunities to engage brand relationships that have mutual benefits. Product placement companies will make these arrangements for a modest fee.

The makers of most brands, from private aircraft to bottled water, are eager to establish these relationships. A call to most corporate headquarters will put a staffer in touch with the company's executive directing product placement. With a little research on prior pictures, the producer can use comparable brand relationships to assist in negotiations for his or her picture.

All of these relationships must be documented, and the producer's attorney should review all of the documents and address a variety of questions. For instance, who is the insurer in the event of loss or damage to the designer luggage or other product? If the contract language is "a minimum of five seconds of brand name recognition" and the picture delivers three seconds, what are the provisions for how this affects the relationship? Is the payment reduced, and if so, by how much and who determines the amount? Working through these details up front may seem like a bother at the time, but it will seem like a dream when problems arise.

Premium Tie-ins

Like product placement, premium tie-ins are related to consumer brands becoming more dominant through their association with a motion picture. A fast-food restaurant chain gives away or sells products related to the motion picture. The public can receive the products only through these outlets. They include character figures, special cups, hats, T-shirts, and toy tractors or spaceships. Whatever they are, these products must mobilize the picture's target audience to come to a brand outlet primarily through wide television or Internet advertising. As they do this, they also sell the picture.

How much are the producers paid to participate in such a promotion? Usually, not anything directly. They are paid indirectly, however—$5 million or $10 million or more—when they engage a television ad or Internet campaign that simultaneously markets the picture. Some of these relationships have more than doubled the amount of advertising that would have been spent launching the motion picture. In 2009, the strongest opening picture of all time was *Avatar*. With an amazing number of promotional tie-in partners, the picture grossed more than $77 million its opening weekend. Promotional partners with kid-, youth-, and family-target audiences received reciprocal benefits from the producers, whose picture grossed $749 million in the United States and more than $1.9 billion in international territories.

Sound Tracks and Music Publishing

The sound track for certain motion pictures can become a substantive income-producing product, as well as high-impact promotion element, especially with active Internet using target audiences. For some pictures, including *O Brother,*

Where Art Thou and *Moulin Rouge!*, these earnings can rival income from traditional motion picture categories. In India's Bollywood, music is the primary sales and marketing element for most pictures' theatrical releases. Music is released and heavily promoted before each picture's release. By the theatrical premiere, target audiences, high on the music, are easily motivated to see the movie. The powerful effect music has on each picture's marketing should inspire how producers do the following:

- Select the composer and needle drops (use of already released music in the picture).
- Create a separate sound track production and distribution plan.
- Set the sound track duplication and release schedule.
- Handle contract deal points with the composer and other related music contributors to enable the promotion and earnings plan.
- Negotiate the sound track distribution and music publishing license(s) to enable the promotion and earnings plan.

Sound tracks are especially powerful earning and marketing elements of a motion picture when one of the picture's primary target audiences is youth.

Again, the most reliable approach to managing these rights is researching recently released pictures with similar target audiences that have well-managed sound track marketing and licensing. Producers should study the successful deals that have been made, with whom they made them, and how these relationships were managed. From this information, the producer should create the model he or she is confident best serves the picture and will be served by it. After consulting with an attorney, the producer should then move forward with the marketing and licensing plan.

Sound track and music publishing normally is licensed to one or two highly skilled and experienced companies. The producer's task is to understand the earnings and promotion power of this license area, evaluate the license, negotiate and manage the license relationship, and set a schedule that allows these rights to be exploited to the maximum earnings and promotion benefit for the picture.

Toys and Merchandising

Even motion pictures that appear unlikely candidates for toys and merchandising should be carefully considered. Often, there are toys or other merchandise items for adult, youth, or children's audiences that seem like an amazing stretch. As producers become more involved in this licensing area, the wide appeal of movie merchandise for extensive global audiences becomes more apparent.

Each picture should be examined exclusively from the perspective of this license category. After a potential product list is made, research ought to be performed using films with comparable target audiences. After the producer prepares a basic merchandise plan, approaches should be made by, through, or after consulting with a producer's representative, who specializes in this licensing area. Though it is best to give them more time, these licensing companies will need 14 to 18 months prior to the motion picture's theatrical release to prepare their licensing arena.

Retail Game Sales and Electronic Games

For some pictures, this category of products may have a substantially larger earnings capacity than all other earnings areas combined. Companies specializing in the game industry understand the power motion pictures have in launching games of all kinds. This category includes paper-based role-playing games, board games, electronic handheld games, console games, computer games—all sold at retail—as well as arcade games, motion control rides, the ever-expanding massively multiplayer online games (MMOs), and games specifically for mobile phones—which may become the single largest game player base and the most market influential.

Producers and their representatives specializing in this licensing area should analyze a picture's game licensing prospects for the opportunity of representing the picture to this industry. It is best to have each picture reviewed by at least two competing representatives and have an attorney review the representative agreement, as well as the licenses.

In-Flight

One of the most important and valuable audiences for almost every theatrically released motion picture is made up of air travelers, whose numbers will continue to grow for the foreseeable future. Especially on flights longer than two hours, airlines have learned that time passes fastest for passengers while they sleep or view entertainment. Whether they are offered an individualized selection or a passenger group screening, a theatrically released motion picture is the first entertainment preference for most passengers. Airline licenses represent an important incremental income and crossover promotion that builds additional ancillary audiences and income.

There are only a handful of excellent and very competitive in-flight distribution companies. Each studio also has an exceptional in-flight department. Producers should meet with competing companies and, with the support of an attorney, enter a distribution relationship.

Planning for this version in development and preproduction allows the producer to budget for cover shots (additional material that will be uniquely required in one or more territories outside the core territory for which the picture was produced; for example, less violence for Europe, no profanity for in-flight screenings, and so on), postproduction time, and to deliver a print at the opening of this market, which is after a picture's premiere but during its theatrical release.

Hotels and Motels, Military, Schools, Indian Reservations, Ships at Sea, and Prison Systems

It is common for independent producers to use the studio that is theatrically distributing their picture to distribute these rights. Each of these rights areas is a small, five- and six-figure income category, but together they can earn a seven-figure income. Understanding that these ancillary earnings niches exist allows producers to plan for them, enter relationships with studio or ancillary rights distributors, exploit these rights, and expand the audience and earnings for their pictures.

PRODUCING COVER SHOTS NEEDED FOR ANCILLARY WINDOWS

During preproduction, every picture should be reviewed separately for cover shots that may be needed to optimally service its ancillary markets. These additional elements increase expenses during principal photography and post, but they save much more money and time later. They also increase the picture's ancillary value and allow the producer to deliver a seamless version of the picture to each participating licensee. Cover shots may be needed for unique international versions, airline audiences (in-flight versions), and the network version that must comply with network time and standards. Planning for and executing these during the production process can allow for elements that are most acceptable to the director, producers, and other creatives that otherwise may not be possible.

CHAPTER POSTSCRIPT

The most powerful producers are exceptional creative and business strategists. They are deeply involved in planning and managing the ancillary rights preparation and release of their pictures. They understand that these are the rights that deliver each picture's largest audiences and profits.

Producers are the parents and ultimate stewards of each picture. To optimally deliver to their far-reaching global audiences, they need to understand these audiences, the earnings dynamics of each picture, and its full array of ancillary products. They will also measure them, plan them, and enter into relationships with strategic partners to dynamically create, exploit, manage, and ensure the best possible performance within each of these release windows.

To succeed in each rights area, the producer must plan early, value each rights area separately, do the research to discover each picture's potential value for each right, consider the beneficial orchestration of these windows and rights with one another, use industry specialists, and always include an attorney in negotiations and documentation.

CHAPTER 6
Motion Picture Financing

This chapter reviews the primary processes of motion picture financing. It explores the many sources most-often participating in this funding process. Further, it demonstrates how balanced producers use their bank relationships to provide capital through financing collateral instruments that include production incentive programs, licenses, and presales, as well as to provide gap financing.

Beginning with the end in mind is a life practice of many successful people. Creating each picture's unique financing architecture from today's broad variety of financing sources, and using a bank as a financing participant with a strong entertainment department to aggregate capital and finance sophisticated collateral, provides producers with a solid plan to which they can subscribe contributors.

Establishing a fully functional independent production entity involves (1) understanding the formidable challenge of financing each unique project, (2) being committed to producing pictures that can fulfill their creative impact, and (3) structuring financing so that each picture fulfills the investment return objectives expected by financing partners. It also includes knowledge of and access to the many foundational production financing sources and having a relationship with a bank able to provide full entertainment services to exercise these relationships.

Although it is less expensive, motion picture *development* is usually more sophisticated, takes longer, and is a less predictable process than motion picture *production*. Consequently, motion picture development is typically financed separately from production financing. This process is reviewed in Chapters 11 and 12.

Perhaps not since the beginning of the motion picture industry has motion picture production and distribution financing been as challenging and sophisticated to secure. The restriction of bank credit facilities around the world has limited the typical capital resources for motion picture projects, from multinational entities to high-net-worth individuals. Fortunately for producers, the performance of the entertainment industry, despite the recent overall credit crunch, remains buoyant, in stark contrast to most other industries. Though

DOI: 10.1016/B978-0-240-81463-6.00006-1

some sectors within the industry have fallen (mostly because of the pervasive Internet, the ever-easier consumer consumption of digital media, and the emergence of streaming and downloading movies and television through iPods, iPads, iPhones, Xboxes, PS3s, and numerous other devices), the overall income from a motion picture has remained steady throughout the breath-catching constriction of major world economies.

As long as overall credit restrictions continue, the total amount of production and distribution capital released will be less. Consequently, to qualify for this capital, producers will have to be more thoroughly prepared if they hope to successfully pass through tighter scrutiny from all financing sources and programs. The primary qualifying elements will remain the same, including a quality, marketable script; a competent producer and director; and a reasonable cost compared with the picture's lowest income estimates.

Each year, an increasing number of motion pictures are entirely financed by private investors. Some of these pictures are from solid independent producers who smartly prepare their pictures' release, as well as their production. However, private financing is (1) often the most expensive cost of money, (2) provides no creative or marketplace check and balance for the producer, and (3) is often a sign of the producer's lack of business sophistication.

Fortunately, today's producers have a broader array of production financing sources available to them than ever before in motion picture history. In addition to private investors, these sources include the following:

- Production incentive programs (see Chapter 7).
- International territory presales—A presale is a contract whereby a distributor agrees to buy or license certain rights in a specific territory for the film for a preagreed amount, of which typically 10 percent to 20 percent is payable upon signing and the remainder upon delivery.
- Ancillary presale—Like an international presale, but with an ancillary participant such as television or electronic game.
- Gap financing—Estimates from a qualified/bankable international sales agent on the value of each international territory, not presold, is discounted by the bank (typically to 50 percent of its value) and is loaned to the producer (some banks have a maximum of $2.5 million or 20 percent of the budget, whichever is less).
- Talent profit/equity—Key talent compensation converted to picture profit or equity participation.
- Vendor profit/equity—Commonly referred to as "contra deal," in which key vendor compensation is converted to picture profit or equity participation.
- Corporate sponsorship or brand tie-ins.

The entertainment lender, the bank, remains the single most important participant when arranging structured financing for production. Regardless of the combination of financing sources, the bank is almost always used for each picture's depository, cash disbursements, and loans against the broad variety of collateral and guarantee contracts. It must be stressed that banks provide loans, not equity capital. They take "no risk," charge interest as well as fees for their services, and expect full repayment within a specific period of time. Every bank financing arrangement requires a completion bond. The two main U.S.-based bond companies are Film Finances and International Film Guarantors (IFG). Neither will bond a film whose budget is less than $2 million dollars. Completion bonds are necessary for producers to access presales, gap financing, or other bank collateral sources.

Balanced producers typically receive and exercise most, if not all, of their production financing through their bank. Knowing that a picture's production financing is managed through a bank's full-service entertainment department indicates that the picture's financing has likely been derived from sources that provide the greatest creative and marketplace benefits.

THE BANKING BUSINESS

Banks are often referred to as institutions. They are certainly governed by more agencies than most other businesses, but banking is a business. Banking decisions are profit motivated and predicated on sound business principles.

Every time the trade papers carry a story stating that a specific bank has supplied production funding to an independent producer, that bank's entertainment department receives calls from naive producers. They set up appointments and arrive, armed with a script and a budget, ready to pitch to the bank as if it were a studio or an equity financier. But banks make decisions with different criteria than those used by studios.

Knowing someone at a bank, like knowing someone at a studio, is helpful, but it has little effect on the bank's lending decisions. The similarity between banks and other financing sources is that to obtain their support, it is critical to understand their unique criteria for making decisions and the way in which they operate.

Every bank's inventory is its money. Banks principally earn profits by lending this money at interest. Like most businesses, banks sometimes have shortages or excesses of inventory. Though lending decisions have limited elasticity, when a bank's lending reserves are low, its lending decisions become more restrictive. When lending reserves are high, its lending decisions are more relaxed. It is an important question, and proper form, to ask your loan officer the status of the bank's current lending reserves.

Banks with strong entertainment divisions will always have the capacity to lend, even if they are not primarily lending their bank's funds. If the division is making "good" loans, then the loss ratio is low, the loans serviced according to terms are high, and overall profits are high. With a strong loan portfolio, these divisions can perform as the lead (syndicating) bank with other participating banks, as well as engage other outside lending-capital scenarios.

When choosing the lead bank that will manage your production borrowing, dealing with one that has a sound, experienced entertainment banking team is very important. Bank lending in most markets is very conservative, as banks typically lend only on premium collateral. When business losses in general are high, commercial and personal savings and average daily balances reduce, naturally restricting lending and tightening lending criteria, as was the condition in most global markets in 2008 and 2009. Under these conditions, it is all the more crucial for producers to follow the funding planning and documentation set forward in this chapter.

As of January 2010, there are only five major banks with entertainment departments active in motion picture financing: Comerica, Union, National Bank of California, Bank Leumi, and JP Morgan. All of these are active in the United States.

Each bank has loan amount preferences. There are small banks seeking loans in the six- to low-seven-figure amounts, midrange banks seeking loans in the seven- to low-eight-figure amounts, and more sophisticated banks seeking loans in the mid-eight- to low-nine-figure amounts. It is important to know a bank's loan size criteria.

BASIS OF LENDING DECISIONS

Banks make their lending decisions based on a combination of elements that must be represented clearly and completely in the loan package presented in this chapter. For loan approval, the loan package must demonstrate that the bank has collateral assurance for its return of principal, fees, and interest and that the loan can be reasonably debt-serviced through the production company's regular course of doing business.

The ultimate assurance of repayment to the bank loan is the strength of the producer's pledged collateral. Collateral alone, however, is not sufficient for loan approval. Banks do not want to lend if there is even a modest probability that they will be forced to call on collateral to recover a remaining amount due. Producers must demonstrate their ability to produce on budget and on schedule as assured by a completion bond, which is part of the loan package.

Each loan memorandum submitted to a bank should include, and its approval is substantially determined by, the following items.

Cover Letter

This letter provides a brief summary of all elements in the bank package. It describes the production company, a brief description of the motion picture being produced, the requested production loan amount, the expected interest rate, the production timing and loan term, and the plan and timing for loan processing. The collateral is summarized and may include (1) production incentive program(s) and their portion of production budget contribution;

(2) writer, director, or actor payment offset for profit participation or picture (special effects) equity ownership; (3) SFX (special effects) entity or other production participant payment offset for larger payment from profits, profit participation, or picture equity ownership; (4) presales and their entities, amounts, and terms; (5) major brand participants and their amounts and terms; (6) gap or other funding requested by the bank and these amounts and terms; and (7) private equity participants and their amounts and terms.

Table of Contents

The pages of the bank memorandum should be numbered, and there should be a table of contents following the cover letter, which will assist the bank in reviewing the completeness of the package and in easily locating information in the memorandum.

Application

The bank's loan application should be completely filled out, signed, and made a part of the memorandum. Some parts of the application may be referenced by "see page number" if the information is completely set forth in another section of the package.

Activity and Cash Flow Projections

Each of these projections should be month-to-month for the first year and cover at least six months beyond the anticipated active loan period. Each of these projections should have narrative "Notes to Projections," which describe important characteristics about the projections that are not self-evident. The cash flow projection must include the loan proceeds and debt servicing, calculated at the rate represented in the cover letter.

Distribution Windows and Liquidation Breakdown Summary

This section reveals the picture's planned distribution windows and a conservative version of the liquidation breakdown estimate, including the producer's share of gross receipts. This is especially important, in backup to international sales estimates, if the bank is requested to provide gap or related financing.

Collateral

In the initial loan memorandum, this is a descriptive list of the license agreements, international sales estimates, production incentives or equity, brand tie-in relationship(s), talent or vendor offset relationships, private equity relationships, and any other parties associated with providing collateral or direct investments in the project. Even if the bank is not managing these elements, it and the completion guarantor will need to verify that the production entity has access to the picture's complete production budget.

Conditional Documents

The bank will not take any substantial risk. If the license agreements used as collateral specify any conditions not satisfied by the completion bond, these further conditions must also be satisfied. The most common additional condition in international presale or domestic ancillary license agreements is that the picture must be released in a specific territory (for instance, the United States) by any one of a specified list of distributors. If this is a condition, a copy of the distribution agreement or a binding commitment letter acceptable to the bank must also be included in the loan package.

Collection Account Commitment

Often the bank will require that a collection account manager be secured to protect all parties. The collection account manager monitors the revenue collection process, the allocation and payment of revenue, and the exploitation of all potential revenue streams. There are two companies whose services we recommend: Freeway Entertainment and Fintage House. Both have been the collection account manager for hundreds of film and television productions, and 99 percent of the independent world works with them: Woody Allen, Relativity, Summit, Lionsgate, to name a few. The collection account manager computes revenue streams, provides the relevant parties with regular reports, and splits revenues between each party in accordance with the party's contractually agreed entitlement. Knowing the producer is using a collection account manager provides confidence and security to potential investors, talent, and other profit participants.

Completion Bond Commitment

In the initial loan memorandum, this may be in the form of a conditional commitment letter that will be replaced with the bond commitment in the final loan documentation.

Production Financing Worksheet

To simplify your understanding, a sample worksheet is included as part of this chapter. To further assist producers in preparing these forms, a worksheet is also included on the website. It includes a financing sources planning section to be filled initially with placeholders of intended participants and eventually with the actual sources and amounts. It also includes an assumption section to list the bank's interest, fees, and collateral discounts. The main body of the worksheet automatically calculates and fills in, revealing the individual collateral amounts, the respective discounts, bank fees and interest for each form of collateral, each category's subtotal, the net loan value applied to production cost, and the total gross loan and license proceeds. These are compared with the motion picture's total production budget (including the completion bond, 10 percent contingency, and reserve for residuals if required by applicable guilds or unions), and a "Yes" is revealed when the plan yields sufficient to produce the picture.

The Picture's Creative Information

This section should include the picture's title, a brief story synopsis, a list of the picture's primary talent and their referenced credits, the picture's production dates and locations, and the projected core-market theatrical release date.

Business History

The production company may be new, a resurrection of a prior company, a merger of companies, or something else. Regardless how short or long, the bank needs to know about the company's genesis and progress.

Organization Chart

This is a simple chart that reveals the members of the production company team by their responsibilities and relationships to one another. There is a production company chart in Chapter 11 and a worksheet on the book's website.

Principals' Biographies and Balance Sheets

The operators of the business are a key factor in a bank's loan review. The bank looks at the experience of those who manage the business and the experience and balance sheets of those who substantially own the business. The bank may not ask for owners to guarantee the loan, but the owners' financial profiles demonstrate their combined experience and success in asset management. This information typically is presented to the bank through brief, but specific, biographical summaries and in some instances a recent balance sheet of each individual.

Company Financials

These are the production company's current balance sheet and, if applicable, a recent profit-and-loss statement. These should be signed by either an in-house accountant or, preferably, reviewed and signed by the company's certified public accountant.

References

This is a list of references that importantly points to the way in which the producer does business and with whom. This list typically includes the completion guarantor (the firm and the producer's contact); the producer's law firm and primary attorney; the producer's current bank and officer; the producer's accounting firm and primary accountant; substantial trade references and contacts; and clients, studios, distributors, and licensees with whom the producer has dealt, along with each of their contacts.

THE LOAN APPROVAL PROCESS

Producers usually work with a bank loan officer. This officer helps the producer to do the following:

1. Identify the strongest international sales agent and international distribution companies.

2. Complete the loan package. The package must be complete before it can be reviewed.
3. Perform a preliminary review. If the loan package underperforms in the loan officer's evaluation, it is rejected. Common reasons for underperformance include insufficient or unstable collateral, an unstable management team, or an unpredictable repayment plan.
4. Present the package to the bank's loan committee. The bank loan committee then reviews the package and approves or declines the loan.
5. Deliver the decision to the producer.
6. Prepare and process the loan documentation.
7. Open the funding facility to the producer.

FINANCE PLAN: PRODUCTION FINANCING WORKSHEET

Starting at the development phase of every motion picture project, the producer should prepare a production financing worksheet that is the basis for the presale plan and the bank financing package. At the development phase, most if not all of it will be estimated. As the producer continues through the financing process, the estimated numbers will be replaced with actuals and the financing plan will be adjusted.

Throughout the motion picture's development process, global distributor relationships should begin early and intensify as development proceeds (see Chapters 1, 3, and 14). These relationships should include the core-territory distributor(s), typically providing at least theatrical and home entertainment (DVD or video-on-demand) distribution; distributors in the leading international markets; as well as prospective premium cable, network television, and other key ancillary licensees. As these relationships advance, it becomes increasingly apparent which of these licensees will enter presale contracts.

Before the producer ever approaches the major international territories for their initial presentation and consideration, the producer will have prepared the first cash flow analysis for the picture (a global gross and net earnings forecast for all major windows and ancillary earnings), compared the picture to at least five pictures with similar target audiences and campaign elements, and identified the international distributors with the greatest propensity to garner the highest gross for this picture in their particular territories.

If fewer than four distributors in the major international territories respond positively and agree to correlate with the producer as the picture continues its development (see the nine distribution relationship points listed in Chapter 3), then producers should either replace their commitments with alternative distributors or not commence development at that time. Though there is no license agreement during this time, all the participating distributors will be involved in the development and preproduction of the picture and will eventually place the picture on their release schedule. The producer will exclusively correspond with and give press, promotion, and advertising materials to these distributors.

However, the picture will likely not be licensed to these distributors until development is close to completion.

At the very first distributor contact, these distributors have little motivation to tie up the picture's rights. But as the picture becomes more substantive—with a shooting script, director, cast, locations, production design, film and printed promotion materials, representation at the major markets, firm release dates, and as novelization and other rights mature—each of these distributors becomes increasingly motivated to secure the picture's presale license for its territory.

The production financing worksheet becomes an extension of the cash flow analysis and places on paper the various financing scenarios, allowing the producer to select the most advantageous course. This financing strategy becomes the basis for the finance plan.

Examine the production financing worksheet in Figure 6.1. A copy of this worksheet is on the website. It is formula based, allowing producers to see the net results of their various contemplated financing scenarios. Producers who have not used such a tool before will find it exceptionally empowering. It allows the producer to apportion a picture's budget among several participants, considering crucial elements, including probabilities of securing them, cost of money, and timing.

[Core-Territory Distributor's Name]

Instructions:

Fill in the shaded areas. Cells will auto-fill.   Picture Budget: $12,000,000

Assumptions		Financing Participants	Percentage	Amount
Borrowing Period in Months	18	Production Incentive Programs	19%	$2,280,000
Presale, Brand Tie-In & LC Interest Rate (LIBOR + 4)	6.00%	International Territory Presales	25%	$3,000,000
Presale, Brand Tie-In & LC Bank Fee	2.00%	Ancillary Presale(s)	10%	$1,200,000
Presale Discount, International Territory Presale	30.00%	Talent Profit/Equity	10%	$1,200,000
Presale Discount, Ancillary Presale	0.00%	Vendor Profit/Equity	13%	$1,500,000
Production Incentive Discount	20.00%	Brand Tie-In	9%	$1,080,000
Production Incentive Interest Rate (LIBOR + 4)	6.00%	Bank Gap Unsold Territories	25%	$3,000,000
Pre-Sale Payment Advance	20.00%	Private Equity Participant(s)	20%	$2,400,000
Brand Tie-in Advance	10.00%	**Total Participatants**	**131%**	**$15,660,000**
Gap Lending Interest Rate (LIBOR plus 4)	6.00%			
Gap Discount	50.00%			
Gap Bank Fee	5.00%			

FIGURE 6.1
Production financing worksheet.

(Continued)

Description	Amount	Reference
Production Incentive Program(s)		
Production Incentives Total	$2,280,000	No. Carolina 19% Tax Credit
Production Incentive Discount	$456,000	Bank Collateral Value Reduction of Production Incentives
Net Bank Collateral Amount	$1,824,000	Net Loan Collateral Amount Before Interest Reserve
Production Incentive Lending Interest Rate	$164,160	Interest Reserved For Bank Loan (LIBOR + 4)
Net Loan Value Applied To Production Cost	$1,659,840	Net Amount applicable to production budget
International Territory Presales(s)		
Gross Presale Amount	$3,000,000	All International Territory Presales
Presale Payment Advance	$600,000	Amount Distributor Pays Producer At Signing
Gross Bank Collateral Amount	$2,400,000	Gross Collateral Value To Bank
Presale Discount	$720,000	Non-Prime Pre-Sale Distributors Bank Discount
Net Bank Collateral Amount	$1,680,000	Net Collateral Value To Bank
Presale Lending Interest Rate	$151,200	Interest Reserved For Bank Loan
Presale Bank Fee	$33,600	2% Fee to Bank
Net Loan Value Applied To Production Cost	$1,495,200	Net Amount applicable to production budget
Ancillary Presales(s)		
Gross Presale Amount	$1,200,000	All Ancillary Presales
Presale Payment Advance	$240,000	Amount Distributor Pays Producer At Signing
Gross License Bank Collateral Amount	$960,000	Gross Collateral Value To Bank
Presale Discount	$ –	Non-Prime Pre-Sale Vendors Bank Discount
Net Bank Collateral Amount	$960,000	Net Collateral Value To Bank
Presale Lending Interest Rate	$86,400	Interest Reserved For Bank Loan
Presale Bank Fee	$19,200	2% Fee to Bank
Net Loan Value Applied To Production Cost	$892,800	
Talent Profit/Equity		
Total Talent Offset Amount	$1,200,000	Total Talent Profit/Equity Amount
Net Value Applied To Production Cost	$1,200,000	Net Amount applicable to production budget
Vendor Profit/Equity		
Total Vendor Offset Amount	$1,500,000	Total Vendor Profit/Equity Amount
Net Value Applied To Production Cost	$1,500,000	Net Amount applicable to production budget

FIGURE 6.1—CONT'D

Brand Tie-In		
Gross Brand Tie-In Amount	$1,080,000	Total Brank Tie-In Amount
Brand Payment Advance	$108,000	Amount Distributor Pays Producer At Signing
Net Brand Tie-In Bank Collateral Amount	$972,000	Collateral Amount To Bank
Brand Tie-In Lending Interest Rate	$87,480	Interest Reserved For Bank Loan
Brand Tie-In Bank Fee	$19,440	2% Fee to Bank
Net Loan Value Applied To Production Cost	$865,080	Net Amount applicable to production budget
Gap Financing		
Sales Agent Unsold Territory Estimates	$3,000,000	Sales Agent Unsold Territory Estimates
Gap Discount	$1,500,000	Lending Value Bank Gives to Collateral
Net Gap Bank Collateral	$1,500,000	Bank Valuation/Risk Analysis Fee
Bank Gap Fee	$75,000	Bank Loan Secured by Unsold Territories
Gap Lending Interest Rate	$135,000	Gap Interest
Net Loan Value Applied To Production Cost	$1,290,000	Net Amount applicable to production budget
Private Equity		
Private Equity LC	$2,400,000	Letter of Credit (LC) Provided by Equity Financier's Bank
LC Lending Interest Rate	$216,000	Interest Reserve
Net Loan Value Applied To Production Cost	$2,184,000	Net Amount applicable to production budget
Production Resources		
Total Net Loan Value for Production	$8,386,920	Total Collateral, Less Discounts and Reserves
Cash Collected from License Advances	$948,000	License Advances Collected For Production Budget Use
Talent and Vendor Profit/Equity Budget Offsets	$2,700,000	Fully Applied To Their Respective Budget Allocations
Total Gross Production Loan and License Proceeds	$12,034,920	Applicable to Budget From Bank Loan, Advances and Budget Offsets
Actual Production Budget (including contingency & interest)	$12,000,000	Physical Production Budget of Picture
Collateral Sufficiency?	Yes	Is There Sufficient Loan Proceeds and License Advances?

FIGURE 6.1—CONT'D

At the bottom of the worksheet is the question-and-answer section, as final proof that the financing architecture configuration provides sufficient collateral and capital to fully fund the production. The cell shifts from "No" to "Yes" when there is sufficient collateral to produce the film.

When producers can represent that over half the funding is provided by multiple participants, most of them from the entertainment industry, they are much more likely to engage private equity investors. Approaching each picture's financing by this method spreads the responsibilities and risk in a manner that makes the investment much more accessible to each participant and often retains major creative and business decisions for the producer.

Using the worksheet enables producers to analyze and configure each picture's production funding plan, early in development, and to adjust the worksheet as the picture matures to the point of production, based on the final commitment of each participant. The final worksheet will reflect the actual elements provided and will be part of the bank loan memorandum submitted for approval. This sample worksheet is configured to deliver the picture's production budget of $12 million from the proceeds of the collateralized loan, cash advances, equity, and production cost offsets.

Let's now walk through each section of the production financing worksheet. All areas highlighted in gray need to be filled in, which will then automatically calculate and fill in all other amounts and percentages.

ASSUMPTIONS

The producer fills in this section as accurately as possible. Initially these will be estimates, but as financing coalesces, this section will be completed with actuals:

- The borrowing period of the loan should be listed in months. This will typically be 12 to 24 months.
- Presale, brand tie-in, and letter of credit (LC) interest rate is estimated at 6 percent (4 percent over LIBOR [London Interbank Offered Rate], here assuming LIBOR is 2 percent). This is a reasonable percentage spread with which to begin for fully secured collateral.
- Presale, brand tie-in, and letter of credit (LC) bank fees are estimated at 2 percent.
- Presale discount, international territory presale. If the distributor issuing the contract is not financially strong, the bank will discount the value of the contract anywhere from 10 percent to 50 percent. Our sample is a 30 percent discount. If the distributor is financially strong, no discount will be necessary, and then this line item would be at 0 percent.
- Presale discount, ancillary presale. If the distributor issuing the contract is not financially strong, the bank will discount the value of the contract anywhere from 10 percent to 50 percent. Our sample shows a 0 percent discount.

- The bank typically discounts production incentives 20 percent for U.S. programs, 10 percent for Canadian programs, and 10% to 25% for most international programs. In our example, because we are assuming a shoot in North Carolina, we are discounting by 20 percent. Also, please note under Description: Production Incentive Programs–Amount, we are only taking a total of 19 percent of the full 25 percent, because not every line item in the budget will be considered a North Carolina spend.
- The incentive programs lending rate is calculated at 6 percent (4 percent over LIBOR, here assuming LIBOR is 2 percent).
- The presale payment advance is usually required by the bank to be a minimum of 20 percent of the total amount for licensing of all rights in a specific territory.
- The brand tie-in advance is usually required by the bank to be a minimum of 10 percent of the total amount for licensing of those rights.
- The gap lending interest rate is calculated at 6 percent (4 percent over LIBOR, here assuming LIBOR is 2 percent).
- The gap discount is typically 50 percent and terms currently with some banks are a maximum $2.5 million or 20 percent of the budget, whichever is less.
- The gap bank fee is calculated at 5 percent, as this is much higher risk collateral.

FINANCING PARTICIPANTS

This section sets forth the eight primary production budget financing categories. First the producer enters the picture's production budget at the top. Then, in the financing participant section, each of the eight funding categories is engaged by entering an amount. This will automatically formulate a percentage of the budget entered at the top of the worksheet.

Production Incentive Programs (See Chapter 7: Production Incentives)

There are numerous program variations worldwide, most covering 10 percent to 30 percent of the budget. Regardless the plan, their rebate or tax credits comes after the picture is produced, allowing the final accounting to be done according to how much money verifiably was spent in the city, state, province, or country, this spending being the incentive source's motivation. Banks and private funds such as 120 db in the U.S. and Ingenious in the UK (see Chapter 7) are typically engaged to advance these incentives for the production budget.

International Territory Presales (Reviewed in Chapter 3)

Especially with the entity consolidations of the late 1990s, most participants financially strong enough to advance a presale are major distributors whose contract will be bank acceptable as collateral. If they are not rated high enough for your bank, the bank will either discount the value of the contract from

100 percent to as low as 50 percent or it may require a letter of credit from the distributor. In our sample, we are securing only presale contracts from "A" list distributors and no discount or letter of credit is required.

Ancillary Presales (Reviewed in Chapter 5)

These are rights presold, similar to international territory presales, and may be any of the participants reviewed in Chapter 5.

Talent and Vendor Profit and Equity Offsets

Typically, writers, directors, and star cast members are a part of each picture's major cost. Negotiating with one or more key talent to be chiefly paid alternatively with an increased amount based on the picture's projected profits (sometimes including picture equity) can potentially increase a talent's earnings and likely enhanced tax advantages while providing the picture with a significant amount of its budget. This allows talent to earn appreciably more income if the picture meets or exceeds its global projections.

Brand Tie-In (See Chapter 5)

For many brands, motion pictures represent their highest impact and most reasonably priced marketing expenditures and strategies, especially global brands. As pictures proceed through each successive release window to increasingly larger audiences, motion pictures become the ever more effective and price-efficient marketing tool. For producers, these brands can also increase a picture's creative integrity and cross-promote/market the picture. These negotiations typically need to conclude a year before a picture's theatrical release, but they have and continue to provide a picture's significant production or distribution funding.

Gap Financing

Gap financing is calculated based on the estimates received from a qualified/bankable international sales agent on the value of each international territory that was not presold. They are discounted by the bank up to 50 percent of the territories' aggregate value. This discounted amount is then lent to the producer as part of the production financing (typically capped at $2.5 million or 20 percent of the budget, whichever is less). Gap financing is a risky model, and banks that do lend on these international sales estimates are constantly assessing the credit worthiness of international sales agents and distributors worldwide. Typically a bank will only accept a handful of sales agents' estimates. Producers must approach the bank early to be sure they are working with an international sales agent acceptable to the bank.

Though the bank loan fee is high, the producer's advantages to gap financing are primarily that fewer presales are made, allowing these licensees to earn higher after-film-completion licenses, and the producer does not have to do the presale work for these territories. The bank will require two and many times three presales from the top 12 territories before doing gap financing. These sales enable the bank to more closely evaluate the estimates supplied by the international sales agent. The top 12 territories are the UK, Spain, Japan, France, Italy, Germany, Australia, Benelux, Scandinavia, South Africa, Canada, and the Untied States.

Private Equity

The private equity sources in this example use collateral (CDs, treasury bills, securities, and so on) rather than cash. This example uses $2.4 million in private equity secured by a letter of credit, which therefore requires the bank to charge both an interest rate and a fee. If, however, the equity is in the form of cash, neither of these charges will be required.

TYPES OF LOANS

If the production loan is in the form of a line of credit, the producer has access to the entire loan amount but is charged interest only on the loan amount actually drawn. With more than $500,000 in potential interest, even a 20 percent interest savings (which is very possible with prudent cash management) will save more than $100,000.

WHEN TO APPROACH THE BANK

Using bank production funding strengthens many aspects of producer operations. The bank relationship and its other related benefits should become integrated into and affect many aspects of the producer's business.

New producers should meet with their bank of choice before completing development of their film(s). Producers should be comfortable with their bank before there is a need for production borrowing. Initial meetings introduce the bank to the producer's business plan, establish the producer's development and production schedule, and clearly show the bank's essential participation in the overall process.

Producers should ask the loan officer for permission to use the bank and the officer as references to others relative to the producer's intention to use the bank as the production funding source for pictures. Most bank entertainment divisions are willing to allow producers to do this, as long as their representations are in keeping with the relationship. Using the bank as a reference to potential licensees and other sources in connection with the producer's finance plan lends substantial positioning strength, especially for producers introducing new production entities.

In addition to production financing and later operating capital funding, bank officers can be well used as business consultants and mentors, contributing excellent business expertise to the production company and opening the way for expanded business relationships.

PRIVATE EQUITY: THE BENEFITS OF A SOLID BUSINESS PLAN

Securing private equity partners as part of each picture's financing has become more essential than ever. The financing sources of recent years (Wall Street, German film funds) have been replaced by new sources such as Abu Dhabi, India, and Qatar. China, Singapore, and Russia appear to be the sources next in line to become regular film financing participants.

Equity partners expect a return of investment (ROI) of 100 percent and in many cases an additional kicker of between 10 percent and 25 percent, plus a percentage of the net profits. Typically, all talent profits are deducted only from the producer's share of profits.

To secure private equity partners, producers need to have a sophisticated and well-thought-out business plan with financial projections (sometimes referred to as a waterfall) that is tightly structured within an offering that is compliant with the securities laws of the areas in which it is offered (see Chapters 9 and 12). The business plan should include the following elements:

Executive Summary. One or two paragraphs that gives a concise overview of each of the following: the motion picture, the company, the management and advisor team, the goals of the company, the finance plan, the marketing plan, the distribution plan, the investment opportunity, and risk mitigation.

The Motion Picture. Give more detail about the genre; include a synopsis; explain the stages of development, production, and distribution; identify your target audience; and delineate your budget and how you intend to control costs. Explain the Finance Plan (how all the financing collateral will come together).

The Company. Explain the legal entity that has been or will be formed to produce the project. Include narrative bios on the managers/producers.

Marketing. Explain who your target and secondary audiences are; describe how you intend to engage them, even during development, preproduction, and production of the film (prerelease marketing), and explain any other methods you intend to use to develop and grow awareness of the film.

Securing Distribution. Without distribution, your investors have no opportunity to receive a return on their investment. Describe your clear and concise model and explain how you intend to implement it to offset the financial risks involved. An overview explaining the different media and ancillary markets, as well as a breakdown of fees and costs, is also recommended to be included in this section.

Investment Opportunity. Include detail about the financing sources that you will utilize and what you are offering the equity investors (i.e., rate of return and profit participation).

Risk Mitigation. Include an explanation of all the balanced-producer models this book advocates: some form of distribution in place before beginning production, bank loan for collateral agreements, bond company, production incentives, and collection account.

The Production Team. Attach résumés for all production talent on the film.

Advisory Team. Attach résumés for all advisory team members on the film, and explain how they will assist management.

Appendices. These should include, but are not limited to, a budget top sheet, picture comparables or greenlight analyses (see Chapter 14), a finance plan, financial projections, a production incentives program outline, talent attachment verification(s), letters of intent for distribution or agreements, and any other research information pertinent to the film.

To write a solid business plan, the producer must first develop a financial plan showing how the investors will receive a return on their investment based on buyers' estimates, presales, and a smart marketing plan.

The mantra of James Steele, CFO of Magnet Media Group, is that a minimum of 70 percent of your budget should be covered by the gross-take-value (gtv) of your international sales estimates. If it does not, then your film budget must be adjusted downward. Our term for this process is "reverse engineering into the budget."

CHAPTER POSTSCRIPT

The challenging financial markets have opened new production, distribution, and funding opportunities. Regardless of how we use the major eight funding participant categories presented in this chapter, our engagement of a solid bank entertainment department is vital to pulling all the funding elements together. Understanding how banks operate prepares producers to approach them with confidence and wonderful predictability.

Banks are powerful allies. In addition to production financing and operating capital, they can provide helpful international and domestic data (useful in many areas, including liquidation breakdowns, international evaluations, international currency, and global industry trends), as well as other information. Producers should engage their bank relationships early and keep them well exercised, as banks are vital strategic operating team participants.

CHAPTER 7
Production Incentives

Currently production incentives are a key component of the finance plan of almost every film made. This chapter concisely and clearly reviews the entire U.S. and most of the major international production incentive programs available as of May 2010. Go to book website for updates.

Although tax incentives, subsidies, and other forms of governmental support have become an increasingly important feature of both domestic and foreign film production, *uncertainty* related to a state's fiscal health, liquidity, or legislative prerogative can make it difficult to fully convert your incentive into cold, hard cash with which to produce the film. We recommend securing an insurance policy to protect this key investment. Aon/Albert G. Ruben offers an exclusive insurance solution that facilitates film finance by insuring against the following causes of loss:

- Bankruptcy and insolvency
- Legislative amendment (rules change during the game)
- Repudiation (refusal to acknowledge or pay)
- Protracted default (late pay, issuance of IOUs, warrants, and other illiquid instruments that won't timely repay your lender or investor)
- Additional accrued interest charges resulting from a declared and covered cause of loss

In addition to the risks associated with governmental prerogative and financial stability, coverage addresses the risks of:

- Loss or destruction of sets and locations, which prevents or precludes filming in the territory offering the incentive
- Cast or crew accident, sickness, or disability, which prevents or precludes filming in the territory offering the incentive

For more detailed information about this production incentive coverage, contact Aon in the U.S. at (818) 742-1400.

DOI: 10.1016/B978-0-240-81463-6.00007-3

ABOUT ENTERTAINMENT PARTNERS*

An employee-owned company, Entertainment Partners (EP) has been the leader in payroll and production services for the entertainment industry for more than 30 years. EP offers a full range of payroll solutions and services for film, television, commercials, music, residuals, and more. EP's Residuals department processes more residuals payments than any other company. The Vista accounting applications are the industry's most widely used production accounting solutions. EP's Virtual Production Office (VPO) is an Internet-based application for users anywhere to access a variety of production documents. EP's Petty Cash Card streamlines the petty cash process through debit card purchasing and online tracking/handling. Movie Magic Budgeting and Scheduling are the industry standard productivity software products, now with new feature sets and architecture. Casting/payroll for background actors is handled through EP's legendary Central Casting division. Finally, comprehensive expert advice and a host of valuable services are all part of the full suite of offerings in the area of Production/Tax Incentives.

PRODUCTION INCENTIVES

What Are Production Incentives? Where Are They Available?

Production incentives are offered as cash rebates, tax credits, or up-front/back-end production funding. In addition, numerous jurisdictions offer sales, use, excise, and gross receipts tax relief in the forms of deductions, credits, exemptions, and waivers. In the U.S. the federal government and most U.S. states offer production incentives for motion picture and television productions. A number of jurisdictions also offer incentives for commercial ad production, digital programming, postproduction, video game production, animation, and other production types. More than a dozen international jurisdictions offer production incentives open to producers from around the world.

Why Are They Granted?

Governments have long used incentives to foster economic growth, build infrastructure, and create jobs. Incentives are used to attract industries that are viewed as important to the local community. Production of filmed entertainment is especially amenable to incentives because it is highly mobile, environmentally "clean," capital and labor intensive, and effective in promoting tourism.

TYPES OF INCENTIVES

What Is a Production Rebate?

A cash *rebate* or *grant* is a sum of money paid to a *qualifying* production company based on the amount of qualifying expenditures or jobs created in the jurisdiction on a qualifying project. These funds do not require a tax return to be filed. They are often administered by the departments of Trade and Industry, Commerce, or Economic Development.

---

*This section is courtesy of and written by Entertainment Partners.

What Are the Different Types of Tax Credits?

Tax credits can be refundable or nonrefundable, and transferable or non-transferable.

Refundable tax credits. A *refundable tax credit* functions in the same way as a production rebate, but it is administered by the local taxing authority and claimed by filing a tax return. The production company must file a tax return regardless of whether it has any income or owes any tax in the jurisdiction. If the production company does owe tax, a refund will be granted for the excess of the credit over the amount of tax owed. In some cases, banks or other lenders can monetize refundable tax credits so that the production company can get the money earlier. Generally speaking, a cost is associated with an advance of the funds.

Transferable tax credits. A nonrefundable tax credit may be transferable or non-transferable. A *transferable tax credit* is one that may be sold or assigned to a local taxpayer. This transfer can be handled directly by the production company or indirectly through the use of brokers. Brokers will generally charge a commission. In addition, the production company will need to discount the credit from its face value to entice local taxpayers to purchase them. Jurisdictions vary in how they regulate these transfers. Some jurisdictions permit a single credit to be divided among multiple transferees. Others permit multiple transfers, allowing transferees to sell all or a part of the credit they purchased to another taxpayer. Note that tax credits may be recaptured by states after audit. Some states have recapture provisions with recourse to the buyer of a credit.

Nonrefundable, nontransferable tax credits. A *nonrefundable, nontransferable tax credit* can be used to offset a current tax liability of the production company. The excess can generally be carried forward and used to reduce taxes in subsequent years. Each jurisdiction sets forth the period of time within which the tax credit can be carried forward.

What Is Up-Front or Back-End Funding?

These funds are made available to qualifying productions from local taxpayers in exchange for advantageous tax treatment from the local jurisdiction.

International Production Incentives

This guide summarizes only those international incentives designed to attract U.S. and other foreign productions. We do not address incentives around the world designed for local content production, although they may be accessible to U.S. and other foreign producers. Some of those incentives may require that copyright be held locally, or that local distribution rights be held locally. This guide summarizes only those international incentives that have no such requirement.

ELIGIBILITY CRITERIA
What Is an Eligible Production Company?

Each jurisdiction defines which type of business entity is eligible to apply for and claim its production incentives. Many jurisdictions require that the company be exclusively engaged in the business of film production. Some jurisdictions specify the legal structure and/or residence required for eligible production companies.

What Is an Eligible Project?

Each jurisdiction defines the types of projects eligible for the incentive benefits. In some jurisdictions, television projects are excluded. In other jurisdictions, the scope of eligible projects is very broad, including film, TV, video, digital programming, interactive games, commercial advertisements, animation, and so on. Some pilots and treatments qualify. There are frequently exclusions for "adult programming," news, weather, sports events, infomercials, reality shows, and the like. In addition, many jurisdictions require that the project be intended for commercial exhibition and/or that a distribution deal be in place.

What Is a Qualifying Project?

Most jurisdictions have a minimum spend test; some have a minimum number of local shooting days/stage days, resident employee requirement, or some other test so that the project will satisfy the jurisdiction's goals in building its local industry, revenue base, employment, and so on.

What Is a Qualifying Expenditure?

Each jurisdiction defines the goods and services that constitute qualifying expenditures for purposes of calculating the incentive benefit. In most jurisdictions, local goods and services directly used in the production are included in the benefit-calculation base. Some jurisdictions allow expenditures incurred in other jurisdictions, but used for local production, to qualify. In some cases, both pre-production and postproduction will be included. In most cases, marketing and distribution expenses will be excluded. Entertainment Partners' handling fees and workers' compensation insurance fees are qualified expenditures in many jurisdictions.

BENEFIT LIMITS

Many jurisdictions have an annual cap on the amount to be awarded under the incentive program. Others have a cap on the amount that can be awarded to a specific project. For TV, there may be episode caps and series caps. Many jurisdictions also have qualifying expenditure caps on salaries. For some jurisdictions, salaries paid to highly compensated individuals, usually $1,000,000 or more, are excluded from the benefit calculation.

KEY ISSUES TO CONSIDER

Funding

For jurisdictions with annual funding caps, it is important to know the fund balance and amount appropriated to date. Find out what is necessary to be certain that the amount needed by your project will be committed to it. Determine which jurisdictions with funding caps allocate funds to productions either on a first-come, first-served basis or on a discretionary basis. Some jurisdictions carry over unused incentive funds to the following year, and some jurisdictions do not carry over any unused funds.

Employment Issues

Are the cast and crew subject to tax in the jurisdiction where the filming occurs? If so, what steps must be taken to ensure compliance? If any members of the cast or crew have established personal service or loan-out corporations through which their services are provided, is the corporation required to register to do business in the local jurisdiction? Are payments to the corporation subject to tax and/or withholding in the local jurisdiction to qualify for the incentive benefits? Is the corporation subject to tax at the entity level in addition to the tax imposed on the talent?

Residency Requirements

Is there a test for qualified residents? When is the test applied (e.g., date of payment, date of services, date of claim, and so on)? How is it proven? Can a local company be used to qualify goods and services that are unavailable or do not originate within the jurisdiction as eligible spend? If so, what requirements must be met?

Confidential Financial Information

If confidential financial information is required as part of the application and/or certification process(es), how can it be protected from public disclosure?

End Credits

Does the jurisdiction require an acknowledgement of support as a condition to receipt of the benefit? If so, what are the requirements?

Local Advice

Local film offices are set up to enhance local production. Contact with the local film office will enable you to find locations, coordinate crews, and access local goods and services. Find out which local auditing and legal services will be needed.

Sunset Dates

Many production incentive statutes are limited in duration. The statute will have a termination date or "sunset date" after which the benefits are no longer available. Will your project be qualified before the incentive expires?

Qualifying Production Expenditures Matrix

This matrix provides a general listing of qualifying production expenditures—specifically purchases and rentals of tangible production equipment and supplies for U.S. jurisdictions. These expenditures are broken down into in-state vendors (as defined by local law) and out-of-state vendors.

The matrix also lists U.S. jurisdictions that qualify fringes (e.g., pension, health, welfare, vacation, and holiday) and taxes (e.g., FICA, FUTA, SUI, and Medicare). However, the matrix does not address all production-related costs, such as services, financing costs, and insurance premiums. Jurisdictions may qualify certain fringes (e.g., taxable per diems versus nontaxable per diems) and certain taxes, but the matrix does not provide a detailed listing of all qualified fringes and taxes, if applicable.

Some jurisdictions require qualified expenditures to be subject to taxes (e.g., sales, gross receipts, income, and excise taxes) for these expenditures to qualify. The matrix does not address each jurisdiction's taxation requirements.

Most jurisdictions do not qualify marketing, advertising, and development expenditures. Note that some jurisdictions provide a detailed list of qualifying expenditures, as noted on the matrix. In addition, certain jurisdictions may qualify out-of-state vendors on a case-by-case basis, even if the matrix indicates "No." Please consult with the local Film Commission to confirm qualifying vendors.

The matrix should be used as a starting point for your production incentives research on qualifying production expenditures. Please contact your legal or tax advisors to confirm how a particular incentive will apply to your project.

| State | Equipment/supplies** | | Fringes paid for qualified payroll | Taxes paid for qualified payroll |
	In-state vendors	Out-of-state vendors		
Alabama	Yes	No	Yes	Yes[2]
Alaska	Yes	No	Yes	Yes[2]
Arizona	Yes	No[6]	Yes	Yes
Arkansas	Yes	No	Yes	No
California[1]	Yes	Yes[1]	Yes[1]	No
Colorado	Yes	No	Yes	Yes
Connecticut[1]	Yes	No	Yes[1]	Yes[1]

State	Equipment/supplies**		Fringes paid for qualified payroll	Taxes paid for qualified payroll
	In-state vendors	Out-of-state vendors		
Delaware	N/A	N/A	N/A	N/A
District of Columbia	Yes	No	No	Yes
Florida[1]	Yes	No	Yes[1]	Yes[1]
Georgia	Yes	No[6]	Yes	Yes
Hawaii[1]	Yes	No[6]	Yes[1]	Yes[1]
Idaho	Yes	No[6]	Yes	No
Illinois[1]	Yes	No	Yes[1]	Yes[1]
Indiana	Yes	No	Yes	Yes
Iowa	N/A	N/A	N/A	N/A
Kansas	N/A	N/A	N/A	N/A
Kentucky	Yes	No	Yes	No
Louisiana	Yes	No[6]	Yes[7]	Yes[8]
Maine	No	No	No	No
Maryland[1]	Yes	Yes	Yes[1]	Yes[1]
Massachusetts	Yes	Yes	Yes	Yes
Michigan[1]	Yes	No[6]	Yes	Yes
Minnesota	Yes	No[6]	Yes	Yes
Mississippi	Yes	No[6]	Yes[6]	No
Missouri	Yes	No	Yes	No
Montana	Yes	No	Yes	No
Nebraska	N/A	N/A	N/A	N/A
Nevada	N/A	N/A	N/A	N/A
New Hampshire	N/A	N/A	N/A	N/A
New Jersey	Yes	Yes	Yes	Yes
New Mexico	Yes	No	Yes	No
New York[1]	Yes	Yes	Yes[1]	Yes[1]
New York City[1]	Yes	Yes	Yes[1]	Yes[1]
North Carolina	Yes	No[6]	Yes	No
North Dakota	N/A	N/A	N/A	N/A

(Continued)

| State | Equipment/supplies** | | Fringes paid for qualified payroll | Taxes paid for qualified payroll |
	In-state vendors	Out-of-state vendors		
Ohio	Yes	No	Yes	No[6]
Oklahoma	Yes	No[6]	Yes	Yes
Oregon	Yes	No	Yes[3]	No
Pennsylvania	Yes	No[6]	Yes	Yes
Rhode Island	Yes	No	Yes	Yes
South Carolina[1]	Yes	No[6]	No[4]	No
South Dakota	N/A	N/A	N/A	N/A
Tennessee[1]	Yes	No[6]	Yes[1]	Yes[1]
Texas	Yes	No	Yes	Yes
Utah	Yes	No	Yes	Yes[2]
Vermont	N/A	N/A	N/A	N/A
Virginia	Yes	Yes	Yes	No
Washington	Yes	No	Yes	Yes
West Virginia	Yes	No[6]	Yes	Yes
Wisconsin	Yes	Yes	Yes[5]	Yes
Wyoming	Yes	No	Yes	No
Puerto Rico	Yes	No[6]	Yes	Yes[2]

[1] See qualified expenditures listing for more details (contact local Film Office).
[2] Local taxes qualify.
[3] Fringes for payroll employees are rebatable under the 10% wage rebate only.
[4] Only vacation and holiday qualify.
[5] Excludes employer contributions.
[6] Confirm with local Film Office.
[7] Only taxable fringes, sourced or apportioned to the state, qualify.
[8] State or local taxes do not qualify.

Qualifying Compensation Expenditures Matrix

This matrix provides a general listing of qualifying compensation for U.S. jurisdictions. Compensation categories include above-the-line payroll (e.g., cast, directors, and producers) and below-the-line payroll (e.g., crew). Each of these categories contains information for both resident (as defined by local law) and nonresident payrolls. The matrix does not address compensation and project caps. (Please refer to the "Compensation and Project Caps" section for each jurisdiction.)

The matrix does not differentiate between compensation paid directly to an employee and payments through a personal service corporation or a loan-out company. Many jurisdictions require compensation to be subject to federal or state income taxes and/or withholding taxes for these expenditures to qualify. The matrix does not address each jurisdiction's taxation requirements.

Most jurisdictions do not qualify compensation for marketing, advertising, and development expenditures. Some jurisdictions have a listing of qualifying expenditures available that will provide more detail than what is listed on the matrix.

The matrix should be used as a starting point for your production incentives research to determine qualifying compensation expenditures. Please contact your legal or tax advisors to confirm how a particular incentive will apply to your project.

State	Above-the-line**		Below-the-line**	
	Residents	Nonresidents	Residents	Nonresidents
Alabama	Yes	Yes	Yes	Yes
Alaska	Yes	Yes	Yes	Yes
Arizona	Yes	No	Yes	No
Arkansas	Yes	No	Yes	No
California	No	No	Yes	Yes
Colorado	Yes	No	Yes	No
Connecticut	Yes[1]	Yes[1]	Yes[1]	Yes[1]
Delaware	N/A	N/A	N/A	N/A
District of Columbia	Yes	No	Yes	No
Florida	Yes	No	Yes	No
Georgia	Yes	Yes	Yes	Yes
Hawaii	Yes[1]	Yes[1]	Yes[1]	Yes[1]
Idaho	No	No	Yes	Yes
Illinois	Yes	No	Yes	No
Indiana	Yes	No	Yes	No
Iowa	N/A	N/A	N/A	N/A
Kansas	N/A	N/A	N/A	N/A
Kentucky	Yes	Yes	Yes	Yes

State	Above-the-line**		Below-the-line**	
	Residents	Nonresidents	Residents	Nonresidents
Louisiana	Yes	Yes	Yes	Yes
Maine	Yes	Yes	Yes	Yes
Maryland	Yes	Yes	Yes	Yes
Massachusetts	Yes[1]	Yes[1]	Yes[1]	Yes[1]
Michigan	Yes[1,2]	Yes[1,2]	Yes[1,2]	Yes[1,2]
Minnesota	Yes	No	Yes	No
Mississippi	Yes[2]	Yes[2]	Yes[2]	Yes[2]
Missouri	Yes[2]	Yes[2]	Yes[2]	Yes[2]
Montana	Yes	No	Yes	No
Nebraska	N/A	N/A	N/A	N/A
Nevada	N/A	N/A	N/A	N/A
New Hampshire	N/A	N/A	N/A	N/A
New Jersey	Yes[1]	Yes[1]	Yes[1]	Yes[1]
New Mexico	Yes	Yes[1,3]	Yes	No
New York	No	No	Yes	Yes
New York City	No	No	Yes	Yes
North Carolina	Yes[1]	Yes[1]	Yes[1]	Yes[1]
North Dakota	N/A	N/A	N/A	N/A
Ohio	Yes	Yes	Yes	Yes
Oklahoma	Yes[1]	Yes[1]	Yes	No
Oregon	Yes[1]	Yes[1,2]	Yes[1]	Yes[1,2]
Pennsylvania	Yes[1]	Yes[1,2]	Yes[1]	Yes[1,2]
Rhode Island	Yes	Yes	Yes	Yes
South Carolina	Yes[1]	Yes[1]	Yes[1]	Yes[1]
South Dakota	N/A	N/A	N/A	N/A
Tennessee	Yes	No	Yes	No
Texas	Yes	No	Yes	No
Utah	Yes	No	Yes	No
Vermont	N/A	N/A	N/A	N/A
Virginia	No	No	Yes	No
Washington	Yes	No	Yes	No
West Virginia	Yes	Yes[1,2,4]	Yes	No[2,4]

State	Above-the-line**		Below-the-line**	
	Residents	Nonresidents	Residents	Nonresidents
Wisconsin	Yes	No	Yes	No
Wyoming	Yes	No	Yes	No
Puerto Rico	Yes	No	Yes	No

1 See Loan-Out Company Considerations within the state incentives overview.
2 Withholding requirements must be met for payments to qualify.
3 For performing artists only.
4 Non-residents only qualify if they are paid through a locally-based business.
**These materials have been prepared by Entertainment Partners for informational purposes only and should not be construed as tax advice or relied on for specific projects. The materials were updated as of May 26, 2010. Though every effort has been made to remain current, laws and incentives change and therefore this information may have been revised. Please contact legal and tax advisors to confirm any laws or the effect of incentives on your project. For updates and more information, please visit: www.epincentivesolutions.com.

Nontraditional Programming

This matrix provides a general overview of the types of nontraditional programming eligible for the production incentives summarized for the U.S. jurisdictions. Nontraditional programming categories covered in the matrix include talk shows, reality shows, game shows, documentaries, news, webisodes, animation, commercials, industrials, music videos, interactive media/video games, and sporting events.

Some jurisdictions require wide or national distribution/syndication to qualify some or all programming categories. The matrix does not address specific distribution/syndication requirements for any nontraditional programming. The matrix does not address minimum spend or criteria required for any nontraditional programming category. (Please refer to the "Project Criteria" section for each jurisdiction. Note however that the "Project Criteria" section may not include information for each nontraditional programming category, so please review the applicable law for specific requirements).

Most incentive statutes address film, television, and video projects but do not specifically address each of these 12 types of programming. Many statutes address some but not all of these categories of programming, while other statutes are very general. Finally, some states have specific incentive statutes for specific types of nontraditional programming (e.g., commercials or animation).

In order to assist our clients in evaluating the best location for their particular project, we have compiled information from the underlying statutes, regulations, rules, and guidelines, including the published "policies" or guidance on the respective film office websites. The information obtained from these sources is noted. To further assist our clients, we have corresponded with each of the film offices to supplement the information found in the statutes, and so on.

The matrix should be used as a starting point for your production incentives research to determine eligibility of specific projects. Note that the project criteria may vary for different types of programming. Please contact your legal or tax advisors to confirm how a particular incentive will apply to your project.

U.S. DOMESTIC
U.S. Federal*

Type of Incentive: Immediate deduction

Benefit (if eligibility requirements are met): 100 percent of the production cost (for the first $15,000,000 of qualified expense)

Compensation and Project Caps/Funding per Year: Deduction applies to the first $15,000,000 of production costs ($20,000,000 if incurred in designated low-income areas)

Project Criteria: ≥ 75 percent of total "compensation" (does not include participations and residuals) must be for services performed in the United States

Sunset/Review: December 31, 2009

Expired at the end of 2009. A retroactive extension will be proposed in the new extenders legislation, expected to be addressed after the August 2010 recess.

INTERNATIONAL
Australia Federal

Type of Incentive: Location and Visual (PDV) offsets and Producer offset (for "qualifying Australian film")

Benefit (if eligibility requirements are met): 15 percent of qualifying local spend (QAPE), including post/digital/VFX work for Location and Visual offsets; 40 percent for qualifying feature films and 20 percent for qualifying television productions/documentaries for Producer offset

Compensation and Project Caps/Funding per Year: No caps

Project Criteria: For Location offset, if QAPE = A$15,000,000 but <A$50,000,000, it must be ≥ 70 percent of total spend; if QAPE ≥ A$50,000,000, no percentage test; TV series must average ≥ A$1,000,000 per hour; for PDV offset, minimum qualifying PDV spend = A$5,000,000; for Producer offset minimum spend = $1,000,000 for feature films, TV series and telemovies (lower spend test for documentaries and short form animation) and production must pass "Australianness test" (subjective), official co-productions automatically qualify

Eligible Entities: Australian resident company or nonresident with a PE and Australian Business Number (ABN)

Sunset/Review: None

---

*The House passed an extenders bill in 2009, including IRC section 181. Due to timeg constraints, the Senate is expected to pass this year, on a retroactive basis.

New South Wales (NSW)

Type of Incentive: Cash rebate

Benefit (if eligibility requirements are met): The level of assistance offered is determined on a case-by-case basis, based on the local economic impact

Compensation and Project Caps/Funding per Year: No caps

Project Criteria: "Footloose" feature films, telemovies, animation, mini-series, TV series, and unaccompanied post production projects are eligible, with a minimum spend of A$5,000,000 in NSW for production, or A$3,000,000 in NSW for postproduction costs

Eligible Entities: Australian resident company or nonresident with a PE and Australian Business Number

Sunset/Review: None

Queensland

Type of Incentive: Cash rebate

Benefit (if eligibility requirements are met): 12.5 percent of qualifying local labor; A$25,000 per department head and state payroll tax rebate (4.75 percent)

Compensation and Project Caps/Funding per Year: Compensation cap of A$2,500 per week per employee; project caps for drama of A$200,000–A$850,000 based on qualifying local spend, and for nondrama of A$100,000–A$300,000; maximum A$50,000 for two heads of department; subject to sufficient funding being available

Project Criteria: Minimum qualifying local spend of A$5,000,000 for labor credit; A$3,500,000 for one department head, A$5,000,000 for two department heads; must be employed ≥ 10 weeks and hire ≥ four local crew; minimum qualifying local spend of A$3,500,000 for payroll tax rebate; bundling allowed

Eligible Entities: The production company or production services company must have an Australian Business Number (ABN) and be registered for the Goods and Services Tax (GST)

Sunset/Review: None; the State Payroll Tax Rebate is subject to review under the regulations of the Office of State Revenue

South Australia

Type of Incentive: Payroll tax exemption

Benefit (if eligibility requirements are met): Up-front exemption of payroll taxes

Compensation and Project Caps/Funding per Year: None

Project Criteria: Film produced wholly or substantially within the state; production employs South Australian residents; and production of the film will result in economic benefits to the state

Eligible Entities: Australian resident company or nonresident with a PE and ABN

Sunset/Review: None

Victoria

Type of Incentive: Grant

Benefit (if eligibility requirements are met): The Production Investment Attraction Fund (PIAF) Committee evaluates applications for both grants to increase local production, employment, and infrastructure; the Regional Location Assistance Fund (RLAF) is paid in two stages, with 75 percent after commencement of principal photography

Compensation and Project Caps/Funding per Year: A$100,000 project cap for RLAF grants

Project Criteria: "Footloose" projects eligible for alternative locations; ≥ 70 percent of the total production budget will be local spend or ≥ A$3,500,000 local spend; if postproduction project, ≥ three Victoria postproduction services must be utilized; production budget must be secured; the RLAF grant requires ≥ five days in regional Victoria locations during principal photography

Eligible Entities: Australian resident company or nonresident with a PE and Australian Business Number

Sunset/Review: None

The following information on production incentives in Canada and its provinces has been provided by Canada Film Capital. Since Canada's introduction of Production Services Tax Credits in 1997, Canada Film Capital has been the leading provider of tax credit administration and financing services to the United States and other foreign producers. Find out more at www.canadafilmcapital.com.

Canada Federal

Type of Incentive: Refundable tax credit

Benefit (if eligibility requirements are met): 16 percent of qualifying Canadian labor expenditures, net of assistance (which includes provincial credits)

Compensation and Project Caps/Funding per Year: No caps

Project Criteria: Costs must be > C$1,000,000 on worldwide basis within 24 months after start of principal photography for feature film or video; > C$100,000 per episode for series or pilot < 30 minutes; and > C$200,000 per episode for series or pilot ≥ 30 minutes

Eligible Entities: An "eligible production corporation" must have a permanent establishment in Canada whose primary activity is the production of films or videos or the provision of film or video production services *and* must own the copyright throughout production in Canada or must contract directly with the copyright owner; private broadcasting/cable subsidiaries are eligible

Sunset/Review: None

Alberta

Type of Incentive: Cash grant

Benefit (if eligibility requirements are met): 20 percent to 29 percent of qualifying Alberta (AB) spend (goods and services); there are three "streams" of AB ownership, which determine the amount of the benefit available: Stream I: Majority AB-Owned Productions = 27 percent to 29 percent; Stream II: Equal or Minority AB Ownership = 25 percent to 27 percent; Stream III: No AB Ownership (foreign ownership is permissible) = 20 percent to 22 percent; bonuses: each stream can earn an additional 1 percent to 2 percent of production expenses by employing additional Albertans in key creative positions

Compensation and Project Caps/Funding per Year: Cap per project = C$5,000,000; no annual funding cap

Project Criteria: The production must be supported by a broadcast license of FMV (fair market value) or a distribution agreement and be shown within two years of completion; must be an eligible genre; minimum local spend of > C$25,000; production must provide evidence of 65 percent confirmed financing for projects > C$1 million, and 45 percent confirmed financing for projects < C$1,000,000; the projected grant may be included as part of the confirmed financing; must also provide either (1) audited financial statements for productions > C$500,000, (2) an engagement review for productions between C$200,000 and C$500,000, or (3) an uncertified final cost report with a statutory declaration for productions < C$200,000; application must be submitted prior to the start of principal photography

Eligible Entities: The production company must be incorporated in Alberta or registered to do business in Alberta and be in good standing with Corporate Registry; distributors/broadcasters are ineligible

Sunset/Review: None

British Columbia

Type of Incentive: Refundable tax credit

Benefit (if eligibility requirements are met): 33 percent of qualifying British Columbia (BC) labor expenditures; Digital Animation or Visual Effects (DAVE) Credit bonus: 17.5 percent additional credit on qualifying DAVE labor (principal photography commenced after February 28, 2010); Regional Tax Credit bonus: 6 percent of qualifying BC "regional" labor when > 50 percent of BC principal photography is done outside Vancouver area (pro rate number of regional days by total BC days), minimum 5 regional days required; Distant Location Credit: additional 6 percent of qualifying BC "distant" labor (calculated by pro rating number of days shot in "distant location" by total BC days; must first qualify for Regional Tax Credit); 17.5 percent of qualifying BC labor for the Interactive Digital Media tax credit for video game development for projects that begin after August 31, 2010.

In addition, the BC incentive is stackable with Canada's Federal Tax Incentive which is 16 percent of qualifying Canadian labor expenditures, net of assistance (which includes any provincial credits attributed to qualifying labor spend)

Compensation and Project Caps/Funding per Year: No caps

Project Criteria: Production budget must be > C$1,000,000 worldwide for feature film or video; > C$100,000 per episode for series or pilot ≤ 30 minutes (exception: productions that consist of all or substantially all digital animation or visual effects); > C$200,000 per episode for series or pilot > 30 minutes

Eligible Entities: The production company must be a Canadian taxable company with a permanent establishment in BC whose primary business is film or video production or provision of production services; broadcasting/cable subsidiaries are eligible

Sunset/Review: None

Manitoba

Type of Incentive: Refundable tax credit

Benefit (if eligibility requirements are met): 30 percent of qualifying Manitoba (MB) labor and MB purchases/rentals OR 45 percent of qualifying MB labor expenditures (which can also include labor paid to non-MB residents who work in technical, below-the-line positions, to a maximum of 30 percent of total actual MB labor expenditures if two MB residents trained per nonresident; nonresidents do not have to deliver the training); Regional Tax Credit bonus: 5 percent of qualifying MB labor expenditures if ≥ 50 percent of MB production days shot at least 35 km from the center of Winnipeg; Frequent Filming bonus: 10 percent of qualifying MB labor expenditures on third film shot within two-year period (producers can access bonus by co-venturing with a company that has frequent filming status); MB Producer Incentive: 5 percent of qualifying MB labor expenditures for productions where an MB resident receives credit as a producer. In addition, the MB incentive is stackable with Canada's Federal Tax Incentive which is 16 percent of qualifying Canadian labor expenditures, net of assistance (which includes any provincial credits attributed to qualifying labor spend)

Compensation and Project Caps/Funding per Year: No caps

Project Criteria: ≥ 25 percent of salaries and wages paid by production company must be paid to eligible MB employees for work performed in MB

Eligible Entities: The production company must be a corporation taxable in Canada, with a permanent establishment in MB, primarily carrying on the business of film, TV, or video production; broadcasters are eligible

Sunset/Review: None

New Brunswick

Type of Incentive: Refundable tax credit

Benefit (if eligibility requirements are met): 40 percent of qualifying New Brunswick (NB) labor expenditures; labor caps at 50 percent of total production costs

Compensation and Project Caps/Funding per Year: Project labor caps at 50 percent of total production costs; no annual funding caps

Project Criteria: ≥ 25 percent of salaries and wages paid by production company must be paid to eligible NB employees for work performed in NB

Eligible Entities: The production company must be a corporation taxable in Canada, with a permanent establishment in NB, primarily carrying on the business of film, TV, or video production; broadcasters are ineligible

Sunset/Review: None

Newfoundland and Labrador

Type of Incentive: Refundable tax credit

Benefit (if eligibility requirements are met): 40 percent of qualifying Newfoundland-Labrador (NL) labor expenditures

Compensation and Project Caps/Funding per Year: Tax credit caps at the lesser of 25 percent of the total production costs or C$3,000,000 per 12-month period

Project Criteria: ≥ 25 percent of salaries and wages paid by production company must be paid to eligible NL employees for work performed in NL

Eligible Entities: The production company must be a corporation taxable in Canada, with a permanent establishment in NL, primarily carrying on the business of film, TV, or video production; broadcasters are ineligible

Sunset/Review: None

Nova Scotia

Type of Incentive: Refundable tax credit

Benefit (if eligibility requirements are met): The lesser of 50 percent of qualifying Nova Scotia (NS) labor expenditures or 25 percent of total production costs; Regional Credit bonus: 10 percent of qualifying NS labor expenditures for productions shooting outside metro Halifax; tax credit caps at 30 percent of total production costs; Frequent Filming bonus: 5 percent of qualifying NS labor expenditures on third film shot within two-year period (not capped)

Compensation and Project Caps/Funding per Year: No caps

Project Criteria: ≥ 25 percent of labor costs paid to NS residents (including personal service corporations); also qualifying are wages and salaries paid to Nova Scotians for work performed outside province; projects with budgets

> C$500,000 require an audited cost report; budgets > C$100,000 require a review engagement report; budgets < C$100,000 require a producer's affidavit certifying the final cost report

Eligible Entities: The production company must be a corporation taxable in Canada, with a permanent establishment in NS, primarily carrying on the business of film, TV, or video production; broadcasters are ineligible

Sunset/Review: Subject to review in 2016

Ontario

Type of Incentive: Refundable tax credit

Benefit (if eligibility requirements are met): 25 percent of qualifying Ontario (ON) labor expenditures and production expenditures; bonuses: ON Computer Animation and Special Effects (OCASE) = 20 percent of qualifying ON labor related to digital animation and special effects work

Compensation and Project Caps/Funding per Year: No caps

Project Criteria: Production budget must be > C$1,000,000 worldwide for feature film or video; > C$100,000 per episode for series or pilot < 30 minutes; > C$200,000 per episode for series or pilot ≥ 30 minutes

Eligible Entities: The production company must be a corporation taxable in Canada, with a permanent establishment in ON, primarily carrying on the business of film, TV, or video production; broadcasters are eligible

Sunset/Review: None

Prince Edward Island

The program is currently under review; no incentives available at this time. Responsibility for the *incentive* is also under review and the responsible department and staff members have yet to be identified.

Quebec

Type of Incentive: Refundable tax credit

Benefit (if eligibility requirements are met): 25 percent of qualifying Quebec (QC) expenditures (not limited to QC labor); bonuses: QC Computer Animation and Special Effects Tax Credit = 5 percent additional credit on qualifying animation and special effects QC expenditures (not limited to QC labor); 20 percent qualifying animation and special effects credit for low-budget productions

Compensation and Project Caps/Funding per Year: No caps

Project Criteria: Production budget must be > C$1,000,000 worldwide for feature film or video; > C$100,000 per episode for series or pilot < 30 minutes; > C$200,000 per episode for series or pilot ≥ 30 minutes

Eligible Entities: The production company must be a corporation taxable in Canada, with a permanent establishment in QC, primarily carrying on the business of film, TV, or video production; broadcasters are eligible

Sunset/Review: None

Saskatchewan

Type of Incentive: Refundable tax credit

Benefit (if eligibility requirements are met): 45 percent of qualifying Saskatchewan (SK) labor expenditures (which can also include labor paid to non-SK residents who train a SK resident in all job categories, above- and below- the-line, to a maximum of 25 percent of eligible labor expenditures); labor caps at 50 percent of total production costs; Regional Tax Credit bonus: 5 percent of total SK spend if > 50 percent of principal photography shot in SK and at least 40 km outside Regina or Saskatoon; Key Position bonus: 5 percent of total SK spend for productions that attain > 6 out of 10 points for hiring SK residents in key positions

Compensation and Project Caps/Funding per Year: Project labor caps at 50 percent of total production costs; no annual funding cap

Project Criteria: ≥ 25 percent of salaries and wages must be paid to SK residents

Eligible Entities: The production company must be a corporation taxable in Canada, with a permanent establishment in SK, primarily carrying on the business of film, TV, or video production; broadcasters are ineligible

Sunset/Review: None

Yukon

Type of Incentive: Spend, travel, and training rebates

Benefit (if eligibility requirements are met): Yukon Spend Rebate: TV programs, MOW's (movies of the week), documentaries, and feature films (not commercials) are eligible for a rebate of up to 25 percent of below-the-line Yukon (YT) spend, provided criteria are met; Training Rebate: Productions (not commercials) are eligible for a rebate of up to 25 percent of the wages paid to individuals providing on-set training (techniques and equipment) to eligible YT labor; Travel Rebate: (for productions not accessing the 25 percent spend rebate, i.e., commercials) 50 percent of travel costs, to a maximum of the lesser of C$10,000, or 10 percent of total YT expenditures

Compensation and Project Caps/Funding per Year: No project limits to Spend Rebate

Project Criteria: The labor rebate is available to productions filming in YT with 50 percent of the person days in YT crewed by eligible YT residents; all elements of the fund must be applied for and approved in advance by the YT Film & Sound Commission

Eligible Entities: The applicant must be a corporation taxable in Canada and registered with YT Corporate

Sunset/Review: None

Cayman Islands

Type of Incentive: Cash rebate

Benefit (if eligibility requirements are met): *30 percent of qualifying local production expenditure and 20 percent to 30 percent of qualifying local labor expenditures depending upon residency status of the employees (the actual percentage is within the discretion of the Cayman Islands Film Commission)

Compensation and Project Caps/Funding per Year: US$100,000 compensation cap per employee, aggregate wage cap per project of US$2,000,000; annual funding cap to be determined by May 2010

Project Criteria: Minimum local spend > US$50,000 for productions of ≤ 29 minutes, > US$150,000 for productions ≥ 30 minutes during the 12 months beginning eight weeks before principal photography through postproduction

Eligible Entities: Film production company incorporated in the Cayman Islands, with copyright ownership during production or direct contract with said owner

Sunset/Review: None; to be reviewed at the end of the year

Fiji

Type of Incentive: Film tax rebate

Benefit (if eligibility requirements are met): 35 percent of qualifying local spend

Compensation and Project Caps/Funding per Year: FJD$8,750,000 per project

Project Criteria: Minimum local spend = FJD$250,000; if the local spend is < FJD$25,000,000, the local spend must be ≥ 35 percent of the total spend; of the local spend is ≥ FJD$25,000,000, there is no percentage test

Eligible Entities: Any film company

Sunset/Review: None

France

Type of Incentive: Refundable tax rebate to the line producer

Benefit (if eligibility requirements are met): 20 percent of qualifying local spend (up to 80 percent of the total production or postproduction costs)

---

*Subject to a 5 percent contribution to the CI Film Industry Development Fund.

Compensation and Project Caps/Funding per Year: €4,000,000 per project; total public subsidies granted for one project ≤ 50 percent of total budget

Project Criteria: Minimum local spend = €1,000,000 for eligible fictional and animation projects, including films, TV dramas, and TV series; minimum shoot (live action) = five days (N/A for animation); culture test

Eligible Entities: French company line producing the project

Sunset/Review: December 31, 2012

Germany

Type of Incentive: Cash (financial aid) grant

Benefit (if eligibility requirements are met): 20 percent of qualifying local spend (up to 80 percent of the total production costs)

Compensation and Project Caps/Funding per Year: €4,000,000 per film (€10,000,000 if local spend ≥ 35 percent of budget or if ≥ two thirds of cultural characteristics awarded; €60,000,000 per year)

Project Criteria: Minimum budgets for feature films = €1,000,000, animated films = €3,000,000, documentaries = €200,000; ≥ 25 percent of budget must be local spend or 20 percent if budgeted > €20,000,000; if €15,000,000 local spend, no percentage test; cultural test

Eligible Entities: German production company or establishment

Sunset/Review: December 31, 2012

Hungary

Type of Incentive: Sponsor tax credit

Benefit (if eligibility requirements are met): 20 percent of qualifying local spend (Hungarian spend and foreign spend, for a maximum effective benefit rate of 25 percent)

Compensation and Project Caps/Funding per Year: Qualifying foreign spend is capped at 25 percent of qualifying Hungarian spend; no other caps

Project Criteria: Culture test requires that 16 out of 32 points be achieved, with at least 2 points in the cultural criteria (versus the industrial criteria); no spend test

Eligible Entities: Hungarian production company

Sunset/Review: December 31, 2013

Iceland

Type of Incentive: Cash rebate

Benefit (if eligibility requirements are met): 20 percent of qualifying local spend, including all EEA spend (European Union plus Norway, Liechtenstein, and Iceland) if >80 percent of the television or movie production costs are incurred locally

Compensation and Project Caps/Funding per Year: No caps

Project Criteria: No spend test

Eligible Entities: Registered production company

Ireland

Type of Incentive: Up-front production funding

Benefit (if eligibility requirements are met): 28 percent of qualifying local spend

Compensation and Project Caps/Funding per Year: Capped at 80 percent of global spend up to €50,000,000 of qualifying expenditure per project

Project Criteria: The amount spent in Ireland on the production must at least equal the amount of investment eligible for tax relief

Eligible Entities: Registered Irish production company

Sunset/Review: December 31, 2012

Loan Program for Productions Available: Yes

Israel

Type of Incentive: Cost reduction

Benefit (if eligibility requirements are met): 20 percent (17 percent, plus VAT (value added tax) of 15.5 percent) of eligible "production payments in Israel"

Compensation and Project Caps/Funding per Year: No project or funding caps

Project Criteria: Minimum local spend of NIS (currency of Israel) 8,000,000 (approximately US$2,000,000)

Eligible Entities: A company resident in Israel that is engaged in the production of films **Sunset/Review:** End of the 2013 tax year

Italy*

Type of Incentive: Up-front reduction in overall costs

Benefit (if eligibility requirements are met): Up to 25 percent tax credit to an Italian executive producer

---

*Awaiting EU approval with respect to measures dedicated to distributors, exhibitors, and outside investors only. The measures devoted to domestic and foreign film producers have been approved.

Compensation and Project Caps/Funding per Year: Euros 5,000,000 per project per year; capped at 60 percent of the overall budget; including up to 30 percent of European Union (EU) spend through an Italian company

Project Criteria: Applies to local spend; must pass a "culture test"

Eligible Entities: Italian executive producing company

Sunset/Review: December 31, 2010

Friuli Venezia Giulia

Type of Incentive: Cash grant

Compensation and Project Caps/Funding per Year: €5,000 for projects filming in the region over one week (six days of filming); €20,000 for projects filming over three weeks; €60,000 for projects filming over five weeks; €140,000 for projects filming over seven weeks

Project Criteria: 150 percent of the regional grant must be spent in the region, with the exception of crews and investment expenses; filming in the region must equal at least 70 percent of the entire external filming of the cut and at least 50 percent of the total filming of the cut, except for productions filming in the region for less than five weeks and for serials of more than two episodes; for the latter, filming in the region must equal at least 10 percent of the entire external filming of the cut

Eligible Entities: Legally and fiscally established European Union (EU) and non-EU film and television companies

Malta

Type of Incentive: Cash grant

Benefit (if eligibility requirements are met): 15 percent to 22 percent of "eligible expenditure"; the rebate percentage is determined by the points obtained in the cultural test

Compensation and Project Caps/Funding per Year: Eligible expenditures are capped at 80 percent of the overall budget; there are caps on a number of specific categories of eligible expenditures as a percentage of the total eligible expenditures, with a €50,000 cap on above-the-line "direct employment" and department heads below-the-line; for films with a budget > €25,000,000, additional labor costs are excluded; annual funding for 2010 = €2,000,000, subject to increases as approved by the minister

Project Criteria: Culture test requires that 40 points out of 100 be achieved, with at least 15 points in "cultural content," and 10 points each in "creative contribution" and "use of Malta's cultural resources"; the rebate is 15 percent if 40 points are obtained and goes up to 22 percent for 72 points and if "Malta features as Malta"

Eligible Entities: Qualifying company

Sunset/Review: December 31, 2012

New Zealand

Type of Incentive: Large Budget Screen Production (LBSP) Grant, cash grant; Post, Digital, Visual Effects Production (PDV) Grant, cash grant; Screen Production Incentive Fund (SPIF), cash grant

Benefit (if eligibility requirements are met): 15 percent of qualifying local spend (QNZPE) for LBSP and PDV Grants; 40 percent of qualifying local spend (QNZPE) on eligible feature films, and 20 percent on eligible television, documentary and short form animation for SPIF Grant

Compensation and Project Caps/Funding per Year: There is no ceiling on compensation for LBSP and PDV; maximum amount eligible for QNZPE for any individual project is NZ$15,000,000 for SPIF Grant; no caps on projects or funding per year for LBSP and PDV

Project Criteria: Minimum QNZPE = NZ$15,000,000 for LBSP; or NZ$3,000,000 in postproduction digital and visual effects work; bundling of productions costing a minimum of NZ$3,000,000 to meet the NZ$30,000,000 QNZPE over 24 months; bundling of episodes (completed within 12 months) averaging NZ$500,000 per hour is permitted to meet the minimum spend; for SPIF Grant, minimum QNZPE = NZ$4,000,000 for eligible feature films, NZ$1,000,000 for eligible series of programs, NZ$1,000,000 for eligible single episode program, NZ$250,000 for eligible documentary, NZ$250,000 for eligible short-form animation, and all eligible projects must contain significant New Zealand content; official co-productions of feature films or television programming produced under one of New Zealand's co-production agreements will automatically qualify as having significant NZ content and may be eligible to apply for an SPIF Grant

Eligible Entities: A New Zealand resident company or a foreign corporation operating with a fixed establishment in New Zealand for the purposes of lodging an income tax return (both when it lodges the grant application and when the grant is paid)

Sunset/Review: Review scheduled for 2011 for LBSP and PDV Grants; review scheduled for 2012 for SPIF Grant

Singapore

Type of Incentive: Cash rebate

Benefit (if eligibility requirements are met): Up to 50 percent of qualifying expenses incurred for filming in Singapore

Compensation and Project Caps/Funding per Year: No caps, but funding is discretionary and will be disbursed in stages, subject to conditions that will be based on a contractual agreement

Project Criteria: Singapore must be showcased in a positive light in the script, and the production must provide an esitmated budget of local spend, track record of the director, producer, and actors, and the financing, marketing, and distribution plan on the initial application to be considered

Eligible Entities: Singapore production company

Sunset/Review: None

South Africa

Type of Incentive: Cash rebate

Benefit (if eligibility requirements are met): 15 percent of qualifying local spend (QSAPE - qualifying South African production expenditure)

Compensation and Project Caps/Funding per Year: R10,000,000 per project; R246,899,000 for 2010/11, R268,873,000 for 2011/12, and R290,305,000 for 2012/13

Project Criteria: Minimum QSAPE = R$12,000,000; for productions with QSAPE of R12,000,000 to R99,999,999, ≥ 50 percent of principal photography for a minimum of four weeks must be local; for productions with QSAPE ≥ R100,000,000, principal photography and shooting requirements may be waived

Eligible Entities: South African production company

Sunset/Review: Decemeber 31, 2013

South Korea–Busan

Type of Incentive: Cash rebate

Benefit (if eligibility requirements are met): 30 percent of the qualifying local spend

Compensation and Project Caps/Funding per Year: KW100,000,000 (approx. US$85,000) per production

Project Criteria: Feature film and TV drama shot in Busan with a distribution agreement or presales agreement signed

Eligible Entities: The applicant must be the producer; there are no restrictions on nationality

Sunset/Review: None

South Korea–Seoul

Type of Incentive: Cash rebate (50 percent up-front)

Benefit (if eligibility requirements are met): 10 percent to 25 percent of qualifying local spend (percentage points above 10 percent are awarded based on a point system for local hires and publicity)

Compensation and Project Caps/Funding per Year: KRW100,000,000 (approx. US$85,000) cap per project; unless more than KRW1,500,000,000 (approx. US$1,300,000) in local spend, or more than 50 percent of the film shot/shown is shot locally, or distribution agreements have been signed in at least five countries

Project Criteria: Minimum local shooting requirement of six days; available for feature documentaries and series, theatrical or television, with a minimum running time of 60 minutes; signed distribution contract or presales agreement, or documented director's invitation to specific recognized film festivals within the past five years

Eligible Entities: A producer of any nationality

Sunset/Review: None

Taiwan, Republic of China (ROC)–Taipei City

Type of Incentive: Cash grant

Benefit (if eligibility requirements are met): 30 percent of total personnel expenses for ROC national cast members; 30 percent of the total expenses for ROC nationals working as crew members for motion pictures filmed partially or entirely in Taiwan; if filmed and preproduced or postproduced partially or entirely in Taiwan, there is an additional grant of 25 percent of local production expenditures; there are also incentives for qualifying animation projects and an additional grant of 15 percent for transport and accommodation expenses and insurance costs for ROC nationals employed as cast and crew members

Compensation and Project Caps/Funding per Year: No caps; annual funding of US$1,000,000

Project Criteria: Minimum local spend > NT3 million, unless produced by globally recognized foreign motion picture production enterprise or directors that will enhance the ROC's international image

Eligible Entities: Foreign motion picture production enterprises with permission from the Government Information Office (GIO)

Sunset/Review: None

Trinidad and Tobago

Type of Incentive: Cash rebate

Benefit (if eligibility requirements are met): 12.5 percent to 30 percent of qualifying local spend

Compensation and Project Caps/Funding per Year: Capped at US$300,000; to be reviewed in 2009-2010

Project Criteria: Minimum local spend = US$100,000; subjective criteria include total local spend, local crew, training, use of interns, portrayal of the country

Eligible Entities: Qualified local production company

Sunset/Review: Fiscal year review

United Kingdom

Type of Incentive: Payable tax credit

Benefit (if eligibility requirements are met): If the "core expenditure" is ≤ £20,000,000, an enhanced deduction of 100 percent may be claimed for a payable tax credit of 25 percent of UK qualifying spend; if the "core expenditure" is > £20,000,000, an enhanced deduction of 80 percent (or the "UK spend" if less than 80 percent of "qualifying expenditure") can be claimed for a payable tax credit of 20 percent

Compensation and Project Caps/Funding per Year: No caps

Project Criteria: Certified "British" film or official co-production; ≥ 25 percent of the "core expenditure" must be "UK expenditure"; intended for theatrical release

Eligible Entities: Qualified UK production company

Sunset/Review: None

CHAPTER POSTSCRIPT

Dozens of global domains actively compete to have productions created on their turf, to reap the related spending, branding/tourism, and tax benefits.

The low cost of money benefits typically far outweigh the necessary planning, location scouting, negotiating, legal, and accounting that are associated with these programs.

CHAPTER 8
Completion Guarantors

This chapter presents the comprehensively beneficial association producers can and should have with completion guarantors, beginning with the initial planning and application process. A completion guarantee sometimes is referred to as a completion bond and is a requirement for bank and other common forms of independent and studio-related production financing. As is reviewed in Chapter 14, producers should engage their completion guarantor relationship during the early development of each of their pictures.

WHAT COMPLETION GUARANTEES DO

A picture's completion guarantee ensures its financier(s)/lender—most often a bank—that the bonded picture will be completed on time, within budget, and delivered to the distributor(s). If it is not, it assures that the guarantor will pay for the related losses. Consequently, the financier/lender does not evaluate the producer's above-the-line talent, production schedule, budget, or other elements, but it relies on the completion guarantor to assure the credibility of these elements.

Completion guarantors are insurers, and the major bonding companies are either owned or backed by large insurance carriers. For instance, International Film Guarantors has the largest bonding capacity, bonding pictures with budgets in excess of $100 million. This very professional bonding company is headquartered in Los Angeles, and its guarantee is backed by Fireman's Fund insurance carrier. Another of the oldest and most well-known insurers is Film Finance. This company is owned by Lloyd's of London, headquartered in London, with its most active office in Los Angeles. The major guarantors also have sister production insurance organizations owned by their parent insurance company.

Motion picture completion guarantors are highly specialized. To assume the risk of production overruns and completion delays, these companies are classically conservative. They insure a picture whose budget is achievable, incorporate margins for the exceptions that will likely occur, and require that an additional overall contingency, typically 10 percent, be part of every film budget they guarantee.

DOI: 10.1016/B978-0-240-81463-6.00008-5

PRODUCERS' PERCEIVED AND REAL VALUE OF COMPLETION GUARANTORS

The motion picture industry has a uniquely demanding production process. Producers create distinctively new products, one at a time. A producer cannot learn about producing a particular movie (even franchise pictures) and then use this experience to produce the same picture again. Every picture is unique in its production chemistry. Production techniques are sometimes similar from picture to picture, but changes in the above-the-line talent (even if they are the same people), the below-the-line crew, locations, and production demands cause these components to perform in a substantially different manner each time.

Each picture's unit production manager (UPM) is responsible for planning and quantifying the physical production process in time and costs. Producers sustain an often painful balance between each picture's creative options and the associated costs. Producers seek production managers who will plan and budget each picture in a manner that will fulfill the producer's vision. Consequently, producers seek and value UPMs who understand and employ economies that allow more production value to be delivered at less cost. This is a challenging balance to maintain, with many offsets negotiated and often renegotiated for exceptions throughout development and production.

Because of often intense give-and-take planning, negotiating, and budgeting, some producers may initially begrudge the cautious scrutiny their production plans and budgets receive during their initial completion guarantor reviews. It isn't that these producers aren't confident in producing according to their preparations. They take meticulous care to achieve a delicate balance between a picture's production quality and its schedule and budget. The concern comes in exposing the producer's sophisticated planning and budgeting work to independent completion guarantor review, whose bonding criteria typically challenges, if not alters, the picture's tightly woven economy.

Although tradition has it that the only reason a completion guarantor participates in the production process is to facilitate financing—and that is its central purpose—guarantors often are and should be invited to contribute more. Each picture's guarantor can be the second set of careful eyes, confirming that the production team, plan, schedule, and budget are sound and achievable. More often than not, the guarantor's observations and suggestions substantially contribute to the picture's overall success.

The guarantor has a fresh evaluation advantage. Guarantors have no political or creative relationships influencing them, so they evaluate from a business rather than a creative position. Because they often have substantially deeper production review experience than even their most prolific producer clients, they are more current in their references of primary production and performing talent, as well as global costs.

Guarantors should be included in the producer's determination of each picture's director, principal cast, and even department heads. They typically are very current on the personal stability and relative performance capacity of all substantial talent. For those about whom they do not possess internal information, they can obtain it from other uniquely expansive and reliable sources. There is no cost for this assistance, and it is exceptionally helpful throughout the planning process. The guarantor will eventually evaluate the bondability of primary talent anyway. It is better for producers to take full advantage of this information and counsel when they are performing this evaluation—enabling the soundest decisions, as well as saving time and needless relationship exploration costs.

COMPLETION INSURANCE RELATIONSHIPS

The completion guarantor's business is based in planning, budgeting, legal interpretation of relationships, translating the details, and comprehensively understanding and being assured the producer will be able to complete each bonded picture within the budget and time allotted. Consequently, completion guarantors are substantially affected by their producer client production history, the thoroughness of the submitted production materials, and experience of the particular production team. It is relationship beneficial for producers to prepare in a manner that anticipates what is important to their completion bond partners.

Typically, there are three participating parties: the insurer, the financier/lender (which is typically a bank), and the producer. These parties participate with a common understanding that, for most pictures, no matter what happens *the picture will not go into default.* This understanding is the single most influential and galvanizing characteristic of the relationship.

When a picture defaults, (1) the guarantor incurs additional expenses and unwanted production takeover, (2) the financier/lender is open not only to potential loan pay-off from sources other than pledged collateral but also to possible litigation and collection activities, and (3) the producer is placed in the potentially compromising position of having to allow the guarantor to assume the governing position in deciding how the picture will be completed and delivered. Because each participant is substantially motivated to avoid this radical upheaval, completion insurance defaults are rare.

When a picture's schedule, budget, or both are threatened, the producers most often lead the restabilization solution. This is typically accomplished by either renegotiating existing collateral or providing new collateral to the financier/lender, enabling amendments with both the financier/lender and the completion bond. Such amendments may include revising collateral agreements with new delivery dates, entering and pledging additional collateral, and adjusting the bank loan and completion bond to conform to these changes. This involves sophisticated maneuvering and is made possible by the confidence of all parties in the producer, the picture, and the fairness of their particular participation.

Schedules and budgets that may have appeared to contain egregiously conservative elements before production are often embraced as very welcome safety nets during production.

THE COMPLETION BOND PACKAGE

In qualifying for a bond, the guarantor must become as familiar with the picture and its production as is the producer. The application for a guarantee should reflect the producer's understanding and empathy for this process. The completion bond package should include the following elements:

1. An introductory letter setting forth the picture's title, its total below- and above-the-line budget, its production schedule, the expected guarantee cost, the anticipated U.S. and leading international territory distributors, the production financing plan, which includes the financier/lender (again, typically this is a bank) and a contact for each of them, and the approximate date the guarantee is needed
2. A copy of the shooting script (hard and soft copy)
3. A copy of the budget (hard and soft copy)
4. A copy of the script breakdown (hard and soft copy)
5. A copy of the production boards (hard and soft copy)
6. Copies of the major talent deal memos with attachments
7. References (these are the same as in the financier/lender/bank package discussed in Chapter 6)

To sustain the highest validation integrity, guarantors traditionally prepare their initial planning and budgeting materials exclusively using the shooting script. If their schedules and below-the-line budgets are close to those submitted by the producer, then the producer's budget documentation is reviewed.

If the plans are close but there are questions, an intermediary meeting with the producer may be set up, or, if it is in keeping with the relationship, a meeting might be scheduled with the line producer or UPM.

After the review is completed, typically there is a meeting with the producer. At this meeting, the guarantor presents the producer with a provisional acceptance letter. Within or accompanying this letter is a list of items to be resolved to the guarantor's satisfaction before the picture's budget and delivery will be insured. The picture and these provisional items are discussed during this meeting. An acceptance letter is sometimes presented following the guarantor's initial review, but producers should not expect this unless the guarantor has been included in reviewing and responding to questionable issues during the planning and budgeting process. This practice provides producers with multiple benefits.

Here are some common reasons for provisional letters:

- Key talent (director or primary cast) are not bondable. Guarantors are necessarily very sensitive to this production aspect. Key talent can cripple a picture. If they are unstable for any reason, they may not be bondable until they restabilize.
- Unstable weather conditions. Most often locations are scouted during a different season than the season of principal photography. In fact, when they are lensed out of natural season, producers can turn the leaves green or amber and crimson, but the challenges and proposed solutions must be listed in the schedule and budget. The big weather challenges, like the need to shoot in tropical clear weather when the picture is scheduled during typhoon season, are more challenging to overcome. Even weather-predictable locations may demand weather insurance for reasonable protection.
- Unstable political or social conditions (insurrection, war, currency problems, and so forth).
- Insufficient time or budget contingencies. Always include a full 10 percent budget contingency.
- Unstable critical talent deal memos or contracts (ability for talent to abandon their commitment for ambiguous reasons, such as benefits or accommodations too sophisticated for the producer's predictable delivery).

COMPLETION INSURANCE COST

Producers typically allow 3 percent for completion bond expense in their budgets, but they usually negotiate less. Producers can suggest bond structures that reduce the insurers' risk and increase their volume, which result in some producers paying close to half of what is commonly budgeted.

Like bank entertainment lending departments, these insurers specialize in pictures with differing budget ranges. Some insure pictures with low to mid-seven-figure budgets, others insure pictures with mid-seven to low-eight figure budgets, and the largest companies insure pictures with mid-eight- to low-nine-figure budgets.

CHAPTER POSTSCRIPT

Completion guarantors are importantly beneficial participants for producers. They are sophisticated organizations that reaffirm and often refine each picture's production plan. These organizations are best utilized if invited to participate early, thus facilitating many development and preproduction processes, including talent evaluation, bondability, and banking. When understood and used effectively, completion insurers are welcome production allies who contribute consistently and positively to each picture's production.

CHAPTER 9

Attorneys, Negotiations, and Entertainment Law

This is an introduction to the relationship producers ought to have with their attorneys and associated firms, how producers should participate in negotiating and documenting, the processes that can limit and protect against litigation, and the valuable extended benefits available to producers from their attorneys and firms.

ATTORNEYS AND THEIR FIRMS

There are numerous excellent entertainment law firms, most of which are headquartered in New York and Los Angeles in the U.S. Some of these are large, multilocation, multifloored firms; some are full-service, one-location firms; and others are specialized, boutique firms. Large firms are not better than small firms or vice versa. The critical factor is the right attorney, in the right firm, who is well matched to the producer's needs and moral compass.

A producer's attorney should be, and typically is, involved in the producer's creative, business, and legal activities. In other words, the attorney is substantially involved in most aspects of a producer's work.

Seasoned U.S. entertainment attorneys bill in the mid-three figures per hour, junior attorneys in the low-three figures. This is not a relationship with which to be penurious. A producer's new-contact credibility, capacity to reach talent and global distributors, and ability to negotiate fair terms and to protect oneself are all largely affected by the attorney's abilities, industry standing, and firm.

It is always best to engage in a relationship with an attorney who has become a well-known presence in the entertainment industry. For the most part, these are also the attorneys who have the experience and understanding that renders them valuable counselors and advisors in all significant business and legal activities. They may also provide exceptional creative counsel. Producers deliver all appropriate matters to their attorney. In turn, their attorney may oversee, yet assign, less sophisticated matters to junior attorneys and staff.

Attorneys and the firms they are associated with should be evaluated separately. Simply being represented by a lead entertainment law firm such as, in the U.S., Loeb & Loeb, Stroock Stroock & Lavan, or Latham & Watkins has a substantial

DOI: 10.1016/B978-0-240-81463-6.00009-7

value. It may not be that the senior-level attorney within this firm is the producer's designated attorney, but even a junior attorney will have access to the firm's impressive team of powerful legal icons. Attorneys have access to the full-service capacities of their firms, including securities, contract, litigation, and business, as well as creative packaging talent. Additionally, many of these larger firms have offices in global business centers where producers may need them most, and not only do they provide producers representation in these markets, but they also provide local business cache and professional commercial working/meeting space. Further, producers have an instant sociability (and consequently more direct access) with their firms' substantive clients.

Producers should settle into a relationship with a law firm and an attorney who functions at optimum for their particular needs. There is a balance of benefits that should be obtained. The smaller the firm, the more important the producer's relationship within it. There are several boutique firms with high-profile partners who are powerhouse attorneys to their producer clients. It is not even essential for a producer's firm to be full service. For instance, if a particular firm does not provide securities work, it may supervise another firm to accomplish this work and fulfill its client's needs in a manner not much different from that of a full-service firm.

The following are the most important considerations for producers in evaluating and selecting entertainment law relationships:

1. Does the attorney have a recognizable, positive reputation in the entertainment industry? Does the attorney communicate pleasantly and clearly with the producer? Does the attorney understand the producer's objectives? Is this person committed to supporting the producer in accomplishing these goals?
2. Does the law firm have a recognizable and positive reputation in the entertainment industry? Is it a full-service firm, or are the firm's services able to address the primary needs of the production company?
3. Do the firm's clients have a business sociability that is complementary to the producer's business?

PRODUCERS PERFORMING AS ATTORNEYS

Producers should never perform the legal aspects of their business without the experience and counsel of their attorney. Having said this, producers should understand that they will be pressed, almost continually, into activities that will demand their knowledge of entertainment law. Further, it is not practical or affordable for producers to have their attorney with them all the time. Consequently, they must obtain a basic understanding of entertainment law to prevent compromising their production company's negotiating power and legal protection.

Contract law is the dominant area of law with which producers are most involved. It is no accident that many powerful producers have either obtained law degrees in preparation for their careers or have hired in-house counsel.

A producer's best legal preparation is a law degree, but even this is not a satisfactory substitute for current experience. A producer's first five years should be spent under the tutelage and coaching of his or her attorney. This is expensive only until it is compared with the damages that will likely occur without the benefit of very involved counsel throughout this time.

Almost everything a producer does has substantial legal consequences. Does this sound paranoid? It is not. The industry is riddled with stories of overconfident, easygoing producers who were either tossed up like tennis balls and whacked out of the industry or were severely bludgeoned, both financially and emotionally, before they learned this important lesson: Producers are almost *always* involved in conversations and correspondence about potential relationships. These are contract-related experiences for which producers are particularly held legally accountable. Lawsuits are levied against producers that to them may appear to be a ridiculous nuisance. These lawsuits eventually come to trial through congested court systems (especially in major entertainment centers such as New York, Los Angeles, London, Tokyo, and Hong Kong) one to five years later. Depositions of verbal conversations overheard by people whom the producer may not even recall were present, along with notes on napkins and casual letters or emails the producer didn't consider or intend to be binding, may be used as evidence. Producers should ask for and keep copies of everything. When asked if they would like a copy, producers should always answer affirmatively, and then file it.

As with most other responsibilities in life, *experience* in legal affairs increases one's power to manage them. However, until the producer obtains this experience, if an attorney is not deeply involved in the producer's early-career legal affairs, the producer may operate in a manner resulting in expensive legal actions.

Contract law is especially slippery and powerful until one understands the language. Verbal representations can be binding, and contract law language definitions do not necessarily correspond with dictionary definitions. What a producer says, writes, hears, and receives—whether the producer intends for an item to be binding or not—may be used as contract evidence. Further, it may even mean something quite different from what the producer meant to communicate. Wise producers become aware early that most of their relationship exploration communications are contract relative.

Producers should do the following:

- Study all phases of entertainment law, particularly contract law (there are several excellent books on entertainment law)
- Have their attorney present during key negotiations
- Review with and be coached by their attorney for meetings they may attend without their attorney
- Immediately report everything potentially litigious to their attorney
- Have their attorney prepare most deal documentation
- Send all other in-house prepared documentation to their attorney for review before it is used

NEGOTIATING

The only good agreement is one that is fair to all parties. Getting excited about acquiring something for less than its value is a sure sign of impoverished ethics. Everyone is best served when the deal is balanced according to the contributions of all participants.

All too common is a negotiating scenario in which both participants, often indelicately, attempt to extract more benefits for their respective position than is fair. These negotiations are typically fiery, confrontational, and most often end with all parties feeling shortchanged and, unhappily, distanced from one another.

Fortunately, this does not always occur. There are producers who refuse to engage in negotiations in this fashion, and they find talent, agents, and attorneys willing participants, though initially they may be understandably suspicious.

It is in the best interests of the producer determined to set the pace toward a gentler path to take hold of this alternative negotiating style and use it. In the final analysis, after production and primary distribution of a picture are concluded, this approach consistently ends up being more financially advantageous than the "me first, you whatever" approach to deal making.

There are three vital principles that may be applied with overall advantages to every negotiation and deal-making relationship that a producer enters into. These principles may be thought of as follows:

- The universal approach to deal making
- The negotiations that are on the same side of the desk
- The decision to weigh a deal in proportion to the scope of the picture

The "universal approach" requires simply looking at the deal without preference to a single party, aggressively considering what is fair from all parties' points of view, and then negotiating to secure the best position for each participant. This approach is often easily derailed by one or more party taking the common "car-buying" position—starting at a higher position than is fair, and still expecting the negotiation to end above what they should reasonably receive. The relationship poison associated with the car technique is that even if this party ends up with a greater than fair portion, this party still may be discontented that he or she did not get even more.

"Getting on the same side of the desk" is waiting to negotiate until all parties are working for the good of the picture. Putting the picture first naturally allies the participants, who are all working together for a common objective. This helps motivate the "universal approach," in which all parties clearly see that from the picture's perspective that the producer is not more important than screenwriter, or the screenwriter than the director, and so on. This puts the negotiators in position to consider the deal elements in light of what is fair and most beneficial for the particular production.

The process of "weighing the deal to the picture" can be accomplished only when producers exercise a balance between their commitment to each picture's creativity, audience, and profitability. This is especially helpful when negotiating deals with potential points participants. The producer uses the picture's sales breakdown and budget to reassess a lucrative cash-only deal as a percentage of the producer's gross profit less the picture's budget. This process is done typically only for the most substantial contributors to the picture—namely, the writer, director, and principal acting talent. This analysis tends to cast a constructive deal-making light on the negotiations. It renders an exceptional deal orientation when participants confidentially review and thoroughly understand these numbers and relate them to their own position. For instance, if a picture has a projected, after negative recoupment, a producer's gross of $30 million, and the cash-only director's fee is $3 million, this percentage "weight" is 10 percent. The participating point application should not be proportional to the fee amount, as there are risks and time-related-to-point income. With this ratio as a reference, this example could yield the director a $2 million fee plus five points (5 percent of $30 million being a forecasted $1.5 million). If the picture achieves its projections, this agreement will provide the director with an additional $500,000 in earnings, compared with the fee-only relationship—that, along with long-term earnings from the picture's continuing rights sales. The plus-points terms also deepen the director's relationship with the picture, naturally motivating the director to make the greatest contribution possible in creating the film, as the higher the earnings, the greater the director's points income.

Using this approach to deal making strengthens each individual relationship and establishes a universal integrity among all participants. No talent wants to think another talent cut a better deal because the other party negotiated more shrewdly. Rather, there is a spirit of fair play and common good. This has a substantial resonant effect on all participants, the work they do, the level of sanity sustained, and, consequently, the picture itself.

How is this achieved? The producer is largely responsible for setting the tone of every relationship. When producers focus first on the picture along with the universal application of the fairness of the deal to all parties, they always influence all other parties associated with the deal. If they haven't dealt with the producer before, agents, attorneys, and business managers initially may be suspicious of this approach. However, it is our experience that engaging these principles has an exceptionally positive effect on establishing solid relationship foundations and arriving at deal parameters that are of high integrity and as close as possible to being unshakable.

VITAL LEGAL ASPECTS RELATING TO THE STORY

A producer's first and constant goal is to discover stories worth telling as motion pictures; the net goals are to evaluate, acquire, develop, produce, and sell them. Literary rights searches, property reviews, negotiations, acquisitions, and rewrites are a roiling pot of potential litigation!

Literary Releases

Writing is the genius art. Skilled writers may complete five finished screenplay pages a day. For them, a screenplay may represent several weeks of research and five to eight weeks of writing for the first draft, which may be 10 to 20 drafts from being ready to actually submit. If this is a "spec" script, it typically will represent at least six to nine months of work and perhaps much more. The screenplay is the writer's most valuable asset and must be protected.

However, the protection issues relating to stories appear much different from a producer's perspective. A producer's literary department may review 30 properties a week just to keep up with submissions. These come in many forms and typically from a variety of sources. As unlikely as it may seem to writers, producers soon realize their story department may receive two very similar stories, from completely unrelated sources, within a similar time period. Topical stories may even have several similar submissions during the same month.

Most stories fall into one of the following three categories, from most to least prevalent:

1. Stories that are poorly written and not worth being told/optioned.
2. Stories that are well written but not worth being told/optioned.
3. Stories worth being told that are not well written or not in screenplay form.

The third category is the stories most often optioned and put into story development.

Studios and successful production companies are excellent negotiators for literary rights. They are well funded and often prepared to spend more than a fair amount to purchase the all-too-rare great properties. They have every motivation to acquire material from writers—yes, especially first-time writers—employing ethical and respectful business practices. They do not and will not steal stories. In the unfortunate and rare instances when individuals working for these companies are found abusing the creative trust and operating policies of these organizations, they are immediately released.

In recent years, the studios have severely cut back on development costs and associated producer/talent overhead deals, unless the property is a franchise or has a branded marketing hook already established. The producer and their production company are now expected more than ever before to advance those development costs, which are recoupable line items in the production budget.

Before submitting their material, writers protect themselves by various registration, copyrighting, or other means, only to be presented with a literary release letter before agents, studios, and producers will accept their unrepresented material or pitch. These release letters substantially limit the writer's legal recourse against the producer and, in their various versions, the writer releases the reviewing producer from legal liability, under certain conditions, and from using "material containing features similar to or identical with those contained in" the material submitted by the writer.

Some writers complain that this gives producers license to steal their material. In fact, these letters substantially limit the legal recourse of the writer. But without literary release letters, producers would be subject to relentless litigation.

A copy of a sample literary release letter is shown in Figure 9.1, as well as on the website associated with this book. After a review, it should be abundantly clear why writers might be reluctant to sign. However, considering the high volume of story material reviewed by producers, the similarity between many of these stories, and the predominance of rejections, it becomes clear that producers must adhere to this fundamental legal process for their own protection.

The Step Deal

Writing is a delicate craft. Consider this scenario. Writer A recently won the Best Screenplay Academy Award for a romantic comedy script. A producer has had a promising meeting with this writer to creatively perform a major rewrite of a romantic comedy script optioned by the producer. A relationship is negotiated that is satisfactory to all parties; it is documented, and the writer commences. The producer is enthusiastic to see the script. The writing proceeds on schedule. Two months pass, and the producer receives the first draft. The producer rated the writer's previous Academy Award winning script a 9 out of 10. The producer rates this first draft as a 4 out of 10. The producer and writer have a tense but seemingly productive story meeting. The producer is convinced that the writer now embraces the fire of the story the producer wants to tell.

Three weeks later, the new property has been substantially rewritten, but it is no closer than the original draft to what the producer envisions. Two more increasingly tense meetings take place, each without an improved draft. The drafts are different but not any better in the producer's eyes. After three drafts, everyone is testy and uneasy. The writer has worked diligently, probably employing the maximum craft possible on this story. The producer realizes that this writer will never write the story needed for that particular production. Sadly for the producer, next year, this same writer may well write another romantic comedy script that, in the producer's evaluation, will be a 10 out of 10.

Exceptional writers may not always be able to exercise their considerable craft to the producer's satisfaction. This rarely has to do with the writer's craft, effort, or diligence; rather, it is often simply that the writer and story do not connect. Although this may not happen even half the time, it happens enough for producers to approach relationships with writers in a fashion that facilitates the best experience possible.

In the preceding example, the writer and producer entered into their relationship with good intentions, but now a new writer must be engaged, and fees, writing credits, and other deal points must be renegotiated to accommodate the new relationship. This forces the restructuring of the development schedule. Because of the additional development time and writing fees, development and production budgets increase. And because the writing budget may not have been configured to accommodate two writers, the new writer negotiation is often entered with less advance cash than the original development plan.

Submission Release Agreement

Date

(Party Submitting To)

(Their Address)

RE: (Title of property)

Dear Sir/Madam:

I realize that many ideas, programs, slogans, scripts, plans, suggestions, and other literary and/or dramatic and/or musical material (hereinafter, for convenience collectively referred to as "material"), which are submitted to you, are similar to material previously used, previously submitted by others, or already under consideration by you. I further realize that you must protect yourself against any unwarranted claims by refusing to examine any material submitted to you unless you are assured that you shall have the unqualified right to finally determine whether such material or any part thereof is in fact used by you or your successors, assignees, or licensees, and what compensation or consideration, if any, should be paid for such use.

I am submitting certain material to you herewith. In order to induce you to consider this material, I hereby irrevocably waive, release, and relinquish any and all claims that I or any person, firm, or corporation claiming under or though me, may now or hereafter have against you, your successors, assignees, or licensees, and your and their respective officers, employees, and representatives, for any use or alleged use, that you, or your successors, assignees, or licensees may make of any such material. I also expressly agree that your decisions as to whether you, or your successors, assignees, or licensees have used all or any part of such material and as to the compensation or other consideration, if any, which should be paid to me therefore, shall be conclusive and binding upon me and all persons, firms, and corporations claiming under or through me. In the event that I bring any claim in violation of the foregoing sentence, I shall reimburse you for your costs and attorneys' fees in defending such claim, along with any damages you may suffer as the result of such claim.

I further understand and agree that you are not responsible for the return of any material submitted, and I acknowledge that I have retained a duplicate copy of such material in my possession.

Very truly yours,

(Signature)

(Print name)

(Address)   (Telephone/e-mail)

Relationship to material (i.e., Author, Producer):

Brief story/concept/idea description:

FIGURE 9.1
Sample literary release letter.

Because of this common phenomenon, producers often protect themselves from these time and legal exigencies through entering "step relationships" with writers. Step relationships compartmentalize the writing processes into progressive steps. Each step has a fixed fee value and provides for evaluation and complete pre-agreed-upon exit remedies that allow the producer to be able to terminate the relationship following the review of each initial step.

To assure a development schedule will likely be met, though it is initially more expensive for the producer, two or three writers may be sought, entering completely separate step relationships, and independently begin writing. Of course, it is essential to the integrity of the relationships that the writers know that multiple writers are being used.

The agreement's first step typically calls for the writers to author a synopsis of the story. Whether or not their synopsis is acceptable to the producer, the writers are all paid for their work. If a synopsis from one writer is not accepted, that writer does not proceed. As most writers are Writers Guild of America (WGA) members, credits are eventually determined according to the guild agreement.

The writers whose synopses are accepted then author a comprehensive step outline or script treatment. It is possible that all the writers will proceed with this step. Again, the writers are paid for their treatments, regardless of whether the treatments were accepted. If particular drafts are not acceptable, a writer may not proceed to the next step. Typically, following the step outline or treatment, there is a single writer selected to continue, writing the first-draft screenplay.

Producers should always do their best to enter step writing deals, even if it is with each single writer in succession. This relationship allows for reevaluation at each step and curbs costly development costs. This does not imply a lack of confidence in the writer. It clearly indicates the producer's seasoned understanding of the delicate fundamentals of the writing craft and the preparations necessary to manage this relationship propitiously.

Multiple-writer step deals always are initially more expensive than single-writer relationships. But they may actually cost less in time and expenses in the long run, especially if the original single-writer relationship does not succeed.

If there is one place a producer should risk overspending, it is on script development. Producers are most often best served by a multiple-writer step deal approach to screenplay development. This prevents the high probability of being pushed off development schedule and over budget, and it provides greater assurance that the writers will craft the ultimate story.

Literary Greenlight Review

After producers discover literary properties they are interested in, they proceed through a discovery phase before they are prepared to commence development. This period is called the producer's "internal greenlight" of each project (see Chapters 1 and 14). Before outside participation in the analysis of the story of a proposed picture, producers should receive written permission from the story's author before they refer to the story in any way to those outside the producer's organization.

A simple deal memo may be prepared, expressing the producer's interest in the property and willingness to invest in a creative and marketing feasibility study to discover the viability of the producer's eventual acquisition of the story. The letter should state that the producer is prepared to proceed with the project research investment pending the writer's approval. The producer warrants that contact will be expressly limited to those needed for the study, will be strictly confidential, and will clearly represent that the story rights have not yet been optioned or acquired by the producer, that this is exclusively an evaluation inquiry, and that the intent of these meetings is to determine project feasibility, not the financing of the picture or acquisition of the property. In this memo, the producer further represents that the research and analysis may include confidential discussions with a limited number of partners relative to their valuation of the proposed picture. The producer acknowledges that this nonexclusive evaluation will not continue longer that a set time (for instance, three to five months).

This deal memo protects the writer and producer from misunderstandings and clearly sets forth the speculative, arm's-length nature of the relationship. It also warms the writer and agent to the producer's serious interest in the property.

Literary Rights Option/Acquisition

After a picture has obtained the critical in-house greenlight (determining that the ratio between the producer's share of the picture's income compared with its estimated all-in cost is acceptable), the first development move is typically to option all rights to the literary property. If a literary review memo is in force, an initial rapport will already have been established among the producer, the writer, the agent, and the attorney(ies).

Mature production companies have internal development funds, allowing them to negotiate and acquire or option properties in a more unregulated fashion than new producers, who may be using development funds from investors, possibly for a fixed number of pictures. Whichever is the case, the producer's best approach to deal making is to reveal the production company's position to the writer or the agent.

The picture already will have a summarized budget, prepared during the internal greenlight. This budget's story purchase price should represent the producer's estimation of a fair acquisition price for the property. This should be affected by how closely the property being acquired resembles the actual shooting script of the picture. Often scripts optioned represent little more than a compelling story concept. Many writers are excellent imagineers but not very skilled screenwriters. A separate, detailed story budget, which reflects a conservative and predictable activity and expense schedule for taking the acquired story to a shooting script, should be prepared. These projections should be the centerpiece for negotiating the option/purchase agreement.

There are two budgets typically at play in this process. The development budget has a fixed elasticity for the option advance and writing steps. The production budget has a more flexible capacity for the actual purchase price.

The genesis writer may participate in a step writing arrangement with other writers—the difference being that the genesis writer will have continuing benefits that will not be offered to the other step-deal writers (i.e., story by credit and the strength perceived by the WGA by being the first writer on the project).

Each writer will need payment allocations relative to his or her option/writing steps and purchase price payments. The producer needs to have development funding sufficient to pay for option/writing steps and will have substantially more funding through production financing to pay the purchase price.

Achieving a successful greenlight is no small feat. Producers should move into the literary rights negotiation with a clear understanding of each picture's creative and global earnings potential. They should be further motivated by the fact that their distributors are looking to them for positive reassurance that their pictures are in active development. Producers want, of course, to realize benefits from the initial development time and money invested. However, first-time producers are subject to the check and balance realities of fixed development budgets.

The success of most literary rights negotiations are driven by these crucial elements:

1. The strength of the story.
2. The flexibility of the literary rights development and production budgets. If development funds are exceptionally tight, the purchase price should be proportionally increased to offset the front-end shortfall.
3. The strength of the producer and other creative players. Everyone wants to play on a winning team. A strong story, along with a powerful director, producer, or acting talent, will have a drawing effect on all other participants.
4. The initial global enthusiasm for the picture. The findings of the in-house greenlight should be shared with all primary participants. The stronger the picture's feasibility, the greater each player's enthusiasm.
5. The willingness of the negotiating parties to be flexible between the deal points. Everything should equal out. Deal points are necessarily rigid. If one creates an unfair position for a participant, then, in offset, one or more other deal points should be added or increased. When all parties are determined to move the pieces until they are fair and acceptable to each participant, then negotiations typically succeed.

Typically, producers deal with literary agents in the negotiation and acquisition of properties. First-sale screenwriters who are not represented by an agent are especially vulnerable during the deal-making process. Therefore, such relationships are always best served if the producer acts as a protector and tutor. Especially as these transactions are most often less than that budgeted, it is better for producers to at least slightly overcompensate these writers, in offset of their susceptible position. First-sale screenwriters may have a script similar in creative value to that of a more experienced writer, but because they are new to the bargaining table, they could be paid much less for their property. Nevertheless, assuring they receive a full measure of all the benefits they are due consistently turns to the producers greater good.

DEAL MEMOS, LETTER AGREEMENTS, AND LONG-FORM CONTRACTS

Of the three forms of deal documentation, deal memos are by far the most prevalent form used for most of the producer's relationships. In fact, many relationships never get documentation beyond the original deal memo. Often longer, more formal documents are in the process of being negotiated as development proceeds, but negotiations become protracted, pictures get completed, and, finally, it is often the deal memo that remains the only signatory document defining the relationship. The notable exceptions are most distribution and license agreements, which typically are done in the long form.

Deal Memos

Deal memos are the workhorse deal documents of the entertainment industry. These typically come in letter form, originating on the producer's letterhead and containing the following information:

1. Identification of the parties involved in the deal.
2. What each party is specifically contributing to the relationship.
3. What each party will get for that party's contribution.
4. Anything else relating to the basic understanding of the parties.
5. Any specific representations from the parties, examples being "I am the sole, original author," or "There are no liens or encumbrances."
6. The city/county/province/state/country of legal jurisdiction.
7. How disputes will be settled.
8. The term (length) the deal will be in force.
9. That this is a binding agreement.
10. A place for the parties to acknowledge by signature that the deal is acceptable to them, along with a signature date.

Although deal memos often contain some casual letter language, they are enforceable contracts and are contract-language structured and exercised.

Letter Agreements

These agreements are more formalized than deal memos. They are also prepared on the producer's letterhead and are in letter form, but they use more formal contract language, though in a more relaxed format than long-form contracts. These agreements typically use contract titles (Bruce Joel Rubin, herein "Writer") and contain limited casual letter remarks. The ten contract elements referenced in the previous deal memo are included in the letter agreement, but in more formal contract language.

Long-Form Agreements

These agreements are neutral-party constructed, so they are not on any party's letterhead. They use an agreement title header (Literary Rights Option and Purchase Agreement) and are written to equally express the position of all participants. They are long, often impressive by their sheer weight, and, frankly, many times the girth is extremely helpful when troubles arise, clearly defining to legal counsel what the parties have agreed.

THE BENEFITS ASSOCIATED WITH THE PRODUCER PREPARING DEAL DOCUMENTATION

As negotiations come to a close, one of the deal-making parties will take the responsibility to prepare the first-draft deal documentation. Producers should never succumb to the temptation of allowing someone else to prepare this documentation on the basis that it would be one less thing they need to do or that it may save their legal fees. The document origination benefits far outweigh these or other considerations.

Whether the original draft is prepared by the producer or by the producer's attorney, it allows the producer the opportunity to encounter and propose terms for deal elements that will reveal themselves in the details of documenting that are often not dealt with between the parties during predocumentation negotiations. This enables the producer's deeper understanding of the deal's architecture and allows the producer to establish the deal-making integrity between the parties.

DEAL REVIEWS

One of the best ways for producers to learn contract language and to interpret all forms of deal documentation is for them to review and annotate documents before they meet with their attorneys.

If there are any terms you do not understand, or conditions that are not what you agreed to, you should make notes of these items. It is at this point that you are ready to meet with your attorney; ask your questions, review concerns, and direct your attorney to prepare an appropriate response. Remember, there are no unimportant phrases or words. Producers should find out what they mean. They may be benefits or pitfalls important to the deal.

THE ATTORNEY AS COUNSEL

Some time ago we closed a preliminary production financing relationship between a producer client and a distributor for an animated feature. Both parties warmly received the deal, and a precontract closing meeting was arranged.

The attorneys substantially took over the meeting, and, within a half day, had all but ruined the good feelings that before existed between the parties. At that point, documenting the deal appeared improbable.

One of the attending producers was a wonderfully creative writer and animator. He slipped us a sketch. It was a picture of a cow. We were pulling its horns, the distributors pulling at its tail, and the two attorneys had reached under the cow and were milking.

This is a bit unfair, as the attorneys for both sides were doing their aggressive best to achieve the finest deal and the greatest protection for their respective clients. However, the picture serves as an excellent reminder that although it is important for the parties of every agreement to allow their attorneys to make their contributions, it is most beneficial for those parties to continue to sustain control and responsibility for their relationships and transactions.

Attorneys are often the voice of their producer clients. Consequently, it is always appropriate for producers to apologize to other deal participants if their attorneys say something damaging to those with whom they are dealing. Producers should be careful to treat their attorneys with respect, especially in front of others. If producers want to redirect a meeting, it is most appropriate for producers to stop the meeting, take a break with their counsel, and then reconvene, moving in the direction they have decided, in light of their attorney's advice.

DISPUTE RESOLUTIONS

Every form of documentation should declare how disputes should be resolved, if they arise. The primary choices are mediation, arbitration, or litigation.

If the document simply states that it will be governed according to the laws of a certain jurisdiction, then disputes will be settled by traditional litigation. In major metropolitan areas around the world, because these matters will not be heard for months at the best—and in most major markets it is years—this resolution process could be expensive and the outcome determined by judgments of fact, legal points, and case precedents that may be substantially disassociated with what is a fair resolution by either party's evaluation.

Either of the other two options, arbitration or mediation, referred to by the court systems in the United States as alternative dispute resolution (ADR), are preferred by most producers. The more formalistic of the two ADR methods is arbitration. This process calls for a mutually agreed-upon or appointed arbiter (or arbiters) to hear the case, much like a judge who makes a determination that the parties have agreed in advance they will adhere to. Perhaps the most effective and exercised entertainment industry arbitration organization is the Independent Film & Television Alliance's Arbitration Tribunal, which serves the entire international film industry and is serviced mostly by attorneys or retired judges.

For many disputes, the best resolution is mediation. A mediator is like an arbiter, except a mediator explores the issues. There is a resolution only when both sides agree to a proposal. Mediated cases differ most substantially from litigation and arbitration in that it is typically not the case that only one side wins and the other side loses. Both sides participate in the solution. Both must agree, and the solution often improves the relationship between the parties or at least provides for a future one. Though some become protracted, most mediated issues are settled in one day. As in most disputes, each side has contributed at least somewhat to the disagreement, so mediation is often both the most fair and the most likely to foster a continued relationship between the parties.

CHAPTER POSTSCRIPT

The development, production, and rights sales of motion pictures engage the producer continually in the process of representations, negotiations, and documentation. The producer's attorney should be thoroughly involved in the producer's business. Consequently the selection and use of an attorney and law firm are critical factors in the producer's success and protection. Further, the producer should be deeply involved and increasingly experienced in all manner of legal matters.

CHAPTER 10
Talent, Agents, and Agencies

This chapter reviews the delicate business aspects associated with producers' vital relationships with talent and their representatives. Two effective metaphors for the relationship between a picture's producer and its talent are the relationships that exist between a general contractor of a construction project and the craftspeople, and that between a symphony's conductor and the orchestra.

Like a general contractor, the best producers are familiar with, and consequently respectful of, the many talents necessary to create their pictures. The talent the producer attaches will add as many, if not more, of the creative contributions as the producer does. Writers, directors, actors, cinematographers, composers, set designers, special effects, unit production managers (UPMs), editors, assistant directors (ADs), costumers, make-up artists, casting directors, transportation specialists, and many other critically important people are needed to contribute their creative brilliance to each picture.

Each of these talents is like a subcontractor in many respects. The artist maintains independent relationships with the producer—each responsible for performing according to the terms of the relationship—and contributes a crucial service that affects the picture as a whole. Further, just as a building project would be hurt if the general contractor personally handled the plumbing, electrical, or some other building aspect, so would producers hurt their film projects if they did not delegate critical responsibilities, such as directing, acting, and editing, to others.

The producer-talent relationship is also like an orchestra whose performers must be sensitive to each other in addition to the conductor. At certain moments, the brass section has to sound like one overwhelming instrument, not the trumpet section sounding distinct from the baritones or the French horns from the trombones. Brilliance, if it is out of harmony with other creative elements, fails miserably. A stunning set design that is incongruous with its story's action, costumes, and color is counterproductive to the picture. The producer, like the conductor, should balance all the elements of the picture in order to create the highest-impact creative experience. Even during principal photography, though all eyes must be on the director, it is good for all to remember that the director is also a talent who was brought into the picture by the independent producer.

DOI: 10.1016/B978-0-240-81463-6.00010-3

Great motion pictures are created by a team of artists who contribute their personal interpretation, within the story universe and parameters provided by the producer, and are harmonically tempered by all other immediate craft providers. For a producer to engage such a team of talent may seem improbable. Doing it well consistently, under the inevitable creative and financial pressure that accompanies every picture's creation, is a clear indication of seasoned genius. Steady-handed veteran producers like Gary Goetzman, Kennedy/Marshall, and Ron Howard consistently select, inspire, and negotiate great talent teams for their pictures. These producers commence from a foundation of respecting their co-creators and treating them fairly, which naturally draws the best from them.

Creation in its most celebrated form is both intimate and delicate. Losing oneself in the work and celebrating in the personal and collective triumphs is possible largely because of the temper and tenor of the producer. The producer establishes the universe in which everyone works. When producers are committed, skillful, valiant, wise, grateful, patient, merciful, generous, and capable of being a good friend, then the wrenching, chaotic frenzy that seems to necessarily settle in on the creation of motion pictures can actually be sweet when one of the participant's looks back on it.

This chapter focuses on the business aspects of the fragile and crucial task producers undertake to engage talent relationships that stir their enthusiasm for the story, give them the creative freedom to perform, and motivate them both creatively and financially to give the ultimate expression of the story's entertainment fire.

THE RELATIONSHIP EVOLUTION

Because writers were discussed in Chapter 9, this chapter considers other talent relationships, especially those involving directors and principal actors. Director selection usually commences at one of the following development steps:

- The producer attaches a director at the start of their development process, which can be from option of story idea, life rights, treatment, or screenplay. At this beginning point, the director becomes a creatively intimate partner with the producer in the visionary development of the material.
- The producer attaches the director after development of the material. The selection of the director at this point is based on matching the producer's vision with that of the director and, as important, the value in the marketplace of that director, based on distributor consultations and greenlight analysis.

Previous to either option being implemented, the potential directors' prior pictures should be screened and studied in the context of the picture in development, and discussions/meetings with the bond company and distributors concerning these referenced directors and their pictures become important sources of information:

- The primary purpose of the bond company discussion/meetings is to vet the reliability of the directors to come in on budget and schedule and to discover any problems past producers might have had working with them.
- The two primary purposes of the distributor discussion/meetings are (1) to inform the producer relative to the marketing and relationship advantages that each director being considered could bring to each major territory and (2) to advance each distributor's commitment through each one's participation in the selection process.

Producers should have five or more selections on their directing lists.

The process with attaching actor talent is similar, but it typically happens later in the development process than attaching the director. The director is the producer's key visionary to create and deliver the picture. The producer and director must be in synch with the actor talent to be attached, as advised through the distributor relationships. The director usually is the major component to attracting the actor talent and giving actors the comfort they need to know they will be treated with respect and given the freedom to create their characters and add substance to the film through their interpretation of the role.

Attaching the actor talent needs to be closely aligned with the distributors and the values of the potential actor in each territory. This is a creative and business/ marketing analysis that is closely aligned with the existing brand, if any, of the project and other marketing elements that will empower the viability of the project in the worldwide market, ensuring the investors will have every opportunity to recoup their investment.

Meetings with Talent, Agents, and Managers

Agents deliver many essential benefits to their talent clients; among them are negotiating and documenting fair deals and assisting their clients in both the search and evaluation of pictures that will advance their careers.

Creative protectionist producers are classically undercapitalized. One of the consequences of this chronic condition is their aggressive attempts to attach talent to their pictures without the agents' participation or to represent that talent are interested/attached before the producer, in fact, has a documented relationship. These predeal attachments most often are used to assist these producers in their attempt to obtain production funding for their pictures.

Agents have, therefore, become fierce guardians of their clients against the abuses associated with this approach. As a consequence, agents save their clients from misrepresentation and having to defend themselves in associated legal actions.

Fortunately, balanced producers typically use both development funding and some form of bank facilitated production financing, which allows them the ability to make pay-or-play contingent offers or holding fee deals to attach talent.

Because each motion picture is a new story, a unique creation, and a new business venture, its producers must assemble a new team of co-creators. Therefore, producers need to test each major talent's creative affinity for the picture, especially the director and lead cast, before negotiating the financial aspects of the relationship. Producers want to know, in strict confidence, whether a particular director or actor has both the vision and passion essential for a critically important creative contribution for the picture in question. So it is during the creative meeting process that the producer and talent must "fall in love" around the picture. It's comparatively easy to agree on a convenient schedule and monetary amounts, but if this is the primary basis for the relationship, it yields a thin, incomplete foundation among the picture, the talent, and the producer.

Most producer-talent creative meetings are delicate, especially if they are a first-time alliance. Fortunately, these meetings are often accomplished with the cooperation and blessing of their respective agents. If not, producers should be prepared for a well-deserved, testy agent response.

If, for any reason, there is a meeting with talent before an agent is called to participate, the producer should immediately assure the talent and agent, in writing, of the following:

1. No representation will be made to anyone outside the production company that the talent has been contacted regarding the picture or that any relationship exists between the talent and the picture, the producer, or the production company.
2. The producer will not talk with the talent about money or other deal points without the agent's participation.
3. Should there be future discussions about the picture, these will be accomplished with the agent's participation.

If such a meeting takes place, this letter or any form of later repentance on the part of the producer will not placate most agents. It is not easy to receive, but it is always best to take creative meetings before business meetings with the knowledge and participation of the talent's agent.

The purpose of the creative meeting is to obtain the most essential element in the producer's evaluation: how the talent feels about and envisions the story. Beyond reviewing their preceding pictures and discussions with prior producers, it is in these creative meetings that producers can receive a clear revelation of a picture's director and lead cast.

Talent manager/management companies are increasingly important and valuable participants in this process. They are more unrestricted in their ability to assist their talent in project participation and are often uniquely beneficial links to talent. Managers have the legal freedom to attach themselves as producers to projects they secure for their talent. For projects in which they feel their talent should participate, they may even assist in securing further financing.

Once creative meetings are finished, the producer prepares to negotiate the deal.

ATTORNEYS AS AGENTS

Talent with brand-significant names may use their attorneys in negotiations along with their agents. Other major talent may use only their agents or managers, and still others use only their attorneys. Just as agents become expert in the legal aspects of deal making, some attorneys develop an affinity for the creative aspects of these negotiations. And for some talent, their attorney may be their agent.

PLANNING THE DEAL

Some members of the production team join during development. These include writers, directors, production designers, and others busy developing the project often months before preproduction begins. This includes lead acting talent who may be attached early to assure their schedule and for the producer to receive the benefit of their project commitment for presale purposes. When planning the proposed talents' deal structures, it is best for producers to create the production portion of the deal terms first, then the development terms. The producer first discovers what may be a fair fee for the performer's production services, keeping in mind the talent's current quote (usually what they were last paid for ether a studio-level picture or an independent picture), in context with the picture's projected gross, its budget, and the services demanded of the talent. The talent's fee, then, should be within the bounds of the production budget, or that talent should not be considered unless he or she is willing to take a deal under their current quotes.

DEVELOPMENT NEGOTIATION

It is essential that the production terms are agreed upon first, including the schedule, the payment amount (including points), the talent's credits, and all other associated benefits. Once the production terms are agreed upon, the stage is set for development terms. The production portion of the relationship will not commence until after the motion picture has been completely developed.

The agreement's development period typically will last somewhere between 6 and 12 months. Producers should add a contingency period to the actual development schedule to provide for unforeseen scheduling and other unexpected issues. These are often associated with script problems or talent schedule conflicts. As the greatest talent earnings are usually paid during production, negotiating these first allows much less pressure negotiating the development terms. These deal points include how long the development period will be; if there are to be extensions (and if there are, how long) and how much the fees will be, if any (sometimes referred to as a holding fee); and if this is an exclusive or non-exclusive deal (if it is exclusive, it actually will bind the talent to a specific performing schedule).

If the deal is nonexclusive and has an unspecified start date, then it will have a significantly lower development fee or none at all, because it does not interfere with other talent activities. Nonexclusive development deals are easier to negotiate and have lower upfront fees; however, they can be challenging in terms of schedule coordination as the development of the picture matures.

If the producer binds the talent to a set performance schedule, the producer should assume that during the picture's development, the talent will turn down other offers that conflict with the agreed-upon schedule. Consequently, the producer should include a fair "pay-or-play" payment guarantee or a holding fee, which ensures that the talent will be paid, regardless of whether or not the talent actually performs the production services.

Advance fees cover two general categories: the expenses incurred by the talent and representatives to investigate and negotiate the deal and talent compensation for the value the producer receives in attaching the talent to the picture.

Development fees are largely affected by talent participation during development. If they are hardly involved, these fees typically begin at 1 percent of the production performance fee and are often much higher than this. For example, if a director's production fee is $3 million, the corresponding development fee would be at least $30,000. Most directors and writers also provide services in a picture's continuing development and will be paid fees commensurate with their services and guild requirements.

Mature production companies typically have generous financial elasticity to match the demands of their deals. In contrast, newer production companies may be limited to rigid development budgets. In every case, though, talent should receive fair value for their participation. Especially producers with budgetary restraints will likely need to entice their talent with additional profit participation. The critical producer objective in these negotiations is not to end up with the maximum points or dollars but to attach the ultimate team who feel appreciated, well treated, and confident in their relationships.

POINTS PARTICIPATION

It can be an advantage to the picture to have the director and principal cast receive part of the fees as profit participation in the picture. Nothing can take the place of the talent commitment and enthusiasm that comes with being a central participant in the telling of a great story.

Because points are most often represented by a percentage, producers should first calculate the projected value of these points in future income by applying the points percentage to the sales breakdown of the producer's gross profit. This provides talent and their representatives a critical point of reference when evaluating their offer. Such representations should always be given with the explanation that these are projected figures and cannot be guaranteed.

Definitions of long-form contract profit participation are typically 10 to 20 pages long. The fairest position for profit participants to partake is in the producer's actual gross profits. This is all the money that the producer earns from a particular picture before any of the producer's overhead is deducted. This is the amount from which talent who have points in the picture should participate.

Producers may finance in-house distribution units that directly license some of their pictures' rights. It is therefore fair for such producers to deduct distribution fees and actual out-of-pocket direct distribution expenses from the producer's gross profits, before talent profit participations. This fee should be competitive with industry-independent distributors. The fairest deal is the one in which all the parties participate at the same level.

PREPARATION OF A FAIR DEAL

Like the genius strategist Napoleon, who is known for "winning his battles in his tent," the industry's most prosperous producers owe much of their success in every area to studied tent work. Before talent and their representatives are approached, producers should become thoroughly familiar with all of the important aspects of each of the players under consideration. They should clearly measure the deal points and ensure they are in balance with the unique contributions of the talent, the demands of the picture, and its budget.

All the producers' research, analysis, and presentation preparation combine to assure them of the ultimate creative team attachment. In addition, it serves to reassure the talent and their representatives that they are appreciated, appropriately valued by the producer, are receiving a fair deal, and are beginning a relationship that is well planned. The beginning of this relationship should be reaffirmed in the producer's documentation and deal performance.

AGENTS AS CREATIVE RESOURCES

Agents, managers, talent, and attorneys can be exceptional creative resources, both inside and outside their agencies and firms for producers. In seeking to make allies of these important resources, a studied approach will yield a producer easier negotiations, fairer deals, and pictures with talent who are more content to deliver their maximum creative capacities. This approach will also help the producer to avoid difficult negotiating deadlocks and development delays.

TALENT RESERVE

Before producers should begin their first-choice talent negotiations, their secondary talent offers should be completely prepared and ready to negotiate. Having done this, producers create at least two advantages for themselves: they won't be negatively influenced in the negotiations because they rely exclusively on a single talent, and if the need arises, the producer is prepared to segue into a secondary talent approach without loss of time. It often seems like the secondary choice would be a distant second. But this is not necessarily so, particularly when you look at the long list of distant seconds—many of whom consistently become absolute genius selections—in comparison to the producer's first choice.

THE PARTICIPATION OF THE PRODUCER'S ATTORNEY

Following the preparation of a talent proposal, producers should present a written summary of the deal proposal to their attorneys for review and comments. For even the most experienced producers, these reviews are often very beneficial.

Further, new or obscure producers often benefit by allowing their attorneys to make the initial talent-agent contact. First impressions are important, and the point-of-reference of a substantive attorney and law firm is often more beneficial in the establishment of the relationship.

CHAPTER POSTSCRIPT

Although there are personal objectives involved, the strongest tie that binds producers and talent is the fact that together they may turn great stories into wonderfully entertaining motion pictures. The most effective beginning for the producer-talent relationship is in initial meetings, in which each party is allowed to test the other's creative affinity for a particular picture, followed by deal-making meetings that have the blessing and participation of the talent's agent, manager, or attorney. Research, planning, and preparation will help render talent attachment a more predictable experience.

CHAPTER 11

Development, Production, and Producing Company Structures

This chapter presents the basic business structures of and the relationships between the operations and companies producers use to manage their motion picture development and production operations.

THE POWER OF COMPANY STRUCTURE

The purpose of company structure is to do the following:

- Provide the business entity with a legal identity recognized by governmental bodies (city, county, state, province, federal, etc.) tax authorities, and other businesses and individuals
- Establish an independent, tangible, tradable business presence with the capacity to increase in value
- Deliver company owners increased business/trading capacities, legal protection, and expanded taxation options

An actor who owns three screenplays and functions as an individual from a fully operational home office is treated substantially different from this same actor, with the same assets, who forms an independent production company around these assets. However, that individual's capacity to communicate does not automatically increase, nor, unfortunately, do the screenplays become better; but the individual's deal-making power and the responsiveness from other businesses may be more immediate and serious than they are when applied to the actor as an individual.

If a talent wants to co-produce a picture with a production company, a talent/ company deal naturally transpires. If a production company wants to co-produce with another production company, a company-to-company co-production deal transpires. The deal point array and relative benefits of the company-to-company transaction are much more extensive and potentially more beneficial to the talent than is the talent/company transaction.

THE PRODUCER'S OPERATIONS AND COMPANIES

Producers achieve maximum structure benefits by managing three separate levels of operations. Each level is accounted separately. The advantage of having multiple

DOI: 10.1016/B978-0-240-81463-6.00011-5

operations is that they deliver the producer operating clarity, clear accounting separation for all profit participants on each project, and critical picture-to-picture legal protection.

As represented in the chart in Figure 11.1 these three levels are the production operation, the development operations, and the producing operations or the single picture producing companies. Though these operations are accounted separately, typically each production company's group of operations exists in the same offices and are operated by the same people.

As these operations result in individual productions, most independent production entities form at least two of these operations into separate companies. (1) The

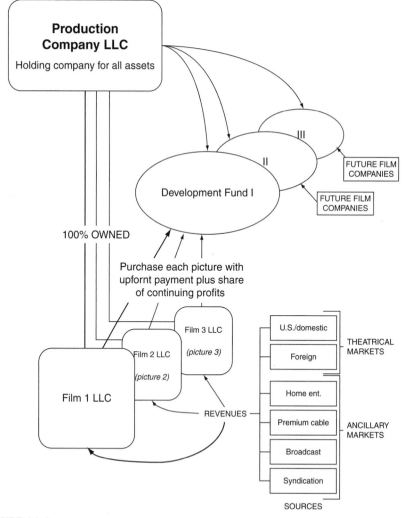

FIGURE 11.1
Business structure and revenue flow.

production company becomes a holding, asset management and overall operations governance company, (2) the development operations are either part of the production company or can be beneficially operated from a separate entity for funding and operating clarity, and (3) each picture is placed in its own separate producing entity.

Production Company

The production company is a holding company for the producer's interests in all the development and producing operations/entities. The production company is the producer's brand presence. Spyglass Entertainment, New Regency Productions, and Hyde Park Entertainment are examples of these production companies.

The production company is the business entity for its owners, administrative team, permanent creative team, marketing team, distribution group (unless operated as a separate entity), story department, producer's support team, and accounting operations. Producers may also manage their development operations within their production companies, and they produce their motion pictures through their individual producing companies.

The production company is the producer's command central. It is a strategic planning entity and manages all the assets. Through this entity, the executive team defines, develops, and manages the producer's objectives. This company retains continuing relationships with all studios, distributors, talent, banks, completion guarantors, and other entertainment organizations. It also reviews all literary properties, receives all pitches, and handles all the advertising and public relations for the companies.

The production company is most often a corporation or limited liability company (LLC), which historically provides the producer with the most legal and tax protection. For an excellent and concise explanation of the different types of legal entities, see Schuyler M. Moore's book, *The Biz*, Chapter 3: Entities.

Development Companies

Many production entities fulfill their development operations within their production company. However, having one or more separate development companies provides producers with cleaner costing and taxation separation, as well as more flexible development financing options.

Development companies fulfill all the creative and business development of the pictures that the producers have selected. For these development companies, the producers are typically the senior development directors, supported by other members of the production company's staff.

If producers use private investors to fund some or all of their development, more than one development company is sometimes used. In such case, each development company may be established to develop a fixed number of pictures, usually at least three and less than ten. For instance, the development company referenced in the company diagram is organized to develop three pictures.

If the producer uses private investors in the development companies, these companies are normally LLCs, delivering investors the greatest protection and taxation benefits and offering the producer the greatest operating flexibility. Investing in a slate of pictures developed by each of these companies enables beneficially specific investor recoupment and returns structures.

Producing Companies

Because, in many ways, each picture is substantially a separate business, it is highly advantageous for accounting, tax, and legal reasons to form each picture as a separate business entity. This is the only picture this company will ever produce. The single company status isolates both the picture's accounting and its liability from the producers' other pictures. Each producing company is wholly owned by the production company and typically is structured as an LLC.

OPERATION AND COMPANY INTERRELATIONSHIPS

The permanent office location for each of the producers' operations/companies is most often in the production company office. As the producer's holding company, the production company usually owns all or the producer's share of each operations/company.

DEVELOPMENT COMPANY FINANCING

Development is that creative gestation precursor essential to motion picture production. Producers financing their development should consider structuring this through a separate entity. Each new development company could be launched around a specific business and investment return plan, prepared by the producer, to develop and produce a specific number of pictures over several years (for instance, three pictures over four years). This plan is set forth in a month-by-month activity projection. The capital need for this company is discovered through the preparation of a cash flow projection that corresponds with the company's activity projection. These projections are presented in Chapter 12.

Seasoned production companies typically finance project development from their own profits. Studios and co-production relationships are also common resources for part or all of development financing. Balanced producers may also consider using private financing for their pictures' development. Depending on structure, there can be financial advantages unique to motion picture development financing for both production companies and investors.

Investors evaluate investment offerings primarily by each offering's risk, term until potential investment recoupment, investment amount, and earnings potential. Consider these qualities in the following risk evaluation comparing investing in motion picture development and motion picture production.

Description	Development	Production
Risk	Development completion	Development, production, and distribution
Term until recoupment	18–24 months	36 months
Investment amount	$150,000 - $2 million per picture	$5 - $70 million per picture
Earnings potential	300% gross yield over 5 years	(assuming achieves major theatrical distribution) Break even to 200% gross yield over 7–9 years

FIGURE 11.2
Motion picture development vs. production investment risk evaluation.

Companies with solid development performance can give investors opportunities with a lower investment amount and higher income in a shorter return period—qualities that investors typically prefer. Production companies seeking private investors for their development companies may offer their investors 50/50 ownership in the company 100 percent of the first proceeds received paid to the investors until they have recouped more than their original investment (i.e., 120 percent to 150 percent), and thereafter an equal sharing (50 percent/ 50 percent) of the company's profits.

Earnings can flow into the development company from its sale of all rights, title, and interest from each fully developed picture to one of the production company's producing companies. The amount of each of these sales can be preset as part of the development company's offering. This amount is equal to or greater than the amount necessary to return all the investors' capital plus an additional 20 percent to 50 percent.

For example, the development company could be structured (1) to develop three motion pictures, (2) with a total capitalization of $2 million, (3) with the investors to receive 100 percent of all income until they recoup 120 percent of their investment, with 50 percent profit share thereafter, (4) and the sale of each developed property from the development company to each of the single picture producing companies set at $1.2 million, (5) plus receiving 20 percent of 100 percent of the producer's profits of each picture. Within this structure, if the producer succeeds in developing at least two of three pictures, this relationship will recoup the investors' financial outlay, plus a 20 percent return, from the sale of the first two pictures ($2.4 million returned on the $2 million invested). If the producers succeed in developing the third picture, the investors will receive additional earnings from the sale of this picture to a third producing company owned by the production company. Additionally, the development company and its investors participate in the profits of the completed pictures. The inescapable risk in this scenario resides in (1) the ability of the producer's development company to develop and finance at least two of the three pictures. Seasoned producers recognize that development is neither time nor expense predictable. So the risk is real. However, a good match can be made between producers with solid development experience and financiers seeking a return-dynamic motion picture investment structure.

SECURITIES

Regardless of the global territory, investment offerings of all kinds must conform to all securities laws within the area where the solicited investors reside. These laws and regulations are highly sophisticated, and producers should have their offerings prepared by their legal and accounting advisors. The planning and preparation of a development investment memorandum is discussed in Chapter 12.

FORMS OF COMPANIES

There are several forms of company structures, each having several advantages. Producers are best served meeting with their legal counsel, who will lead them through a series of questions, the answers to which should reveal the best company structures for their operating, financing, taxation, growth, and protection objectives.

If just one person is involved, a production company may be commenced as a sole proprietorship. Often, these organizations may commence their legal life by simply filing a fictitious name with a local recording office (in the United States this is usually with the county clerk) according to the directions given by the recording officer. This gives the producer the documentation needed to open a bank account and officially use the name recorded in the area in which it is registered. This is quick and inexpensive, but it does not give the producer the legal protection that comes with more sophisticated company structures.

Once a production company is ready to commence earnest business, most attorneys will suggest that it form an LLC or incorporate. This delivers the owners (partners and stakeholders) personal legal protection from actions that may be taken against the entity. When the entity is still limited in its partners/stakeholders and earnings, it can receive special tax status that will allow the tax liabilities to be passed through to the stakeholders, so they are not burdened with an additional entity taxation.

In the United States, the most flexible and popular structure producers use for protection and single instead of double taxation is a limited liability company (LLC). In most states in the United States, the cost of setting up an LLC and corporation are the same.

CHAPTER POSTSCRIPT

Company structure is important at start-up, and that importance increases as an entity grows. Structure determines asset protection, investor and other partner flexibility, protection of the principals, and limited access to outside entities of the parent entities' various assets. Balanced producers adopt structures that promote and enable their project development, production, and long-term rights sales—structures providing them with the greatest operating power, structural stability, flexibility, investor benefits, and personal and picture protection. Producers who model their operations after this pattern receive these proven benefits.

CHAPTER 12
Development Financing

This chapter discusses the purposes of development financing and the methods and resources from which to secure this financing.

THE ESSENTIAL POWER OF FUNDED DEVELOPMENT

Producers often share a common understanding about the schedule and resources it takes for the average motion picture to fulfill production. However, the schedule and resources for a motion picture to complete development often garner more questions than answers. For example, does a picture's development time include, and should related overhead expenses be charged to, each "go" project for reading scripts and listening to pitches that lead to the discovery of that project's story? And are not most of a motion picture's final development activities and expenses also part of its preproduction and should therefore eventually be allocated to its production budget? The answer to these questions is certainly yes.

Producers should plan, finance, and manage their pictures' entire development process to enable them to move through development at a steady, confident pace that will continue through production and distribution. Every picture has its unique development and production schedule. The following is an example of a typical picture's schedule.

This model demonstrates that, in a well-planned and sufficiently funded independent production entity environment, 24 (two thirds) of the 36 months of a typical picture's complete development and production process is spent in development. As producers invest the majority of their time developing pictures, this should be, as is done in the best-operated production organizations, a finely orchestrated process, adequately financed and performed according to schedules, budgets, and accountability, in keeping with the integrity of each picture's production processes.

Most producers have multiple pictures in development and production at the same time. Multiple pictures sustain a continuous flow of projects and allow their production company to amortize (distribute) fixed development overhead costs over several pictures. Even with amortization, development overhead in the United States typically averages $150,000 to $800,000 per picture

DOI: 10.1016/B978-0-240-81463-6.00012-7

and more depending on how many writers and drafts are required, and if it is necessitated, holding fees to secure the director and lead cast. In addition to these expenses, the accomplishment of all of the development steps typically takes the development team a minimum of 18 months, and often much, much longer.

Description	Approximate months	Cumulative months
Development- prestory acquisition: reading, researching, internal greenlight, first core-territory distributor meetings	5	5
Development - story acquisition	1	6
Development - shooting script evolution: original drafts, rewrites, and polishes	12	18
Development - director and lead talent attachments; physical production prep (all elements including location considerations/site visits/relationship explorations, production boards, budgets, schedules, etc., exploration and determination of production design, visual and sound effects, and other production elements unique to the picture that demand development planning and articulation)	(Done by team during the same 12 months as above)	
Development - finance and sales plan; development marketing material creation and subsequent versions; global distributor meetings and collaborative relationship engagements; presales, completion bond application and preliminary approval, production banking loan memorandum prep and preliminary approval; commence trade/audience PR; execute distribution agreements and presales; publisher and other ancillary product relationship establishment, etc.]	6 Much of this done during above 12 months	24
Preproduction	3	27
Principal photography	3	30
Post-production	6	36

FIGURE 12.1
Motion picture development and production schedule.

Producers should understand that development is the foundation of each picture. A strong foundation allows producers to produce their pictures with predictable confidence. A weak development foundation is the number one reason pictures don't get made, dissemble during production, or have lackluster earning power. Understanding this, producers ought to ensure that each aspect of their picture's development is just as intricately planned, budgeted, and sufficiently funded as its principal photography.

DEVELOPMENT FUNDING SOURCES

Primary sources of development funding include:

- The production company
- A studio
- Private investors

- Co-production relationships
- Government agencies
- Crowd funding

Production Company Financing

Most mature production companies fund at least some, if not all, of their development expenses from cash flow or bank credit facilities. For many of these companies, this funding is only interim and is repaid to the production company when either a separately funded development company is set up or the picture is acquired by its producing company.

Studio Financing

The studios' production departments provide development financing for only the most established independent production companies. Some have a solid history of producing profitable films, like Jon Turtletaub for Disney. Others have a good long-term distribution relationship with the studio, like New Regency for Fox. Then, there are former studio executives that negotiate themselves into independent production structures, like Unique Features for Warner Bros. and Chernin Entertainment for Fox. The chief studio motivation in these relationships is the ownership and distribution of significant pictures.

Investor Financing

Balanced producers often engage in relationships with a limited number of sophisticated private investors who provide development financing for their pictures. Mature balanced production companies sustain cash flows from earnings and maintain bank credit facilities substantially greater than are needed to finance all their development expenses without engaging investment capital. Some of these companies still elect to use development private-investor partners. The primary motivation for this is that development investor partners do the following:

- Promote a more focused management for each picture's development progress
- Provide tighter control of development expenses (which, for many production companies, may easily slip out of control)
- Balance the producer's risk
- Expand capital availability

In Chapter 11, the terms and company structure that best accommodate development investors are presented. Producers should prepare a development business plan and if necessary, a private placement memorandum (PPM or offering) with the assistance and under the direction of an experienced securities attorney.

Regardless of your global territory, there are local and country government securities regulations to which such offerings and investor relations must comply. In the United States there are state and federal securities and exchange commissions (SECs). These regulators both protect investors and provide a structure that governs and identifies investment offerings.

Development offerings are most often prepared for the exclusive review and participation in a securities investor category that in the United States is called *sophisticated* or *accredited investors*. This securities category varies depending on where you globally reside, but it basically refers to investors who are experienced in investments similar in amount and risk to the one being offered and possess a specific minimum net worth that demonstrates even greater sophistication and the investor's ability to risk the investment's failure.

The advantages of using this offering category are that, first of all, the producer has an exclusive relationship with investors who are durable and experienced, thus allowing for less fear of investor impact if the development company, for any reason, fails to achieve its objectives. It also makes for smoother presentations to experienced, business-savvy potential participants. Another important advantage of sophisticated/accredited investor offerings is that they are simpler, less expensive, and less time consuming to prepare than nonrestricted public offerings. Sophisticated/accredited investor offerings are restricted in their content, presentation, and number of participants. Among other minimum requirements, sophisticated/accredited investor offerings must conform to securities regulation language. This language gives investors and their representatives reference to each offering in relation to the laws governing it. It also includes complete and clear declarations of the risks related to the investment. The offerings are typically numbered, and a log is kept of each investor who has been presented an offering copy, those retrieved, and, certainly, the number of investment interests actually purchased. Depending on the securities regulations, the number of participating investors may be limited to as few as 10. This restriction keeps the investor group to a manageable size, but it may result in a high per-investment amount (one tenth for example), which may further restrict the number of potential investors.

A producer's first development offering is often the most challenging to prepare and fund. However, following the initial offering, subsequent offerings are simpler to author and fund. Typically, some of the original investors want to reinvest in one or more of the producer's future development entities, and new investors are now substantially easier to engage, using the first development company as a powerful point of reference. Most producers will find it challenging to obtain their initial development financing. But sophisticated investors are just that. They are skilled investors, looking for exceptional investment opportunities. They wisely tend to shy away from untried management teams and industries in which they are inexperienced.

Co-production Company Financing

Production companies can receive development financing for their projects from other production companies that have development funding and, consequently, are seeking the strongest stories.

The two most desperate development positions for producers to be in are (1) to have one or more sterling stories that have passed their internal greenlight but not to have sufficient capital to develop them, and (2) to have development capital and either only weak stories to choose from or no story that has passed their greenlight.

Producers are generally very receptive to story pitches from other producers seeking funding through co-production relationships. Co-development/production relationships are most often set up for a single picture. One production company provides the story and the development progress related to it; the other company provides the development capital. They both share in the development and production of the picture. Equity is divided according to the value of each party's contributions.

Government Agency Financing

Most countries have an economic development department. The common mandate of these departments is to grow their countries' productivity and enliven their industries. Many of these countries provide a broad variety of support, including tax incentives, rebates, loans, and outright grants. Some of these are exclusive to entities headquartered in or at least residing in these countries; others may be participated in by those globally, if the production entity complies with the specific program's criteria. Countries may be further bolstered by additional jurisdictional government bodies (states, provinces, and territories) with similar incentive programs. Some programs are offered by a collaboration of multiple countries, such as the European Union.

Although information on these programs is readily available (much of which is an astounding bundle of difficult-to-navigate documents) from the agencies that regulate them, as these programs come and go with the government bodies that oversee them, it is most beneficial, safe, and sane to use a legal or accounting group that specializes in the specific program(s) that may apply, allow them to evaluate, recommend the strategy, and apply and manage the relationship. Whereas some countries do not provide any development funding, other countries provide much or all of it, for those who qualify.

Crowdfunding

Crowdfunding describes the collective cooperation, attention and trust by people who network and pool their money together, usually via the Internet, in order to support efforts initiated by other people or organizations. **Crowdfunding** occurs for any variety of purposes, from disaster relief to citizen journalism to artists seeking support from fans, to political campaigns.

— **Source: Wiki**

Crowdfunding films is an alternative model for both development and production financing by going online and soliciting donations. In other words, it does not include investments and only includes the donations, memberships, and preordering of products, giving none of the funders future profits in the film. This online solicitation is called *crowd funding* or *tribe funding*. So far, they seem to work best for documentaries or social issue films because most crowd funders are typically linked by social networks or shared interests. The amounts typically do not exceed $25,000, so it appears to be a limited resource. However, this is a quickly changing environment and obviously only restricted by the size of the crowd and their motivation.

There are two websites worth mentioning that are presently crowdfunding movies through "donations": www.IndieGoGo.com and www.Kickstarter.com. Both of these sites use a donation model that also offers the participants a "reward" of some kind, such as a DVD, a T-shirt, or a poster of the funded project. The rewards for donations from funders are typically tiered, offering larger rewards for larger donations.

Because soliciting investments from the general public is most often illegal unless the opportunity has been filed with an appropriate securities regulatory authority, such as the SEC in the United States, producers should seek legal advice before using this solicitation model.

There is also another unique model we are currently tracking that has not been utilized yet called CinemaShares.com. CinemaShares.com is a website for fan financing, or crowdfunding, major feature films by offering single shares of stock online to movie fans to finance a movie. A proposed movie is posted on the CinemaShares website, and fans can purchase as little as a single $22 preferred share of NASDAQ listed stock in the company owning the proposed movie in order to fund it. When the site accumulates the total required budget, the offering closes, the producers can access the money, and production begins. The CinemaShares.com method of crowdfunding is a complex securities transaction, subject to numerous rules and regulations that make it feasible to only fund large productions, as the cost of complying with these regulations can be considerable. However, the CinemaShares.com method could be the wave of the future, as many funding sources have now dried up and in addition to providing the very scarce film financing, this method has other advantages such as offering investors the liquidity of a publicly trading stock and eliminating the typical loan repayment and interest charges. CinemaShares.com has a business patent on this model, and crowdfunding could very well be the wave of the future in film financing.

THE PROCESS OF SECURING DEVELOPMENT FINANCING

There are seven basic steps to obtaining development financing, described as follows.

1. Develop a Business Plan

This is the cornerstone to success in obtaining the necessary funding. Refer back to Chapter 6 for the elements a business plan needs to address. Producers should evaluate their resources (operating team, stories, cash flow) and recommit to or redefine their mission statement (why they are in business, the kind of pictures they want to make, the way they want to make them, the style of doing business internally and with others, and so on). They should also make decisions about the basic development planning possibilities, including the number of pictures to be developed within the new development company, the stories (if any) that the producer has, and the most logical sources from which to receive development funding.

2. Prepare the Activity Projection

This is a list of the primary activities performed for the company's pictures during their development. These activities are presented in a month-by-month spreadsheet format, showing in a single projection each separate activity for all the pictures developed.

The activity projection shown in Figure 12.2 has been set up for the development of three pictures. Several production companies are currently using this basic form for planning and managing their development operations/companies.

This example is predicated on a particular producer's resources. The activities and format are universal. The layout may be helpful to producers in planning their individual development operations/entities. The timing represented is just an example—producers should not expect their plan to be timed like those in the example. There is an activity projection on the website ready to be filled in.

The chart tracks over five years and is broken into months. The first far-left description row is labeled *Event* and tracks the major worldwide markets and sales events. Various points about how the producer accomplishes the activities referenced in this projection have been presented in previous chapters, are chronicled in Chapter 14, or are presented later.

The initial activities are labeled *Start-up*. Some categories are for new producers who have not previously engaged an attorney, publicist, or entertainment bank, or who have not started trade press releases for their production company.

The *Development: Creative* section primarily charts the producer's story discovery plan. This plan includes developing stories that are internally greenlit, as well as soliciting and reading scripts (as part of the search for new properties). Subsequently, the producer goes through the process of garnering the United States and international distributor greenlights.

For most pictures, *attaching the director*, which includes researching, creative meetings, and negotiating, precedes attaching lead talent and most other development functions. A director is fundamental to each picture's creative life. It is essential that the director be brought in early and allowed to participate in all other facets of a picture's development and production.

YEAR	2011												2012	
MONTH OF OPERATION	1	2	3	4	5	6	7	8	9	10	11	12	13	14
CALENDAR MONTH	Jan	Feb	Mar	Apr	May	Jun	Jul	Aug	Sep	Oct	Nov	Dec	Jan	Feb
Event		BERLIN			CANNES		COMIC CON	GENCON			AFM			BERLIN
Start-Up														
Prepare all legal & busn docs	X	X												
Funding	X													
Retain Entertainment Atty	X	X												
Set-up Office	X	X												
Hire Development & Office Assistant	X			X										
Retain Publicist		X												
Entertainment Bank Open	X													
Development: Creative														
Read Scripts & Lit Properties	1,2,3	1,2,3	2,3	2,3	2,3	3	3	3	3	3	3			
Option Rights			1		2						3			
Internal Greenlight		1	1								3			
Search, meet, negotiate & document writer		1	1	1		2	2					3	3	
Commence Writer on 1st draft						2	2					3	3	
Deliver 1st Draft									2					
Commence Writer on Director Rewrite					1				2					
Deliver Director Rewrite						1				2				
Commence Writer on Talent Polish							1			2				
Deliver Talent Polish								1			2			
Prep / Produce Promo Materials				1		2								
Core Territory & Major Int'l Territory Distributor Meetings			1	1				2	2					
Global Distributor Creative Correlation Begin				1					2					
Director: List Considerations		1	1	1						2	2			
Director: Submissions & Meetings			1	1	1					2	2	2	2	
Director: Select, Negotiate, Document					1							2	2	
Actors: List Lead Considerations		1	1	1	1					2	2	2	2	
Actors: Submissions & Meetings					1	1				2			2	
Actors: Select, Negotiate, Document						1	1						2	
Talent: Story Meetings & Notes						1	1							
Additional Screenplay Drafts							1	1						
Shooting Script								1						
Keys: List Production Talent					1	1	1	1					2	2
Keys: Meet, Select, Negotiate, Document						1	1	1					2	2
Development: Production														
Location Scout								1						
1st Pass Production Budget/Schedule						1							2	
UPM: Meetings/Negotiate/Document				1					1	1				2
Shooting Draft Breakdown/Boards								1	1					
Final Production Budget/Schedule								1	1					
Completion Bond Meetings			1								2			
Completion Bond Set									1					

Picture: Funding

Activity													
Establish Financing Plan	1	1					2						3
Bank Review and Acceptance of Financing Plan			1				2	2					
Equity: Negotiate / Document		1	1	1			2	2	2			2	2
Tax/ Location Benefits: Research & Meetings		1	1	1			2	2	2			2	2
Tax/ Location Benefits: Negotiate & Document			1	1									
Int'l Sales Agent: Meet/Negotiate/Document		1						2					
Int'l Pre-Sales: Submissions / Meetings			1	1		1	1						
Int'l Pre-Sales: Negotiate / Document				1		1	1						
Core Territory: Submission / Meetings		1	1	1		1							
Core-Territory: Negotiate / Document			1	1		1							2
Engage Bank Production Funding			1	1				1					
Sell Picture to Producing Company			1	1				1					

Ancillary Rights Development

Activity													
Establish Rights Liquidation Plan	1			2								3	
Plan Retail, Web, TV, Radio, Print Promotion		1	1					2	2				
Meet/Select/Negotiate Brand/Merchandising Partners				1		1							
Publisher Novelization: Negotiate & Document								1	1				
Soundtrack: Negotiate / Document			1			1	1	1					

Pre-Production | | | | | | | | 1 | 1 | | | 1 | 1 |
Principal Photography | | | | | | | | | | | | | |
Post Production | | | | | | | | 1 | 1 | | | 1 | 1 |

Marketing

Activity													
Website Creation & Installation/Niche & Social Networking						1	1	1	1			1	2
Trade Releases	X							1	1			1	1
Consumer PR								1	1			1	1
Corporate Sponsorship PR & Branding													
Other PR & Co-Promo													

Release Dates and After Market

Activity													
Int'l Rights Licensing								1	1			1	1
No. America Theatrical Release													
No. America Home Ent. Release													
No. America Premium Cable TV Release													
No. America PPV													
No. America Network Television													
Int'l Release													
Paperback Release													
Soundtrack Releases													
Merchandising Release													

FIGURE 12.2

Activity projection.

(Continued)

YEAR	2012										2013	2014	2015
MONTH OF OPERATION	15	16	17	18	19	20	21	22	23	24	Year 3	Year 4	Year 5
CALENDAR MONTH	Mar	Apr	May	Jun	Jul	Aug	Sep	Oct	Nov	Dec			
Event			CANNES		COMIC CON	GENCON	TORONTO		AFM				
Start-Up													
Prepare all legal & busn docs													
Funding													
Retain Entertainment Atty													
Set-up Office													
Hire Development & Office Assistant													
Retain Publicist													
Entertainment Bank Open													
Development: Creative													
Read Scripts & Lit Properties													
Option Rights													
Internal Greenlight													
Search, meet, negotiate & document writer													
Commence Writer on 1st draft													
Deliver 1st Draft	3												
Commence Writer on Director Rewrite	3												
Deliver Director Rewrite		3											
Commence Writer on Talent Polish		3											
Deliver Talent Polish			3										
Prep / Produce Promo Materials				3									
Core Territory & Major Int'l Territory Distributor Meetings					3								
Global Distributor Creative Correlation Begin						3							
Director: List Considerations							3				3		
Director: Submissions & Meetings								3	3		3		
Director: Select, Negotiate, Document										3	3		
Actors: List Lead Considerations											3		
Actors: Submissions & Meetings											3		
Actors: Select, Negotiate, Document	2										3		
Talent: Story Meetings & Notes	2										3		
Additional Screenplay Drafts		2									3		
Shooting Script			2								3		
Keys: List Production Talent											3		
Keys: Meet, Select, Negotiate, Document	2										3		
Development: Production													
Location Scout	2												
1st Pass Production Budget/Schedule	2										3		
UPM: Meetings/Negotiate/Document				2							3		
Shooting Draft Breakdown/Boards				2		2					3		
Final Production Budget/Schedule					2						3		
Completion Bond Meetings							3				3		
Completion Bond Set								3			3		

Picture: Funding

Activity	Timeline values (left → right)
Establish Financing Plan	3
Bank Review and Acceptance of Financing Plan	3
Equity: Negotiate / Document	3, 3
Tax/ Location Benefits: Research & Meetings	3, 3
Tax/ Location Benefits: Negotiate & Document	2, 3
Int'l Sales Agent: Meet/Negotiate/Document	3
Int'l Pre-Sales: Submissions / Meetings	2, 3
Int'l Pre-Sales: Negotiate / Document	2, 2, 3
Core Territory: Submission / Meetings	2, 3
Core-Territory: Negotiate / Document	2, 2, 3
Engage Bank Production Funding	2, 3
Sell Picture to Producing Company	2, 3

Ancillary Rights Development

Activity	Timeline values (left → right)
Establish Rights Liquidation Plan	
Plan Retail, Web, TV, Radio, Print Promotion	1, 2, 3
Meet/Select/Negotiate Brand/Merchandising Partners	1, 2, 3
Publisher Novelization: Negotiate & Document	2, 2, 3
Soundtrack: Negotiate / Document	2, 2, 3

Activity	Timeline values (left → right)
Pre-Production	1, 1, 2, 2, 3
Principal Photography	1, 1, 2, 2, 3
Post Production	1, 1, 2, 2, 3

Marketing

Activity	Timeline values (left → right)
Website Creation & Installation/Niche & Social Networking	2, 2, 3
Trade Releases	1,2 · 1,2 · 1,2 · 2,3 · 3
Consumer PR	1, 1, 1, 1, 2
Corporate Sponsorship PR & Branding	1, 1, 2, 2
Other PR & Co-Promo	1, 1, 2

Release Dates and After Market

Activity	Timeline values (left → right)
Int'l Rights Licensing	1,2 · 1,2,3
No. America Theatrical Release	1, 2, 3
No. America Home Ent. Release	1,2 · 3
No. America Premium Cable TV Release	1, 2, 3
No. America PPV	1, 2, 3
No. America Network Television	1, 2
Int'l Release	1 · 1,2 · 3
Paperback Release	1, 2, 3
Soundtrack Releases	1, 2, 3
Merchandising Release	1, 2, 3

Gen Con – Gen Con Indy is a non-stop place for all things gaming. Hundreds of world-class exhibitors and over 7000 events from RPGs, TCGs,
Comic Con – the largest comic book and popular arts convention in the world with over 125,000 attendees in 2007.

FIGURE 12.2
Activity projection.

Development: Production charts the development of the production budget and schedules that are created from the script and are coordinated and eventually signed-off by the picture's completion guarantor.

Picture: Funding tracks all the financing plan participants. These processes are presented substantially in Chapters 2 through 6. It is each picture's as-detailed-as-possible financing and business definition. Substantially and naturally, it comes from preparing each picture's sales breakdown, finance plan, audience research, and campaign development.

Sell Picture to Producing Company refers to the formal activity of selling all rights, title, and interest of each developed picture to a separate producer-owned producing company, as presented in Chapter 11.

Ancillary Rights Development charts the typical ancillary rights events for an ancillary rights-expansive picture. The sale of these rights is closely correlated with the picture's creative development. Many ancillary rights licensees additionally require time for manufacture, and ideally these ancillary rights' consumer products should be on retail shelves just before the picture's release date or as a day-and-date release (see Chapter 5).

Release Dates and After Market estimate and track the United States theatrical date, then the other distribution dates are laid in according to traditional distribution window timing, as presented in Chapter 1.

3. Prepare the Cash Flow Projection

After the producer has projected specifically how development of a series of pictures will be accomplished, then a cash flow projection may be prepared. This projection applies expense amounts to the achievements chronicled in the activity projection, plus the related overhead, such as rent, phones, salaries, and taxes. Some of the production company's expenses are passed through to the development company. For instance, the producer typically is one of the development directors, so the development company will pay a portion of this salary, office space, and equipment expenses during the picture's development.

A cash flow projection sample is presented in Figure 12.3 Like the activity projection, this is only a sample. Producers should prepare their projections with the assistance of their accountant or business manager and apply expense amounts appropriate for their organizations.

There are two cash flow projections on the website for your use. One is in the sample projection's format but without amounts; it is ready to be filled in. The other has the sample projection's amounts filled in. This projection may assist users with points of reference until they become familiar with these expenses. Extending for five years, this projection indicates expenses incurred monthly with a year-end summary.

The top of this projection lists the sales events attended by the producer, as well as the most significant activity benchmarks from the activity projection. These are not mandatory but are a helpful reference.

Below the activity references are *Cash Receipts,* a listing of all the development company's income by projected receipt date. Each category should be referenced here, including, but not limited to, investments from the producer, private investors, and loans, as well as income generated from the sale of the developed pictures to the subsidiary-producing companies. If this sale includes a development company profits participation in the pictures, the income from this participation should also be shown. The investment amounts are usually left blank until the expenses are completed and totaled. Once the expenses are identified, the producer will know how much is needed to fund each picture's development.

Following cash receipts is a listing of the (development) *Expenses.* The first items listed are rights option and purchase price, retainers for production/performing talent. Following these expenses are professional fees, then overhead items, payroll taxes, insurance, miscellaneous print and promotional materials, and a contingency, followed by the total expenses for that month.

Below *Total Expenses* is the *Monthly Balance,* which is the month's total income less the month's total expenses. On the next line is *Cumulative Cash Flow,* which lists the monthly balance plus the cash remaining from the prior month.

After all expenses are filled in, the preparer can examine the total cumulative cash flow for the month following the first picture's theatrical release date and have a starting point in estimating the amount of development financing necessary to develop the proposed picture. Depending on development duration, it may be necessary to calculate the cash flow projection monthly for the first 24 months in order to determine how much the development company will need until it is self-sufficient.

Typically, development companies (this does not apply to development operations) are set up for a fixed number of pictures, and the highest expense categories terminate after the pictures have sold to the producer's producing companies. After this time, the remaining expense categories substantially diminish.

Following the first expense pass, the producer often will reassess the basic elements of the plan. This includes looking at the number of pictures to be developed, the activity projection timing, and the major category expenses. There must be a balance between a sane development/production schedule, income and expenses, and producer/investor return and earnings motivations. Several revisions typically are made to these two projections before a balance can be obtained with which the producer is content.

	2011													2012	
YEAR															
MONTH OF OPERATION	1	2	3	4	5	6	7	8	9	10	11	12		13	14
CALENDAR MONTH	Jan	Feb	Mar	Apr	May	Jun	Jul	Aug	Sep	Oct	Nov	Dec		Jan	Feb
Event		BERLIN			CANNES		COMIC CON	GENCON			AFM		**YEAR ONE**		BERLIN
Activities	Funding Complete	Internal Greenlight 1	Option Film 1	Distributor Meetings 1	Option Film 2 / Director 1 / Rewrite 1	Budget 1 / Greenlight 2	Polish 1 / Actor 1 / Rewrite 2	Presales 1 / Website 1	Rewrite 2	**Sell Picture 1** Polish 2 Greenlight 3	Option 3			1st Draft 3	Director 2
Cash Receipts															
Invested Funds	$2,000,000												$2,000,000		
Production Sale										$1,500,000			$1,500,000		
Picture Participations													$0		
Total Cash Receipts	$2,000,000	$0	$0	$0	$0	$0	$0	$0	$0	$1,500,000	$0	$0	$3,500,000	$0	$0
Expenses															
Brokerage Fees @5%	$100,000	$0	$0	$0	$0	$0	$0	$0	$0	$0	$0	$0	$100,000	$0	$0
Legal	$10,000	$1,500	$1,500	$1,500	$1,500	$1,500	$1,500	$1,500	$1,500	$1,500	$1,500	$1,500	$26,500	$1,500	$1,500
Rights Option			$3,000		$3,000						$3,000		$9,000		
Producer's Fee	$5,000	$5,000	$5,000	$5,000	$5,000	$5,000	$5,000	$5,000	$5,000	$5,000	$5,000	$5,000	$60,000	$3,000	$3,000
Development Executive Fee	$3,000	$3,000	$3,000	$3,000	$3,000	$3,000	$3,000	$3,000	$3,000	$3,000	$3,000	$3,000	$36,000	$3,000	$3,000
Unit Production Manager						$5,000							$5,000		
Writer's Fees					$32,000		$150,000		$32,000	$16,000			$230,000		
Internal Greenlight		$7,500				$7,500				$7,500			$22,500		
Prepare Business Plan / PPM / Supporting Docs	$10,000									$15,000	$10,000		$35,000		
Director Retainer					$50,000								$50,000		
Actor Retainer							$75,000						$75,000		
Casting Director		$5,000	$5,000	$5,000					$5,000	$5,000		$5,000	$30,000	$5,000	$5,000
Publicist									$5,000	$5,000		$5,000	$15,000	$5,000	$5,000

Line Item													Total		
International Sales Manager				$6,000	$6,000	$6,000	$6,000	$6,000	$6,000	$6,000	$6,000	$6,000	$54,000	$6,000	$6,000
Travel & Ent. / Markets & Shows					$25,000					$10,000			$35,000	$35,000	$17,000
Advertising					$4,500					$2,000			$6,500	$6,500	$2,500
Accounting	$2,500	$500	$500	$500	$500	$500	$500	$500	$500	$500	$500	$3,000	$10,500	$500	$500
Development Assistant/Office Manager					$3,000								$0	$3,000	$3,000
Payroll Taxes @ 18%	$1,890	$1,530	$1,530	$2,610	$2,610	$2,610	$2,610	$2,610	$2,610	$2,610	$2,610	$3,060	$28,890	$2,790	$2,790
Benefits										$550		$550	$550	$550	$550
Rent & Parking	$2,000	$2,000	$2,000	$2,000	$2,000	$2,000	$2,000	$2,000	$2,000	$2,000	$2,000	$2,000	$24,000	$2,000	$2,000
Telephone	$100	$100	$100	$100	$100	$100	$100	$100	$100	$250	$250	$250	$1,500	$250	$250
Office Equipment	$11,000												$11,000	$7,000	$7,000
Printing	$500	$500	$75	$75	$75	$75	$75	$75	$75	$75	$250	$250	$1,750	$75	$75
Supplies, Misc. Office	$250	$250	$250	$250	$250	$250	$250	$250	$250	$250	$250	$250	$3,000	$250	$250
Pstg / Dlvry Service	$100	$100	$100	$100	$100	$100	$100	$100	$100	$100	$100	$100	$1,200	$100	$100
Production Sftwr	$2,500			$75					$5,000				$7,575		
Print Development & Production	$5,000									$5,000			$10,000		$5,000
Promo Development & Production	$25,000	$25,000											$50,000		$25,000
Web Development	$2,500				$2,500						$2,500		$7,500		$2,500
ISP, Web Hosting/Maintenance	$300	$300	$300	$300	$300	$300	$300	$500	$500	$500	$500	$500	$4,600	$500	$500
Insurance (E&O, GL, Travel & Office Contents)	$2,500	$2,500	$2,500	$2,500	$2,500	$2,500	$2,500	$2,500	$2,500	$2,500	$2,500	$2,500	$30,000	$2,500	$2,500
Investment Servicing (Repayment and Return)										$1,000,000			$1,000,000		
Total Expenses	$154,140	$29,780	$57,355	$29,010	$140,935	$36,435	$248,935	$24,135	$86,135	$1,072,635	$59,285	$42,785	$1,981,565	$38,015	$50,515
Monthly Balance	$1,845,860	-$29,780	-$57,355	-$29,010	-$140,935	-$36,435	-$248,935	-$24,135	-$86,135	$427,365	-$59,285	-$42,785	$1,518,435	-$38,015	-$50,515
Cumulative Cash Flow	$1,845,860	$1,816,080	$1,758,725	$1,729,715	$1,588,780	$1,552,345	$1,303,410	$1,279,275	$1,193,140	$1,620,505	$1,561,220	$1,518,435		$1,480,420	$1,429,905

FIGURE 12.3
Cash flow projection.

(Continued)

YEAR	2012													
MONTH OF OPERATION	15	16	17	18	19	20	21	22	23	24				
CALENDAR MONTH	Mar	Apr	May	Jun	Jul	Aug	Sep	Oct	Nov	Dec	YEAR TWO	YEAR THREE	YEAR FOUR	YEAR FIVE
Event			CANNES		COMIC CON	GENCON	TORONTO		AFM					
Activities	Actor 2 Rewrite 3	Polish 3			Sell Picture 2					US Theatrical 1 Director 3				
Cash Receipts														
Invested Funds											$0	$0	$0	$0
Production Sale					$1,500,000						$1,500,000	$1,500,000	$0	$0
Picture Participations											$0	$0	$600,000	$950,000
Total Cash Receipts	$0				$1,500,000	$0		$0		$0	$1,500,000	$1,500,000	$600,000	$950,000
Expenses														
Brokerage Fees @5%											$0	$0	$0	$0
Legal	$1,500	$1,500	$1,500	$1,500	$1,500	$1,500	$1,500	$1,500	$1,500	$1,500	$18,000	$18,000	$6,000	$6,000
Rights Option			$15,000								$15,000	$0	$0	$0
Producer's Fee	$3,000	$3,000	$3,000	$3,000	$3,000	$3,000	$3,000	$3,000	$3,000	$3,000	$36,000	$24,000	$12,000	$12,000
Development Executive Fee	$3,000	$3,000	$3,000	$3,000							$18,000	$0		
Unit Production Manager	$5,000			$5,000	$5,000	$5,000	$5,000	$5,000	$5,000		$35,000	$5,000		
Writer's Fees											$0	$0		
Internal Greenlight		$12,000									$12,000	$0		
Prepare Business Plan / PPM / Supporting Docs											$0	$0		
Director Retainer				$250,000	$25,000	$25,000	$25,000	$25,000	$25,000	$25,000	$400,000	$25,000	$0	$0
Actor Retainer					$500,000	$100,000		$50,000	$50,000		$700,000	$0		
Casting Director										$5,000	$5,000	$5,000		
Publicist	$5,000	$5,000	$5,000	$5,000	$5,000	$5,000	$5,000	$5,000	$5,000	$5,000	$60,000	$60,000	$60,000	$45,000

Item														
International Sales Manager	$6,000	$6,000	$6,000	$6,000	$6,000	$6,000	$6,000	$6,000	$6,000	$6,000	$72,000	$48,000	$18,000	$18,000
Travel & Ent. / Markets & Shows		$25,000				$25,000		$17,000			$59,000	$32,000	$17,500	$17,500
Advertising			$5,000				$5,000		$5,000		$12,500	$7,500	$4,000	$4,000
Accounting	$500	$500	$500	$500	$500	$500	$500	$500	$500	$500	$8,500	$8,500	$8,500	$8,500
Development Assistant/Office Manager	$3,000	$3,000	$3,000	$3,000	$3,000	$3,000	$3,000	$3,000	$3,000	$3,000	$36,000	$36,000	$0	$0
Payroll Taxes @ 18%	$2,790	$2,790	$2,790	$2,250	$2,250	$2,250	$2,250	$2,250	$2,700		$30,690	$20,970	$6,930	$6,930
Benefits	$550	$550	$550	$550	$550	$550	$550	$550	$550	$550	$6,600	$6,600	$0	$0
Rent & Parking	$2,000	$2,000	$2,000	$2,000	$2,000	$2,000	$2,000	$2,000	$2,000	$2,000	$24,000	$12,000	$6,000	$6,000
Telephone	$250	$250	$500	$500	$500	$500	$500	$500	$500	$500	$4,750	$3,000	$900	$900
Office Equipment	$7,000										$7,000	$0	$0	$0
Printing	$75	$75	$75	$75	$75	$75	$75	$75	$75	$75	$900	$900	$900	$900
Supplies, Misc. Office	$250	$250	$250	$250	$250	$250	$250	$250	$250	$250	$3,000	$1,200	$600	$600
Pstg / Dlvry Service	$100	$100	$100	$100	$100	$100	$100	$100	$100	$100	$1,200	$600	$300	$300
Production Sftwr					$5,000						$5,000	$0	$0	$0
Print Development & Production	$5,000										$5,000	$0	$0	$0
Promo Development & Production	$25,000										$25,000	$0	$0	$0
Web Development				$10,000	$10,000	$10,000					$30,000	$30,000	$0	$0
ISP, Web Hosting/Maintenance	$500	$500	$500	$500	$500	$500	$500	$500	$500	$500	$6,000	$6,000	$6,000	$6,000
Insurance (E&O, GL, Travel & Office Contents)	$2,500	$2,500	$2,500	$2,500	$2,500	$2,500	$2,500	$2,500	$2,500	$2,500	$30,000	$2,500	$0	$0
Investment Servicing (Repayment and Return)					$1,000,000						$1,000,000	$650,000	$200,000	$320,000
Total Expenses	$36,015	$73,015	$71,265	$296,265	$1,567,725	$167,725	$62,725	$112,725	$129,725	$60,675	$2,666,390	$952,770	$347,630	$452,630
Monthly Balance	-$36,015	-$73,015	-$571,265	-$296,265	-$667,725	-$167,725	-$62,725	-$112,725	-$129,725	-$60,675	$352,045	$899,275	$1,151,645	$1,649,015
											$0	$0	$0	$0
Cumulative Cash Flow	$1,393,890	$1,320,875	$1,249,610	$953,345	$885,620	$717,895	$655,170	$542,445	$412,720	$352,045				

FIGURE 12.3
Cash flow projection.

4. Select the Development Team and Advisors

The development operation/company will be operated by a team, including the development director(s), an operations person, and development assistants. There will also be outside professionals, including an attorney, banker, completion bond company, physical production specialist (retained UPM), and a publicist. This team is usually populated by a time-apportionment of the production company team members.

The dynamics of the development team are projected into the pictures that they produce. Additionally, many investors look first to the development team when evaluating the development offering. The development team is reviewed in Chapter 13.

5. Formulate the Development Company Investment

Even if the investment is completely internal, separate development operations should be planned and run, and it can even be beneficial for separate entities to be formed and financed from the production company. As this occurs, terms of the investment or loan must be prepared between the companies. The pictures, production company, and investors should receive the greatest amount of protection, along with the most efficient tax consequences possible. If there are private investors, they will need reasonable incentives and protection. The producer's accountant and attorney, who assist in the deal formulation, tax considerations, and securities issues, typically accomplish these functions. Many of the basic considerations relating to this step are reviewed in Chapter 11.

6. Prepare the Investment's Documentation

Even if the production company is the sole investment source, documentation should be prepared and entered into with legal, producer income, and tax consequences that facilitate the plan's formal engagement.

The producer's attorney usually prepares this documentation. If funds are raised from private investors, a securities attorney should be involved. No investment documentation should be distributed until it has passed an attorney's review.

7. Make the Presentations and Fund the Development Company

Regardless of which of the sources of development financing the producer receives, an offering or finance agreement will be written (except for the crowd funding model), and, after acceptance, the documentation will be completed and the funding obtained.

If the funding is to come from private investors and this is the producer's first private offering, it is often constructive to make a list of potential investors, another list of people of influence who may recommend sophisticated investors to consider the offering, and another list of brokers, investment counselors, and securities dealers. The sources in each category should be prioritized and a plan prepared as to how to approach each source.

Raising private capital is especially challenging for a new production entity. For these producers, a strong team (presented in Chapter 13), with exceptional stories under consideration, with at least one picture's internal greenlight analysis completed that indicates a producer's share of earnings that is twice the picture's production cost, making a professional presentation, and offering a motivating investment are critical to success in receiving the necessary development capital.

CHAPTER POSTSCRIPT

Like production, development should be thoroughly planned, completely financed, and precisely executed to ensure each picture's success. Also, like production, development should be helmed by a skilled team to ensure a smooth transition into funded production and then into the hands of the various global territory licensees that are prepared to receive and exploit each picture.

CHAPTER 13

The Team

This chapter reviews the internal and external players who are the operating and advisory teams of the production and development operations. It also presents the primary considerations related to planning the team, as well as evaluating, employing or retaining, and setting compensation and fees for all the players.

THE COMPLETE TEAM

No producer would attempt principal photography without a whole production team, yet some producers operate their businesses without a complete operating team. Producers should have a person handling each of the responsibilities that their business demands. Most production companies begin with a sparse in-house team, supported with outside professionals that may include an attorney, an accountant, a producer's sales representative, an international sales organization, a public relations (PR) firm, or an advertising agency. These may provide critical services at a more reasonable cost than the producer would pay for comparable full-time in-house executives. Regardless of the source, producers should be able to perform all the functions necessary to their business in a coordinated, efficient fashion. The organization charts in Figures 13.1 and 13.2 present the basic positions that are necessary to operate an independent production company and its development operations/companies.

COMPANY STRUCTURE

In the United States, the production organization and producing entity structures are recommended to be (and most of them are) limited liability companies (LLCs) or subchapter S corporations. These structures provide optimal legal protection for the members/share holders and principals and are single taxation entities—as the entities are not taxed separately from the member/shareholders and they provide the optimal flexibility facilitating growth, mergers, acquisitions, and so on. The structure used most often for film companies is the LLC. Always discuss the appropriate structure with your attorney and accountant before setting up the legal entity.

DOI: 10.1016/B978-0-240-81463-6.00013-9

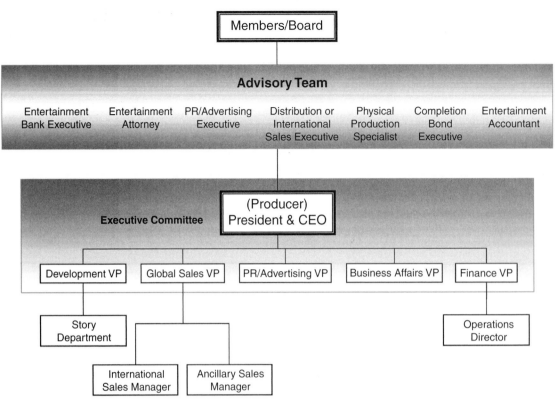

FIGURE 13.1
The production company.

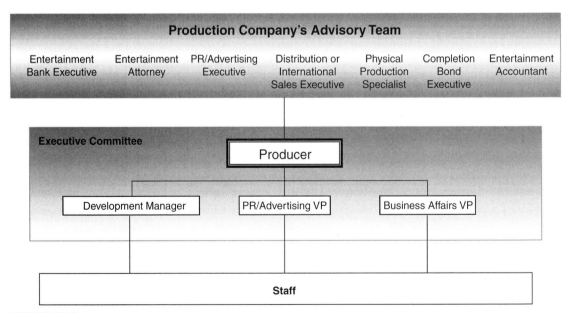

FIGURE 13.2
The development company.

These entities are owned by their members/shareholders, who approve the managers/board of directors who are responsible not only for establishing the company's constitution, policies, and procedures, but also for appointing its officers responsible for operations. On the production company chart in Figure 13.1, the members/board is shown in a separate box, as it is rarely involved in the day-to-day operations. Its members usually just meet annually, when they review annual reports and projections and participate in the review of matters related to mergers, acquisitions, substantial capital restructuring, or changes in company policy and procedures.

THE PRODUCTION COMPANY'S TEAM

The production company's chart shows three tiers of the team. The first tier is composed of a six-member advisory team; the second tier is composed of an operating team with six key players who are the production company's executive committee; and the final tier is composed of the executive committee's staff.

The Advisory Team

The advisory team substantially benefits every production organization. The members of this team are entertainment industry professionals who are rarely available or affordable for executive positions within a production company. They are seasoned industry players, and the advice, counsel, the relationships they have with other powerful people, and their deal influence amplify the production company's industry position, broaden its reach, and sharpen its business and creative focus. These typically are informal, nonpaid relationships. This team is especially important for newer production entities.

The most common members of production company advisory teams are as follows:

- An entertainment bank executive
- An entertainment attorney
- A brand-making professional who is most often an executive in a public relations firm or advertising agency
- A physical production specialist who is usually a line producer or unit production manager (UPM)
- A completion bond executive
- An entertainment accountant
- A distribution or international sales executive

Their primary function is to serve the company individually as mentors in addition to providing more customary paid professional services.

Most potential advisory team members have no natural business motivation to serve as a member of a production company's advisory team except that they are mature in their professional duties in the industry and may be persuaded to guide organizations that need their help. The keys for newer production companies to win the support of these powerful people are the ethics and achievement commitment of the producer, the kind of pictures the producer is committed to create, and the approach the producer is taking to produce and distribute these pictures.

The production company may actually also retain the attorney, a physical production specialist, a PR firm, an international sales group, and an accountant. The services provided by and the process of selecting and engaging a relationship with a bank are reviewed in Chapter 6, completion bond executives are covered in Chapter 8, and entertainment attorneys are discussed in Chapter 9. Though certain loans may be too large or small for the bank with which the advisor is associated, usually legal and bonding services are provided through the organizations with whom the producer's advisors are associated.

The services provided by a physical production specialist are presented in Chapter 12. This person usually is selected by research and reputation. Producers most often become familiar with line producers and UPMs by the pictures they have worked on. Like most industry talent, these professionals are very busy but quite approachable. Producers should meet with the three to five strongest candidates, present their company's purpose, explain the relationship desired, and express enthusiasm for the candidate's advisory team participation.

The Executive Committee

The executive committee consists of the producer and key personnel. These are the people responsible for ensuring that the company's objectives are fulfilled. They are responsible for all earnings and are accountable for all operating expenses. This committee typically meets once a week, where it reviews company progress and revises projections.

The producer's title is usually chief executive officer (CEO), president, or both, and the department heads may be vice presidents. The producer is the team leader responsible for the ultimate creative and business bottom line of the company. The producer's duties are presented more fully in Chapter 14. The producer may have a subordinate officer who is primarily responsible for directing the department heads. This person may also serve as the chairman of the executive committee and have the corporate title of chief operating officer (COO) or senior vice president.

The primary duties of the development vice president are to solicit and discover stories. After the story has been greenlit, the vice president manages its development under the direction of the producer.

The *global sales vice president* is responsible for preparing the initial sales breakdown for each picture that passes the scrutiny of an internal greenlight, as well as evaluating sales strategy, presales, and all initial and continuing rights sales of the company's pictures. This vice president may direct the activities of a staff, including an international sales manager and an ancillary sales manager, as well as the vice president's assistants.

The *advertising and public relations vice president* is responsible for establishing and sustaining the production company's brand to the entertainment global trade and global consumers, and for establishing each motion picture's initial brand with the global entertainment trade and global consumers. This person also manages the continuing brand in conjunction with the various global distributors, reviews and manages the producer's position relative to the media plans and media buys before and during the theatrical and home entertainment releases, and audits media and public relations' expenses fulfilled by distributors on behalf of the producer. This vice president also may direct the activities of a staff of one or two assistants, plus the activities performed by promotions/public relations firms, advertising agencies, and other related vendors.

The *business affairs vice president* typically has a law degree and directs the deal documentation preparation for development and production-related issues, along with sophisticated rights sales and distribution. These vice presidents closely correlate their work with the company's attorney, direct an assistant, and usually participate in development and production negotiations.

The *finance vice president* manages the company's cash flow, accounting, tax management, government agency reporting, management reports, and the company's information systems. This VP also manages the relationship with the company's entertainment accountant and manages the efforts of the operations director and department assistants, if there are any.

The *international sales manager* and *ancillary sales manager* assist the global sales VP in establishing each picture-in-development's global value, by territory and right; preparing promotional, publicity, and marketing materials; meeting with global media and distributors; negotiating and preselling some of these rights if this is part of the picture's production funding plan; and preparing all other rights for future sales. This team also manages all global film market activities. Some of the most critical sales relationships—for instance, those with U.S. studios—may be led and primarily carried out by the producer. But even for these, this team is responsible for ensuring they are planned and accomplished.

Typically, the production company's *operations director* is responsible for keeping the development operation/company on task and holding the entire team accountable in order to sustain balance between the timing allocated for developing its motion pictures and the budget the team has available to achieve this task. This person also fulfills all day-to-day accounting functions, through the delivery of trial balances to the finance VP for the purpose of adjusting entries and preparing interim, monthly, and quarterly reports.

THE DEVELOPMENT ORGANIZATION/COMPANY'S TEAM

The development organization/company at a minimum should keep its own separate income and expense accounting. If it is a separate business entity from the production company, it has its own accounting records and government agency reporting. However, it is most commonly at least half-owned by the production company.

Regardless of whether it is the same or a separate company, most, if not all, of its members are the production company's team, the development team physically resides in the production company office.

Mirroring the production company, the development operation's team has three tiers: Advisory, Executive Committee, and Staff.

After a development operation's first picture has successfully completed its internal greenlight, the producer focuses full-time attention into development. The development organization tracks all the producer's time, as well as the time each other member of the production company spends on each project in development, and it apportions these costs to each project. If the producer uses a separate development entity, this entity pays the producer and each of the production company team members that portion of their income, which otherwise would have been paid by the production company, for serving in their respective development positions.

At least initially, the producer is typically also the development organization's *development manager* and is responsible for story search, evaluation, recommendation, and all aspects of each motion picture's creative development and preparation, in every respect, for physical production. As development manager, the producer uses the development operations and production company staff team as needed, expensing them per project.

OPTIMIZING THE TEAMS

There are as many production companies whose operating temperament is chaos separated by moments of sanity, as there are companies whose operating temperament is steady, progressive achievement. The difference is rarely the amount of work being done but rather the approach the teams take to accomplish the work.

Operating temperament is set more by the producer than by all the rest of the combined team. It is crucial that each producer accept this responsibility. Producers set the pace. They establish the operating style. They determine the stability of the relationship dynamics within the team and with all the others with whom the producer's team relates.

Among the highest achieving and happiest production company teams, there is one management principle observed more consistently than any other. This is the observance by the producer, and subsequently by the rest of the executive team (and therefore the staff), of including these three phases in most things they do:

1. They plan through study and evaluation.
2. They do what is planned.
3. They evaluate what was done and then course-correct.

These phases are deeply interrelated, and employing all of them optimizes the producer's capacity to accomplish every desired task. It also sets the standard for the team members to approach their accountabilities in a similarly constructive style.

Planning our work creates the greatest assurance that the work we do will accomplish our short- and long-term objectives. *Working* moves us forward to the achievement of our objectives. *Evaluating and modifying* our work motivates, makes enlightened planning possible, and inspires more confident and focused work. Sacrifice any one of these three critical phases, and predictable achievement is crippled. Applying these principles is especially helpful when selecting new teams or organizing or reshaping existing production or development teams.

Planning has been emphasized throughout this text. Just as discovering a picture we want to produce is only the beginning of planning how we are going to develop, produce, and distribute it, likewise preparing a mission statement that sets forward why we are in business is only the beginning of planning how we will achieve our objectives. Part of each producer's plan should be identifying the talents and capacities needed and desired in the individuals who will be the advisory, operating, and staff teams. The team members should embrace the production company's mission statement, contribute to its clarity, and share the producer's approach to doing business.

DISCOVERING, NEGOTIATING, AND COMPENSATING

Producers are best served by team members who are not just good at what they do but also have the attributes, character, and operating styles complementary to the producer and the rest of the team.

Discovering

For existing teams that have vacancies, the best approach to filling them is to write a description of the person sought, their duties and accountabilities, and compensation. This description should be circulated among the executive and advisory teams. Additionally, industry personnel agencies and advertising in the trade papers should be used to allow fresh, vibrant talent to have the opportunity to join the team. Set a time for the decision. Include those in the decision-making process who may share duties or parallel positions with the open post. Attempt to adhere to the time, but never select someone less than the position demands. Team orientation and releasing someone are emotionally and financially expensive. It is always better to wait for someone who appears sure.

For new production companies start by bringing on the advisory team. These members are easy to spot, evaluate, and approach. Once they are in place, then use them as resources for the executive committee. After the executive committee is set, use them and the advisory members to recommend staff.

Negotiating and Compensation

Before negotiating, research what is the industry's fair compensation for a particular position, then temper this amount according to the company's projected budget. Negotiate the best relationship possible with the person, and after the negotiation has concluded, agree to start the person at a little more than he or she expects, if possible. Good will motivates a positive attitude and usually increases productivity.

Production companies are naturally rigorous environments. Participating in a winning production team demands everyone's personal excellence. Driving successful pictures is emotionally—and should also be financially—rewarding. It is very good business for producers to set a percentage of pretax profits aside (perhaps 10 percent) in which all employees will annually participate. Some producers require new team members to vest (mature) in their relationship for 6 to 12 months before they qualify to participate. Sharing profits builds team spirit and loyalty, which fosters a happier and more profitable environment.

CHAPTER POSTSCRIPT

New and existing producers are well compensated if they understand all the business and creative functions that must be accomplished to do the work that their production and development teams require. These functions should be defined in terms of the advisory, operating, and staff tiers of the overall team. Producers should have complete teams to ensure their capacity to accomplish the company's goals.

The producer sets the operating style and performance of the team. The producer should demonstrate these in ways that promote the team's satisfied, sure, and successive achievement.

There is an abundance of talented prospective team members. A good plan to discover them, patiently executed and using team resources, will draw them in. Evaluating teams regularly and allowing team members to participate in the company's rewards promote solidarity and mutual success.

CHAPTER 14

Production Company Operation

This chapter presents the operations of production companies and their related development and producing organizations, which may be structured in their own separate entities, but seamlessly operated by the same people and within the same facility. Prior chapters have presented the independent fundamental operating principles of these companies. This chapter demonstrates both how they work together and the business elements that join them.

The chapter also reveals the operations of these companies in their complete forms. For those who have experience with the operating performance of successful production companies, the operations presented in this chapter may seem more cumbersome or thorough than necessary. Consider the performance of a new driver compared with the performance of an experienced one. Seasoned drivers may speed through yellow lights, may turn without using their signals if they don't see any oncoming traffic, and may consistently drive a few miles over the speed limit on the freeway. These are not recommended operating styles but may become entrenched habits of experienced drivers.

As dexterity increases, so does confidence. As this occurs, one has a natural tendency, especially under pressure (and producers operate under extreme conditions), to cut operating corners and increase operating speed. Abbreviating, or especially missing any development or production steps, places the creative and earnings life of a picture at risk. As with experienced drivers, accomplished producers often press pictures through the production process with amazing agility and success. However, like the best race car drivers, fine producers occasionally trash pictures that would otherwise have been successful, simply because those producers slighted certain steps or passed them altogether. Because this natural tendency exists, it is necessary to establish a development and production checks and balance system through which each picture passes. This chapter presents this system.

It falls upon the development chief (vice president in the example organization chart) to ensure each picture accomplishes all the development steps. By establishing this process, a production company can successfully maximize operating integrity, as well as each picture's creative and financial success. To present the most comprehensive operating profile, the example in this chapter is of a new production company.

© 2011 John J. Lee, Jr. and Anne Marie Gillen. Published by Elsevier Inc. All rights reserved.
DOI: 10.1016/B978-0-240-81463-6.00014-0

DEFINING AND ESTABLISHING THE PRODUCTION COMPANY

As presented in Chapters 11 and 12, producers should invest the necessary time and resources, with the help of a seasoned attorney and other business counsel, to devise the optimum business structure and overall strategies. These should include writing a mission statement that sets forth the vision and purpose for creating their company, along with the manner in which they intend to conduct their business. This statement is often several pages long in its expanded reference format for the executive committee, pared down to less than a page for use by other executive-level team members, and no more than a paragraph for published collateral materials.

There are several advantages for two or more principals rather than one to create a production company. Multiple principals typically deliver a better system of checks and balances for the company—each principal reviews and, from a similar position of power, holds the other accountable for performance. If each principal shares the mission of the organization but delivers different experience and capabilities, the company's overall strength and operating ballast are increased. There are several excellent examples of this kind of partnership, including Ron Howard and Brian Grazer with their Imagine Entertainment empire and Gary Barber and Roger Birnbaum with their Spyglass Entertainment powerhouse. With each of these teams, both are producers, but one is more deeply creative and the other has a stronger business background, thus delivering an excellent balance to their respective organizations.

If the organization has more than one principal, these individuals should agree on the company's mission, their respective accountabilities, contributions, equity, operating control, earnings, and profit participations. They should also enter a written agreement or separate management contracts, reflecting these deal elements. (These should include buy/sell terms and the method of dispute resolution.)

It is always best to have the producer's entertainment attorney or some other lawyer involved in both negotiating and preparing the principals' documentation. The attorney should also prepare and file the company's formation documents with the appropriate governing authorities and direct the initial organizing meeting.

THE STORY SEARCH

Most mission statements share one critical common goal—that the production company find and acquire the kinds of stories it is formed to produce and distribute. The search for these stories will be a preeminent activity throughout the life of the production company. This should be the first focus of newly formed companies.

Although there is an abundance of scripts, only a few are worth producing. The search should start immediately and continue in an organized fashion.

Chapter 9 provides information about the legal aspects of story review and the need for literary release forms.

In contrast to the stunning volume of stories presented to producers from traditional trade sources is the smaller but just as vital proportion of stories discovered from nonindustry sources. Usually producers have their private treasure house of folks who may be willing to champion their story search, including family, friends from childhood, teachers, and others. This group can become a pipeline of continuing story discovery. Most of these connections, when asked, will recommend stories they believe will make great motion pictures.

Producers can be benefited by making a list of everyone they believe may be willing to participate as story resources; then they compose an email that can easily be customized for each person, saying they are looking for stories for production consideration that may make great motion pictures. Some of the industry's most notable producers have found this to be a stunningly fine source of story discovery. Great stories from unpublished journals, out-of-print books, and true-life stories from small town newspapers are also some of the most remarkable finds. It is essential that producers commence and continue the story search and review process throughout the predevelopment company preparation. This persistent story search will necessarily continue as long as producers are producing.

Stories of interest to the producer should be represented to investors only as such, *unless* they have been greenlit by the producer, signifying there are business as well as creative justifications to proceed. It should be emphasized to prospective investors that, in large measure, their confidence in the new production company stems from the fact that it will develop and produce only pictures that have a conservative ratio between the producer's share of earnings to their production and distribution costs, and that are closely coordinated with global distributors.

DEVELOPMENT EMPHASIS

Near the end of this chapter is a list of the 25 main activities through which most new production companies pass to produce their first motion picture. These are mapped out in Figure 12.2 of Chapter 12. The first 20 are largely development activities beginning with the story search. As emphasized in Chapters 11, 12, and 13, there are several core operational, profit, financing, tax, and risk mitigation benefits to separating a production company's (1) brand and asset (motion picture) management, (2) its development, and (3) each picture's production and ownership. This separation may be by establishing a "Chart of Accounts" delineation or by forming actual separate entities, which is recommended. However it is accomplished, it must be done in some fashion. As story discovery and development activities come before production and distribution, the first order of business for most production entities is the planning and financing of development—and if they use a separate development company, the financing of this entity. The need for this process and its thorough analysis is discussed in Chapter 12.

Many production companies are launched with only their development financing (whether or not in a separate entity) and teams (these are presented in Chapter 13), because developing their first pictures is typically their entire initial business.

If this is their position, these producers begin by preparing the activity projection for the development of the company's first pictures. This will be the first development entity, if the producer elects to use a separate entity. If not, these are activity projections of the first pictures. Following the preparation of the activity projection is the preparation of the cash flow projection, also presented in Figure 12.3 of Chapter 12, which expresses the costs of the development activities.

Though development expenses will likely be capitalized and made part of each picture's budget, development is the *only* operation until a picture is greenlit and its production is financed. Consequently, each new production entity's initial financing, or seed capital, is its development financing.

Most new production entities start with properties favored by their producers. This is a major advantage, but these still must prove their business viability, be in shooting script form, engage the above-the-line team, receive distributor interest and confirmation, and production financing. All of these are development operations.

Most development operations will at least initially be financed privately, according to the methods referenced in Chapter 12. If this is the case, producers will analyze the cash flow projection in relation to the total operating cash needed and the potential income earned by the development company. If private investors are used, their participation is then applied to the cash flow projection and reviewed for its impact on the producer and its appeal to the investor. This process determines the basic deal points offered to the private investor. Often several operating models are analyzed by passing their criteria through the projections until the producer settles on the ultimate balance among the number of pictures to be developed, the development pace, the total investment amount required, and the appeal to potential investors.

PREPARING THE INVESTMENT DOCUMENTS

With the activity and the cash flow projections prepared and the investment model configured, the producer is ready to commence authorship of the business plan, and if seeking accredited investors, the private placement memorandum (PPM), with the assistance of the producer's attorney and business consultant or accountant. If the investment is being secured from just one or two investors, a financing agreement should be all that is needed, and the time and expense of the PPM is unnecessary.

The business consultant or accountant prepares the following:

- The activity and cash flow projections as they will appear in the investment documents
- The notes to these projections

- The offering's use of proceeds
- The more detailed source and use of funds analysis
- The tax consequences

The producer prepares the introductory letter and the business plan (which should include all the items as discussed in Chapter 6), as well as the production company's mission statement as it applies to the development activities, including the kinds of pictures and properties the development company is seeking, and the development team summary biographies. The attorney authors the PPM, as well as reviews and approves all legal language, especially regarding the risks involved, in all of the business planning materials prepared by the business consultant or accountant and the producer.

ASSEMBLING THE TEAM

One of the most important sections in the investment documents is the producer's management and advisory teams' information. Who will be managing the partnership's business is crucial to prospective investors. They learn early that a great plan is only as impressive as the assembled team's ability to carry it out. Chapter 13 comprehensively presents the producer's advisory team categories and how to approach them.

PRODUCING THE INVESTMENT DOCUMENTS

The producer reviews the materials prepared by the business consultant or accountant and delivers all these materials to the attorney, after which the attorney prepares a final draft of the memorandum for the producer's review. The attorney makes final content polishes and hard and digital copies are given to the producer.

The attorney should have offering samples the producer can review for ideas on the look of the published draft. Having prepared many of these over the years, our suggestion is to focus on the content. The business plan can be glitzy, but keep the PPM clean and simple in presentation.

Some producers use designers to create and coordinate the look of the business plan and PPM. Whatever the cosmetic attributes, the master is then prepared and copies made and numbered for presentation to prospective investor-partners.

RAISING THE FINANCING

Typically, one investor will be enamored with the offering's merits and will get the momentum going and influence one or more investor associates to join in the relationship. The first investor is typically the hardest to secure.

As to the most effective approach, each investor should be considered individually. What are the most compelling reasons for someone to invest? It may be a specific story in your control, the kind or genre of films you will be producing.

Possibly it is the investors' interest in and desire to participate in the motion picture industry. It may even be their interest in the potential high return on investment (ROI). Some investors prefer to be in a group presentation, whereas others prefer a private meeting. Each investor should be approached with their most effective method and setting in mind.

It is well to remember that the person to meet with is the actual investor. Sophisticated investors often have assistants who afford professional courtesy to the myriad offers that barrage these sources. Producers should begin this process by amassing lists of investors, brokers, finders, and people of influence they know who might invest or open the direct doors to them or others who have the means and inclination to invest.

Take these steps when you meet with investors:

1. Make the entire presentation brief (less than an hour). Let them know before the meeting how long it will take.
2. At the beginning of the meeting, let them know that first they will receive an overview of how some of the most successful independent producers do business, then hear how the production company is poised to operate in this manner. Next, do a concise overview of this particular investment, allowing the investors to consider the relationship in whatever manner they may be interested.
3. For most investors, this is a new and fascinating business playing field. They often have questions and comments.

Most investors place their confidence in the person rather than the documentation. Preparing the business plan and PPM is expensive, and the information it contains is critically important. Investors will want to be entirely convinced that the producer understands the industry, knows this particular plan, and is thoroughly committed to do everything possible to assure the venture's success. A producer needs solid confidence that comes from experience, team integrity, a deep understanding of the plan, and a commitment to the plan's success. Many investors have an uncanny sense for this dynamic. If they believe the producer has these qualities, they are more likely to consider the investment seriously. If not, then they will pass. The presenters need to be prepared. The professional production values of the investment documents and even impressive deal points will not overcome a producer's weak presentation.

Before these meetings commence, producers should meet with their attorney and banker. The attorney will review the appropriate legal approach to these highly regulated relationships. The banker will assist in opening an escrow account for the receipt of investment income from the offering.

INVESTMENT PARTNER COMMUNICATIONS

Once a producer has received the investment capital, there is often no immediate motivation to communicate with the private investors, who, before this time, were sought after with the producer's passion, sincerity, and rapt attention.

Though the partnership agreement may not require communication with partners more than annually, it is good form and builds relationship integrity to prepare and send a letter or email, at least quarterly, informing them of development, production, and distribution progress.

Producers build confidence in their investors by beginning this relationship with a letter of appreciation and encouragement. Then they should set triggers in their schedule for similar communications to continue. This will be challenging to do after development commences, but it should be done, even if an assistant prepares the initial drafts.

WORKING THE DEVELOPMENT PLAN

The development activity projection used in the investment documents is the producer's representation to the investors of what will be done and when it will be accomplished. The activities in this projection are the investors' benchmark expectations, which is also what the management team will use to gauge the company's progress.

Each activity in the projections should be accomplished as if it is crucial to the initial and continuing success of the production company and its pictures. Each item should be finely planned, collaborated upon as a team, and accomplished at its zenith.

The producer's activities in order of priority are described in the next sections.

Story

Producers should work on the story every day, including reading and reviewing coverage and analysis reports. In addition, they should send more email requests (referred to earlier), research story leads, and, where appropriate, brainstorm new ideas, as well as receive pitches/spec scripts from qualified writers. Whether from a solid treatment, script, novel, short story, graphic novel or comic book, the number of writers and drafts is hard to determine until the shooting script is in hand. Developing or optioning a script that fulfills the creative demands, and that is business feasible and ready to produce, is a godsend.

Advisory Member Meetings

Producers should meet with each member of their advisory committee immediately after funding has occurred. Each member should receive and review copies of the current development activity projection. Suggestions relative to the plan, story suggestions, and open team candidate recommendations should be elicited. Meeting with the advisory members as a group is often most effective, but because of tight schedules, this may often not be possible.

The banker will transfer all invested funds from the escrow account to the development working and savings accounts. Retainers will be advanced to the attorney, the unit production manager (UPM), and possibly the publicist.

U.S. and Major International Territory Distributor Announcements

After the creation of the new production company, an introductory announcement should be sent to every major global distributor. Because there are so few balanced producers, the most important aspect of this announcement is the definition of the relationship the producer seeks to have with these distributors.

There are multiple distributors in each of the United States and major international territories, and every one of them should receive a personal letter with the announcement. As reviewed in Chapters 2 and 3, all distributors have their unique sales values and characteristics for specific pictures; consequently, every distributor is important to the producer.

The quality of this announcement should demonstrate that the production company operates in the same manner as the finest production entities in the industry. In other words, it should look like it came from a major studio.

The announcement introduces the new motion picture production entity and states that it is fully funded to develop its first projects. The announcement incorporates the spirit of the production company's mission statement and, moreover, presents the company's operating profile as one that develops and produces the caliber of motion pictures these distributors are distributing.

The producer will introduce the company in a personal letter to the distribution chief of each major U.S. theatrical, DVD, and video-on-demand (VOD) distributor, as well as the major international territory distributors. The number of pictures on the production company's first development slate should be listed, along with the producer's intent to make a picture-specific pitch to the distributor for its initial distribution interest consideration in the future. Stated clearly in this letter is the producer's position that the production company will develop and produce only motion pictures that first receive distributor interest. The producer should assert that the company will continue a close relationship with the distributor throughout development and production to ensure each picture's strongest production values, to achieve its maximum audience performance in the distributor's territory, and to assure the distributor of the greatest support of marketing and public relations materials to help prepare each picture's audiences. These letters, with their collateral materials, should be sent to these individuals and their organizations before press or trade ads.

The producer should break trade press releases and publish trade paid advertising three to five days following the distributor's receipt of their packages. The process, overall appearance, and quality of the ads and press releases should continue to appear as if they come from a major independent producer.

The producer will likely feel little effect of this first announcement. However, it is the consistent application of operating as a balanced producer of significant pictures that will enable the eventual meetings to pitch the pictures in order to secure a serious relationship engagement.

STORY SELECTION

The development manager reviews all submitted stories. Stories that the development manager recommends to the producer(s) (who must approve them) are then passed on to the production company's executive committee for its approval for investment in the story's internal greenlight.

Internal Greenlight

The internal greenlight process is the heart and soul of the financial and audience dynamics of the project and its potential in the worldwide marketplace. If the picture's earnings will come predominantly from the United States, then the greenlight process and costs are significantly as set forth here. The greenlight processes presented here will enable the production entity to gather and assess current worldwide data to do the following:

- Reveal its primary and secondary target audiences by approximate weight (the percentage of each major target audience within the picture's unique audience universe)
- Point to the studio or distributors with the highest success profiles in releasing pictures with similar audiences, campaigns, and above-the-line elements in their particular territories
- Indicate at least some of the most likely production funding sources
- Identify the optimal season and release pattern to theatrically release the picture
- Accurately/closely project the picture's gross income from its major earnings windows
- From the terms typically engaged by producers, compute the producers share of income
- Compare the producers income share to the pictures all-in production costs
- Determine if the earnings-to-cost ratio is within the risk parameters that the producer has set

Excellent sources are available that will enable a production company to perform this work in house (see the information sources listed in Chapter 16). If accomplished by an outside greenlight source, this process may cost $5,000 to $50,000. The process may appear time consuming and expensive, but the results are vital in order to reveal critical business aspects of the picture that will inform and enable the producer to succeed in the development phase or to abandon the project until it has a reasonable possibility to succeed.

Greenlight Processes

The most time-consuming and expensive phase is the campaign breakdown process. However, this step will yield the greatest amount of critical information.

1. *Script campaign breakdown.* Like a budget breakdown, the script is reviewed, and all the elements that lend themselves to the picture's 30-second television

commercial that will be used as the primary driver for its U.S. theatrical release are culled from the entire script into the script campaign breakdown form, similar to the one shown here. A version of this form is on this book's website.

Script Campaign Breakdown

Production Company: Over-the-Top Pictures
Picture Title: Spare Parts
Date Prep: 4/22/2010   **Analyst: MCS, ZM**

Page #	Setup	A streamlined spaceship streaks TOWARD CAMERA. The beautiful red and green planet in the distance suffers a series of brilliant, violent explosions high in its atmosphere.
1		
Page #	Setup	The controls and machinery glow and spark ominously. The instruments still working all read in the red danger zones.
1		
Page #	Setup	THREE MEN man the controls, struggling to keep the ship moving.
1	Line	COMMANDER: We're gonna fry if we don't blow up first.

---

2. *Campaign creative.* A professional copywriter, deeply exercised in writing the copy for theatrical release television campaigns for leading campaign creation entities creates the voice-over "spine" for the commercial, and a final 30-second television commercial script is created (see the following). This script is the critical foundation to the greenlight. Using motion picture campaign scriptwriters deeply exercised in this process is critical to delivering valid results.

Sample Script
Major Entertainment
"Film Title"
30-Second Script

Internal Greenlight Draft
              Cumulative Time

Video	Audio (Wild sounds throughout spot)
Charlie in his BMW takes the MLK Blvd exit off the Fwy.	(S.O.) Two drumsticks smack together counting a steady single rhythm about 50% greater than a resting heartbeat. More music cues.

	:02	VO: IN EVERY CITY
Rachel rides with her father through Beverly Hills in the rainy night, police car following them.	:04	VO: THERE ARE PLACES...
Rachel sits with a few girls at a multiracial table, Charlie smiles at her, she hesitates, then smiles back.	:06	VO: WE FEAR TO GO

3. *Campaign beat analysis.* The number of emotional beats in each of the 11 major categories that follow is counted in the 30-second television commercial script. The results are tallied and the emotional beats of the proposed picture's campaign are analyzed. The percentage allocations of the emotional beats are the picture's "campaign signature" and will allow each picture to be defined by its target audiences and their percentage of dominance.

Campaign Beat Analysis
Data Entry Worksheet

Production Company:	**Picture Title:**	
Campaign:	**Date Prepared:**	**Analyst:**
Emotions	**Sci-fi/Fantasy**	**Cultures**

Romance Drama Comedy Action Risqué Supernatural Horror Men Women Youth Kids

---

Directions:

Each beat scores one point.

Drama beats are every visual, VO, or sound that reveals the story.

Culture beats are those that speak directly to that particular target. If a child is in the scene, this is not necessarily a kids' beat. Culture beats have an extreme perspective of that culture. Each beat may not be a particular culture beat.

4. *Campaign signature.* As referenced in the following example, by applying the Campaign Signature quotients to a studio, industry data collection source or an alternative source's audience analysis matrix (see Chapter 16), the picture's target audiences by dominance are computed according to the picture's campaign emotional beats. This report reveals the proposed picture's target audiences as percentages, ranks audience dominance, and reveals studio picture profiles such as Romantic Comedy, Date Picture, Buddy Picture, and so on, as well as major blended audiences.

Great Producer
Amazing Script
Date Prepared: 4/20/2010
Analyst: SP
Target Audiences

Traditional audience profiles	Beat Score translation	Campaign Appeal (as a percentage)	Rank
Women 18+	34.0	29%	1
Men 18+	32.0	27%	2
Youth 12–17	30.0	25%	3
Kids 5–11	23.0	19%	4
Total	119.0	100%	

Major blended audiences	Score	As a percentage	Rank
Youth/young adults 16–25	33.0	28%	2
Older women 25–49	33.0	28%	2

Campaign Score

Emotional category	Number of beats	As a percentage of total beats	Rank
Romance	5	12%	4
Drama	10	24%	2
Comedy	13	31%	1
Action	6	14%	3
Risqué	2	5%	
Sci-Fi/fantasy	0	0%	
Horror	0	0%	
Men culture	2	5%	
Women culture	3	7%	
Youth culture	1	2%	
Kids culture	0	0%	
Total	42	100%	

5. *Preliminary and then final comparative pictures gathered and analyzed.* The development team, or outside vendor under the team's direction, next identifies 20 to 30 pictures released in the past five years that appear to potentially have similar target audience, campaign signatures, and above-the-line elements to the proposed picture. The primary 30-second commercial used in the U.S. theatrical campaign, before each of these pictures' theatrical premieres, then undergoes a campaign beat analysis, revealing each of the campaign signatures. Each of these signatures is then compared with the picture under analysis. Those pictures very close in target audiences, campaign signature, and above-the-line elements are compiled into a report (typically four to eight pictures) showing their composite average earnings, release dates,

releasing studios, directors and lead cast rankings, tag lines, and other information helpful to identify the market and business characteristics of the picture being analyzed.

6. *Global sales breakdown.* The identified comparative pictures are then used to compute a global gross and net earnings forecast of the proposed picture for all major windows and ancillary earnings. This also indicates the final producer's share of profits in relationship to the picture's all-in costs.

7. *U.S. comparative campaign strategy and spending breakdown.* This reviews the media buy for each of the comparative pictures including their total advertising dollars spent and release pattern, providing the team valuable information for evaluating and influencing the U.S. theatrical release pattern, media buy, brand alliances, promotion, and other related campaign aspects.

This information not only reveals the likely feasibility of each project, but it also becomes the producer's vital business bulwark for understanding each picture's business and marketing qualities. The similar pictures' campaigns are also worthy of intense study and can be very informing relative to the most effective marketing approaches. Once a project is greenlit, other beneficial research includes the following:

1. *Brand tie-in ad spending.* This identifies the comparative pictures' estimated total ad dollars spent by brand tie-in partnerships and helps identify likely brand tie-in categories, partners, and relationships.

2. *Director and actor rankings.* The comparative picture's directors and actors may inspire further considerations. During this research, the actors and directors being considered for the picture being greenlit should also be ranked in each major release territory for value analysis.

3. *Distribution executive tracking.* Though distribution executives do not regularly move position, it can be beneficial to track distribution executives at the studios and distributors of the comparative pictures, to see if those responsible for the success of the comparative pictures are still at the studio or distributor in which the producer may be interested.

Greenlight Processes: Outside Services

There are services that offer greenlight processes that might be beneficial for collecting and analyzing the required data. Here is a sampling:

- In 2010, *OTX (Ipsos OTX MediaCT),* the online test-screening service long used by the majors, launched a script evaluation division that will assess the playability and marketability of screenplays. It uses many of the same tools it employs to test-screen and conduct tracking for films before they unspool in theaters. OTX essentially compares a script to other films in its genre and identifies its target demographic and box office potential, as well as potential marketing messages. Creative elements are analyzed and compared with similar films to suggest how audiences might react to scenes, based on a database OTX has assembled based on of years of research. Recommendations are offered to address any negatives. The scripts are also pitched to 1,500 moviegoers to gauge their interest in wanting to see the film. Each report costs approximately $5,000.

- *Gillen Group LLC* (whose CEO co-authored this book) created the Comparables Chart discussed next that takes the project through an extensive comparables/antecedents discovery by analyzing approximately 20 pictures that are similar in genre, budget, level of talent, target audience, prints and advertising (P&A) spend, and release pattern and projects three levels of potential revenue models assessing all rights worldwide and the timing of the return on investment for the investor(s). (www.gillengroupllc.com)

Greenlight Processes: Comparable Pictures

At the absolute minimum, the producer and the executive team should use the Gillen Group Figure 14.1 Comparables Chart at the end of this chapter to research and track approximately 20 to 30 pictures that are similar in genre, budget, level of talent, target audience, P&A spend, and release pattern. This chart is also available on the website as a blank chart to fill in, along with formulas to add and average out the categories.

Some information is available online for free from such websites as IMDb.com, boxofficemojo.com, and showbiz data.com. Other information can be purchased from research sites such as Media by Numbers, Adams Media Research, Baseline Studio System, and Rentrak. Figure 14.1 was charted without purchasing outside numbers so most of the DVD and some of the budgets were not available (NA).

Some important tactics to keep in focus as you chart your list are as follows:

- Only use films released in the past five years.
- The Talent rating should be based on the level of talent the year the film was released, not on how they would be perceived in the marketplace today. Talent rankings are Star, A, B, C, and Unknowns. Track both the director and the lead cast. We suggest working with a casting director or international sales agent to make this subjective call.
- Be sure to chart all levels of performing films, not just successes. You will learn as much, if not more, from the failures. Also, the exercise here is to analyze if your film will have an audience and at what level, so to not track the failures will give you and your investors' inaccurate results.
- If one of the films you are tracking is a well-known brand going into the marketplace—such as a franchise, a film based on a bestselling book, a sequel, a film based on a successful TV series, and so on—you should downgrade all the revenue numbers by at least 50 percent or more.
- If a film you are tracking received important award nominations or wins, be sure to track where in the release of the film this occurred. Typically nominations and awards create a spike in the theatrical revenue, and this revenue should be discounted.

	PRIMER	CODE 46	THE MACHINIST	THE SIGNAL	MOON	TOTALS	AVERAGES
YEAR	2004	2004	2004	2008	2009		
DISTRIBUTOR	ThinkFilm	Warner Indie	Paramount Classics	Magnolia/Magnet	Sony Classics		
GENRE	Sci-Fi Thriller	Sci-Fi Romantic Drama	Drama Thriller	Horror Sci-Fi	Sci-Fi		
TALENT	C	B	B	C-	B-		
BUDGET	$ 7,000	$ 7,500,00	$ 5,000,000	$ 50,000	$ 5,000,000	$ 10,057,000	$ 2,011,400
DOM. BOX OFFICE	$ 424,760	$ 285,585	$ 1,082,715	$ 251,150	$ 5,010,163	$ 7,054,373	$ 1,410,875
FOREIGN BOX OFFICE	$ -	$ 600,442	$ 7,120,520	$ 112,995	$ 4,005,850	$ 11,839,807	$ 2,367,961
WW BOX OFFICE	$ 424,760	$ 886,027	$ 8,203,235	$ 364,145	$ 9,016,013	$ 18,894,180	$ 3,778,836
U.S. DVD	NA	$ 20,170	NA	NA	$ NA	$ 20,170	$ 20,170
SCREENS: OPENING	4	3	3	160	8	178	36
SCREENS: WIDEST	31	21	72	160	251	535	107
RATING	PG-13	R	R	R	R		
TAG LINE	What Happens If It Actually Works?	In the Future…Love is a Dangerous Game	How Do You Wake Up From A Nightmare If You're Not Sleeping?	This Is Not A Test	The Last Place You'd Ever Expect to Find Yourself		
SYNOPSIS	At night and on weekends, four men in a suburban garage have built a cottage industry of error-checking devices. But, they know that there is something more. There is some idea, some, …	A love story set in a Brave New World-type near-future where cities are heavily controlled and only accessible through checkpoints. People cannot travel unless they have "papelles," a special travel permit…	An industrial worker who hasn't slept in a year begins to doubt his own sanity	A horror film told in three parts, from three perspectives, in which a mysterious transmission that turns people into killers invades every cell phone, radio, and television.	Sam Bell has a three year contract to work for Lunar Industries. He is the sole employee based at their lunar station. There is no direct communication link available between the lunar station and Earth.…s		

DISTRIBUTORS	TOTAL
ThinkFilm	1
Warner indie	1
Paramount Classics	1
Magnolia/Magnet	1
Sony Classics	1

RATINGS	TOTAL
PG	0
PG-13	1
R	4
NC 17	0

FIGURE 14.1
Film comparables chart.

- The tag line is the selling line on the film poster.
- Once you have your long list (20 to 30 films), decide on the top 7 to 10 comparables.
- Once you have that final list, delete the highest and lowest grossing film.
- The chart will automatically average out each category, which is typically a midrange projected performance level for your film.

External Greenlight

When producers discover a picture that passes an internal greenlight, they also then have the information they need to proceed in engaging their U.S. and international strategic distribution relationships (external greenlight). If the literary rights have not yet been acquired, then the producer should approach the rights holders or their representatives and either (1) enter an exclusive relationship that allows the producers the right to continue the final steps of development discovery for a short term or (2) enter an option/purchase agreement.

The next step is approaching a U.S. distributor (either theatrical, DVD, VOD, cable, etc.) both to validate that the forecasted earnings rendered from the greenlight analysis appear to be valid and to engage the distributor in a confidential, arms-length, best-efforts, no-obligation, exclusive first-look development collaboration.

In preparation for these meetings, the distributor presentation materials must be prepared. The most critical discovery in this meeting for the distributor is determining (1) if the picture's earnings may be sufficiently high to justify the significant theatrical release costs (especially in the United States) and (2) how easy or predictable the picture's marketing may be. The single element that will answer these questions for them is the picture's trailer/TV commercial.

There are several methods one can utilize to create this all-important trailer/commercial:

- *A professional trailer house.* Hire an organization that works consistency with the major distributors to create it as an animatic (cost: $10,000 to $35,000).
- *Do it yourself (DIY).* Film one or two scenes and edit them together.
- *Ripamatic.* Cut and edit using existing footage from films that are similar to yours in genre, period, talent, and so on, adding your own voice-over and titles.
- *Proof of concept.* Similar to DIY, here you create a trailer that focuses on those issues that might concern the distributor about your film or your ability to deliver the project for the budget, i.e. prove to them you can.

If at all possible, we highly recommend using a professional trailer/marketing house whose team is deeply experienced in creating trailer or commercial campaigns for pictures similar to the producer's and that regularly work with the strongest distributors in creating and delivering their pictures' campaigns. Though the picture is only in script form, the campaign house rewrites and polishes the trailer/commercial scripts, records voice talent, may produce some original visuals, creates titles, creates and captures storyboards, may discover and use some existing footage, identifies music and sound effects, and creates a trailer/commercial that clearly demonstrates the picture's marketing power and story intensity.

After the materials are prepared, the core-territory distributor presentations are made, as referenced in Chapters 1 and 2. If one or more of these distributors concur that, with a director and cast of the level represented attached, they believe the picture could earn similarly to the pictures that are given as comparables and they are willing to give the development collaboration requested, then the international territory meetings are set up, as reviewed in Chapter 3. Should no core-territory or international distributor development relationship be engaged, then the producer moves on to another project. This may seem brutal. However, it is not nearly as emotionally and financially devastating as spending extensive time and funding on projects that do not have sufficient business feasibility to warrant distribution. Especially for new production entities, theatrical distributors naturally take a "wait and see" attitude. Remember at this stage, the objective is not to receive a distribution commitment. It is to follow the nine steps reviewed in Chapter 3. If distributor interest and territory earnings estimate confirmations cannot be received from a theatrical distributor, depending on the picture, the producer may seek a U.S. distributor development relationship with a DVD, VOD,or TV distributor that will suffice in moving forward to international territory meetings.

The core-distributor development relationship can be considered sufficiently engaged after the producer sends a confirming letter to the distributor, referencing the relaxed nine-point relationship commencement referenced in Chapter 3.

As also presented in Chapter 3, after establishing the primary territory distributor relationship, the producer then prepares to meet with the picture's potentially strongest distributor in each of the seven major international territories, as outlined in the plan prepared by the development manager. Typically, many, if not most of the materials prepared for the primary distributor are also applicable to their international territory counterparts. It is always most effective, especially in setting new relationships, to meet with distributors in their own offices, apart from the clutter of a sales market event. However, although meeting with decision makers is challenging at a major global sales markets, meetings can be accomplished at these events if appointments are made well in advance.

Meetings with major ancillary partners such as electronic games, major book tie-ins, music, merchandise, and so on are also important. These meetings introduce the relationship possibility and allow validation of the project, earnings potential, planning relative to the picture's schedule, and terms.

After introductions have been engaged with the major international territory distributors and potential ancillary partners, confirmation letters are prepared and presented to each of them.

An analysis is then taken on the project to assess strong, medium, and weak alliances. The production financing worksheet reviewed in Chapter 6 is used to strategize possible production financing participants. If the team agrees there is strong probability that these relationships will bring about the picture's distribution, funding, creative, and earnings objectives, then further development funds are approved for the project. If not, then a new strategy is commenced that will bring the picture to qualify for the development funds, or the project is placed on hold until conditions change, enabling the picture to advance.

Projects receiving development funding approval continue with a new letter to the distributor in the primary territory, as well as the most preferred distributors in the other territories, and ancillary and brand partner candidates. This letter thanks each of them for their important contributions to the final greenlighting and states that the project is now commencing fully financed development and will be announced in the industry trade papers on the date that is specified in the letter.

These negotiations then proceed as presented in Chapters 9 and 10. The press release should include the literary right's purchase, allow the producer time to first notify each of the global distributors and other developing relationships of the acquisition, then follow this notification with press releases and paid trade announcements regarding the commencement of the picture's development phase. As reviewed in Chapters 1, 2, and 3, this process of distributor participation and trade culture deepens distribution relationships and increases their positive anticipation.

DIRECTOR ATTACHMENT

The earlier the director is attached, the greater the creative cohesion and harmony of every aspect of the picture. Producers who are also directors by craft but who will use another director for the picture are especially well served by the earliest possible director attachment, so that every creative element is a collaboration.

Differences in producer/director creative vision have weakened many pictures and literally destroyed others. Early director attachment naturally establishes a strong producer/director collaborative creative foundation. Once the director is attached, this person substantially drives the physical development and production of the motion picture.

The producer presents a written list of director recommendations, distilled from the management team's recommendations, to each advisory team member for that person's notes and suggestions. Some of the producer's advisory team will have multiple experiences with the directors on this list and will render exceptional counsel relative to the consideration, approach, and eventual relationship with the director. After checking each director's availability and quote, the producer next prepares a final priority list of directors, considering advisory team input, additional creative research, and discussions with producers, bond execs, and others who have experience with these directors.

Then the producer notifies the distributors, confidentially revealing the directors being considered, in their order of priority, and requesting each distributor's preferences and comments. Typically this list is also shared with the international distributors. If appropriate, a director's reel is prepared.

Tempered by distributor responses, the producer creates a final priority list of at least three directors. It is rare that the producer's decision will match every distributor's first choice. The producer now proceeds with director meetings leading to attachment.

As reviewed in Chapter 10, producers should meet about the story with the director before talking about compensation. Most directors comfortably accommodate these initial creative meetings, since they may have their own production companies and businesswise are negotiating their own agreements and using their attorneys and agents primarily for documentation and counsel.

It is during the initial creative meetings with the three leading directors that it often becomes apparent who should direct the picture, because of the director's affinity for the story and the director and producer's natural ability to communicate and respect each other's position, relative to developing and producing the picture.

After the producer reviews the creative meetings' events with the advisory and management teams, a director decision is made and a term sheet is approved. A negotiation meeting or conference call is then set with the director's attorney or agent.

As presented in Chapters 9 and 10, the director's relationship must be negotiated and documented. Part of this negotiation should include a release for this relationship's press announcement. The U.S. and international distributors are then notified of the successful attachment of the director, followed closely by a jointly coordinated press release and paid announcement in the entertainment trades.

THE PRODUCER/DIRECTOR RELATIONSHIP

The producer is the picture's ultimate parent. The producer discovers the story, holds the initial vision of it as a motion picture, provides the environment and resources for the picture to be developed and produced, and even selects the director. However, the producer has simultaneous multiple-picture responsibilities. The final preparation and actual production of the picture is so intense that one person must be exclusively focused on each picture. This is the director.

The producer sustains the ultimate authority and power throughout the process. It is important that the producer exercise this authority only with the director. The department heads and all other production participants are accountable to the director, not the producer. When the producer works directly with any of the team members reporting to the director, it is done only as an adjunct to the director, not as an authority superior to the director.

The director must sustain position integrity with the production team as its ultimate voice. It is standard operating procedure, and everyone knows the director works for the producer. All should also understand that the director has complete power to produce the picture on behalf of the producer.

Most producers are *very* involved in each picture's development and production, particularly when it comes to script development, talent attachment, storyboard creation, location selection, and the final postproduction and sweetening. Even after the producer reviews the dailies, the director may receive a call requesting reshoots, rewrites, and other major alterations. But this is between the director and the producer.

It is always in the best interest of the picture that the producer and director sustain this relationship integrity. To all who work on the picture, the producer creates an aura of respect for the director as the development and production chief of the picture. The director listens and responds to the producer who is, after all, the picture's creator and ultimate authority.

If the picture is going to be infused with the life it needs, the director must feel the creative freedom and the leadership control over all aspects of the picture. Directors must respect that the ultimate creative and financial ownership and responsibility belong to the producer. The director is allowed the opportunity to create the picture, because the producer has put it in the director's hands. The producer is ultimately responsible for the picture's creative and financial success. Consequently, regardless of the extensive genius and energy directors pour into their pictures, the director should respect the producer's position and respond to requests even if they seem unreasonable.

James Cameron created the landmark achievement picture *Titanic*. Tom Sherak at Twentieth Century Fox made suggestions. Cameron listened, considered, and responded. Each was under intense creative, time, and financial pressure. Cameron later credited Sherak with the suggestion for what Cameron said was a better ending for the picture. In the final analysis, it isn't who has the greatest power but rather how well the creative team works together to deliver the most creative and financially successful picture.

SHOOTING SCRIPT

The core development team now is composed of three members: the director in the primary position, along with the producer and the development manager. The producer still has the ultimate control, but the director is rightly the head of and leading this core team.

The first focus of the core team is the story. The picture must have a first-draft shooting script before the intricate and intense planning and budgeting that are essential for its creation. The story will go through further rewrites as other key collaborators are attached, but the basic story will be recommended by the director and finally decided upon by the core team, tempered by executive team review and comment. This review is a key contribution to the picture's success.

Often the director is a writer and may participate in the writing of the drafts leading to the shooting script. Even if this is so, it is best to enter a multiwriter step deal, as presented in Chapter 9. This will ensure the greatest probability for the script's predictable on-schedule completion and the creation of the strongest shooting script. Typically the director and producer will insist on having the first-draft shooting script before they approach potential lead cast talent.

LEAD CAST ATTACHMENT

The producer and development director will have drawn up a proposed list for the lead cast before the director is set. The director and producer will use this list plus the director's suggestions to prepare the final list of lead actors under consideration. Their agents or managers will be contacted to verify their quote and availability.

Following much the same process as the director selection, the U.S. and international distributors are contacted, their responses are weighed (considering the television quotients [TVQs] and marketing values of each performer in the various markets), and a priority list for the final actors is prepared.

The actors are approached, as presented in Chapter 10, and negotiation and documentation engaged. After all that, distributor notifications are sent out before press releases and paid trade announcements.

PREPARING FOR PHYSICAL PRODUCTION

Once the first draft of the shooting script is completed, physical production preparation commences in earnest. This includes attaching the picture's line producer or UPM. These now become the central participants in the physical production process. They will create the original and the many permutations of the picture's production breakdowns, schedules, and budgets. Department heads and others will study and use various portions of these materials, along with the shooting script, in their individual planning and performance decisions.

Production department heads will be recommended by the director and reviewed by the producer, and the advisory and management teams make a final review and recommendations. The director will approach the key department heads in concert with the line producer through creative discussions that will expand into negotiations and then attachment to the picture.

Creative collaboration from the newly added pool of the department heads will deepen the overall creative heft of the picture, further perfecting the script and bringing the picture into clearer focus.

Development of physical production now begins in earnest, with locations being determined, departments making staff arrangements, the balance of the cast being attached, and, of course, the continual enhancement of the script in response to the reality of these elements.

MATURING MARKETING MATERIALS

As talent is attached to the picture, so are their representative reels, including those from the director, actors, cinematographer, production designer, composer, and in some cases specialists such as the SFX designer, fight choreographers, and dance choreographers. Through many of the excellent film commissions, reels are even provided on the picture's locations. These elements, together with print elements, combine to establish a rich resource that can be used to create the picture's enhanced print, film, and video presentations for the major festival/market meetings. When these are presented to participating distributors, they in turn use them to promote the picture within their respective territories.

PREPARING THE PRODUCTION BANK FINANCING FACILITY

Since the completion bond advisor's company usually bonds all of the production company's pictures, and the bank advisor's bank provides the fully collateralized production funding, each of them are regularly brought current on the picture's progress. In addition to the referenced advisory meetings, at least two additional meetings with documented picture plans should be set up before placing bonding and lending requests with these institutions.

Typically 9 to 12 months pass between the story's postgreenlight acquisition and the placement of the production loan request with the bank. During this time, the most aggressive distributors for the picture become apparent. Also, conditions within these territories change from the time of the first greenlight. Mergers, acquisitions, and changes in the economy are largely responsible for these shifts.

Because of these phenomena, the global rights manager should revise the picture's sales breakdown at least monthly, and again just before preparing the picture's finance plan and the presentation draft of the bank loan analysis. A description of how to prepare the plan and analysis is presented in Chapters 3 and 6. The UPM also prepares a revised budget for use with the preparation of this documentation.

Once the bank loan analysis is prepared, it is presented, along with the finance plan, to the management committee for approval. Following its approval, the bank loan memorandum, as described in Chapter 6, which includes the completion bond memorandum, as described in Chapter 8, are prepared by the production company's finance vice president. The bond memorandum is prepared and presented first, since the completion bond company's intent will accompany the bank memorandum.

Each of these memoranda are mature intent documents. Their purpose is to receive a contingent commitment from each participant, so that when the producer provides the imminent elements declared in the memoranda, each respective entity will participate in the picture's production funding. The production company must be bondable to engage the production bank loan, and the bank loan facility must be available to accept the picture's presales, as well as many of the following as are additionally used in production funding: equity purchase agreements from director cast or vendors, brand tie-in agreements, production incentive program materials, and private investor agreements.

The producer meets with the bonding company and receives the completion bond written contingent commitment first, then meets with and receives the bank's written contingent commitment.

THE PRIMARY-RELEASE TERRITORY DISTRIBUTION AGREEMENT

As thoroughly reviewed in Chapter 2, this agreement is typically with a major, mini-major, or strong indie distributor, if the picture's primary release territory is the United States. This agreement affects all other rights, relationships, and earnings and is central to the picture's global success. This is the time when producers should enter their picture's primary-release territory theatrical distribution agreement.

As suggested previously, these distributors, especially the U.S. majors and mini-majors, are excellent marketers as well as negotiators. They understand the value of a picture, and, as they have global sales power, they prefer to acquire all global rights.

Fortunately, there are distributor competitors in most territories. These distributors in all the major territories have become very open to a broad spectrum of distribution relationship configurations. Each wants the valuable inventory, the product with predictable and hopefully substantial earnings power.

As reviewed in Chapter 2, U.S. theatrical distribution rights are usually more of a liability than an asset. Consequently, any theatrical release agreement will also acquire all home entertainment rights (the right with the greatest earnings potential). Each is an excellent offset to the other. Also, the timing of these two distribution windows is close, with home entertainment earnings primarily driven by the picture's theatrical campaign. Though the United States is the most expensive theatrical release territory, because of the close timing of the windows and the theatrical release carrying the primary branding responsibility for both of these windows, in most territories, these are bundled in the same distribution agreement.

Though the theatrical and home entertainment distribution rights bundle is the most common distributor relationship, as the picture matures through development, the distributor may become much more aggressive in negotiating for specific or all international rights, as well as for specific or all ancillary rights. Many of these distribution proposals are extremely competitive with those from other distributors in individual territories that the producer has established throughout the picture's development and preproduction. The producer should analyze the primary distributor proposal and compare its gross potential, distribution fees, and costs, as well as the producer's internal costs, against these factors in the alternative relationships. Then, with the counsel of the advisory and executive teams, the producer must decide the best financial course of action.

To clearly compare the offers, producers must also recalculate the picture's bank financing worksheet, including bankability that may affect borrowing costs, as reviewed in Chapter 6.

THE PRESALES

As reviewed in Chapter 3, presales have always been challenging and are especially so currently. However, given strong target audience potential, sales, and comparables information allowing each distributor to evaluate and project earnings (as well as marketable talent), presale agreements are achievable. The international license strategy and approach is presented in Chapter 3 and the premium and network television rights in Chapter 5.

When motion picture development becomes this mature, the picture is a familiar name among trade participants in the major territories and in the United States, and more often than not, consumer press has begun.

By this time, the producer has been approached by other international distributors who are competitors of the producer's participating greenlight distributors. The producer maintains the integrity of the participating distributor relationships; however, the competing distributors will become increasingly interested in engaging license rights for the picture.

The producer prepares and presents a preferential license opportunity to the proposed presale licensees. In the licensee presentation meeting, the producer first provides the most recent progress and materials, then reveals the name of the bank providing the picture's production funding and the completion guarantor providing its bond. Next, the producer presents the plan for this particular distributor to obtain the rights to the picture for its territory by entering a presale license agreement. This agreement includes an advance, or minimum guarantee, paid against the producer's share of future revenue and profits with the licensee. To secure the presale, if necessary, the producer can offer to discount the advance amount by approximately 20 percent compared to what the producer would be expected to receive for an advance after the picture is completed (most often this is only 5 to 12 months away).

The producer makes this offer only to the distributors that are part of the presale plan. The offer is made at the time when these distributors should be especially motivated to secure the picture's rights and to receive the financial advantage associated with the license advance discount. This is good business for both the distributor and the producer.

The appeal for this relationship is heightened by the licensee's advance amount typically being no more than the lowest amount the licensee may potentially earn from the rights being distributed. If there are U.S. ancillary presales, these are offered in much the same manner, with similar discounts, as discussed in Chapters 1, 5, and 6.

ENGAGING THE COMPLETION BOND

The completion bond (refer to Chapter 8) is necessary for the bank loan and is formally requested by the producer immediately following the securitization of the presale documentation.

The request for the completion bond is made in writing with the most recent shooting script, production budget, and supporting documentation. The completion guarantor's legal counsel will participate in structuring the lending bank, the producer, presale distributors, equity, production incentive and all other collateral, discount and deferral participants, plus the guarantor itself into an interparty agreement. This agreement, when closed, will finalize and cash flow the production funding. Producers should allow at least eight to twelve weeks for the interparty agreement to close.

ENGAGING THE PRODUCTION BANK LOAN

The collateral and completion bond are presented to the bank to engage the production loan (refer to Chapter 6). Processing the loan includes conforming the letter(s) of credit language to language that is acceptable to the bank, should any of these be used. This process may take 5 to 10 working days.

At this time the producer forms a single-picture producing entity for this one project. As presented in Chapter 11, this organization is a wholly owned subsidiary of the production company and will produce and own the picture. After the production loan's line of credit is open, the production company begins making the several advances to this producing company, as it will continue to do throughout the completion of the picture.

The first expense of the producing company will likely be the purchase of all rights, title, and interest of the picture from the production company, or if they have financed the picture's development separately, from the production company's development company, according to the production company's purchase agreement with the development company.

FINAL PREPRODUCTION

During final preproduction, the producer does the following:

- Closely participates with and supports the director. As frenetically paced as this time is, this is the last sane time the producer can participate with the director until principal photography wraps. The creative look of the picture is substantially established during this period. The script receives special producer scrutiny for the apparent creative reasons, as well as special needs that include writing, planning, and budgeting for international territory and ancillary media cover shots (as discussed in Chapters 3 and 5).

- Sets the picture's novelization relationship with a publisher, even if the story has been or currently is in release, as explained in Chapters 1 and 5.
- Continues to mature potential and manage engaged premium tie-in and product placement relationships. To accomplish this goal, the global rights and advertising vice presidents combine their efforts in presentations, relationship negotiations, planning, and execution coordination as reviewed in Chapter 5.
- Prepares, in cooperation with the primary global distributors, the picture's ramp-up consumer public relations and advertising; the print, TV commercials, and trailer title, look, teasers, and long-form element list; layouts; boards; title research and treatment; and home entertainment additional features production, along with related activities. Some of this is for release soon after principal photography begins, and the rest is for the several releases that will escalate as the picture approaches the global marketplace.

PRINCIPAL PHOTOGRAPHY

As principal photography commences, primary location accommodations are made for special production guests, including development partners (if any), primary distributor representatives, presell participants, brand and product tie-in participants, and trade and consumer press. Appropriate invitations are sent to these guests, and as they respond, their individual arrangements are made.

The producer reviews all the picture's dailies, consulting with the director relative to the picture's creative progress, and informing the director about the picture's distribution and marketing. The producer will be on location most of the shoot, as well as with the picture's postproduction team, which most often begins assembling the picture from the beginning of principal photography.

The initial consumer press releases are staged and rolled into the major global territories. Trade press and paid announcements are released.

As the picture is produced, the marketing reel expands; the teaser trailer is assembled and released to the theatrical distributors; the primary trailer(s) start and continue to assemble; and promotional coverage is captured, assembled, polished, and released, according to the marketing plan. Copies of all press releases and promotional materials are sent to the major global distribution participants. The picture's up-to-the-minute promotional reel is exclusively exhibited in the appropriate global markets.

POSTPRODUCTION

The director often supervises postproduction. As this process begins, soon after principal photography commences, assemblies are sent to the director for review. The digital postproduction process and Internet use have been extremely helpful in *fixing it in principal photography,* which is most often much better and less expensive than the traditional method of fixing it in post.

In addition to more traditional postproduction duties, the producer supervises trailers and ad spots that have been produced in house. The producer also reviews the preparation and audience testing of distributor and trade specialist-produced trailers in two or three versions, and television commercials in four or five versions. If the picture's title is in question (this process is often excruciating), it will also be market and audience tested before a decision is made. As postproduction is completed, global sales intensify, and the major global distributors deepen their marketing preparation.

THE PICTURE'S THEATRICAL RELEASE BRANDING

The picture's total theatrical and after-theatrical release audience size and earnings are substantially determined by the effectiveness of the picture's branding during its theatrical release in each territory. The picture's total earnings are not determined so much by the picture's theatrical gross as they are by the power and effectiveness of the picture's campaign, the reach and frequency of its media buys and brand tie-in partners to its target audiences, and the word on the street and Internet among the picture's targets. Box office grosses can also be negatively affected as much as one third by marketplace anomalies including picture release glut, weather, spectacular national news, or sports events.

The producer is never busier than during a picture's postproduction and pretheatrical release. In fact, it is not enough to make an outrageously fine motion picture. Audience reactions to a picture's early trailers are excellent indications of the content and texture that should be used in the picture's strongest television commercials, as well as its trailers that will be shown closer to the picture's release and the clips shown during celebrity show visits.

At the time the final theatrical campaign begins (in the United States this is about three weeks before the first theatrical street date), the picture's novels should have already flooded retail checkout stands with the picture's one-sheet on their covers. Commercials for brand tie-in partners will begin airing immediately before and then into the picture's theatrical release.

The week the picture opens, distributors' public relations and advertising departments are at full throttle, executing release strategies prepared months prior. Theatrical premieres and entertainment, intricately choreographed Internet stories, pictures, and even segments are strategically released; morning news and other television shows are sporting celebrity and picture highlight segments; entertainment and other publications have eye-grabbing photos and articles about the picture; and literally every other promotional and purchasable device is employed to establish and turn up the heat on making the picture a commercial success.

THE GLOBAL TERRITORIES AND ANCILLARY MARKETS

Once the picture is completed, lab access letters are delivered to prebuy distributors and special screenings are set for the other international distributors (as discussed in Chapter 3) and for major ancillary rights media (as presented in Chapter 5). This is the completion of the primary cycle of discovering, producing, and bringing a picture into the market.

A checklist of the big items within the motion picture development and production cycle follows:

- Search for the story
- Plan development operations, forecasts, and funding
- Assemble or tune the team
- Produce the development investment documents
- Present to, negotiate with, and close with the development/production company investors
- Begin and continue investor communications
- Work the development plan
- Review and select the story
- Evaluate the internal and external greenlight criteria to determine the project's creative and business feasibility
- Configure the picture's probable production financing participants by using incentive programs, director/actor and major vendor profit participation/equity, brand tie-ins, bank/bond exercised presales, and private equity
- Complete predirector picture development
- Search for and attach the director
- Cause the first-draft shooting script to be created
- Attach the lead cast
- Prepare the physical production
- Prepare and mature the picture's marketing materials
- Prepare the bank financing facility
- Enter production incentive program relationships, brand tie-ins, equity/profit sharing relationships, major global territory distribution agreements, and private equity agreements
- Engage the completion bond
- Engage the bank loan
- Complete the final preproduction
- Perform principal photography producer's duties
- Perform postproduction producer's duties
- Direct the picture's global branding
- Sell into all remaining global ancillary markets and territories

CHAPTER POSTSCRIPT

Before the production company begins the white-hot demanding process of developing, producing, and liquidating the rights of its motion pictures, the operating plan and the team that will run it should already be prepared and in place.

This team and its organization establish and finance each picture's development plan; discover, qualify, and develop the stories; commence and manage the marketing of the pictures; fund the production of the pictures; produce the pictures; mature their marketing; and manage the pictures' global distribution. These are seven individually critical processes of assuring that the production team produces the pictures it wants and that each picture individually has the greatest opportunity for artistic and financial success.

It is good for producers to understand how all the pieces fit together and how the team accomplishes the work and sustains the critical checks and balances during each picture's search, development, production, and distribution. Thoroughly understanding the whole process and preparing for its successful operation are essential to achieving the team objectives of producing consistently profitable pictures that please their audiences and fulfill the producer's creative passion and the company's overall mission.

CHAPTER 15
The Producer's Business

This chapter presents the producer's role in the process of multiple picture production. It covers the producer's involvement in establishing the production company brand presence with the global entertainment trade and consumers; maneuvering the balancing act between business, artistic, and personal objectives; managing library pictures; and advancing team vitality and allegiance.

MULTIPLE PICTURE MANAGEMENT

As demonstrated in the previous chapter, shepherding a single picture through the complete cycle—from discovery, internal greenlighting, and development through production and distribution—is a wonderfully complex process. When producers plan multiple pictures, their activity projection reveals the hyper-challenge of simultaneously managing a picture in postproduction, starting principal photography on another, moving YET another picture through predevelopment evaluation, and reviewing new stories.

The single picture activity and cash flow planning that is reviewed in Chapter 14 must be done for each picture proposed in the producer's multiple picture development plan. Each picture's planning, management, and resource needs must be considered separately, as well as the beneficial amortization of time, team, and expenses that all the pictures have on one another.

The capacity to manage multiple pictures is directly related to how well the producer understands the entire development/production/distribution process. It also depends on the planning and work ethic of the individual. Similarly, producers must sustain the individual creative and business integrity of each picture while they focus on the creative and business balance among all the pictures.

Seasoned producers adhere to the most successful processes of multiple picture development and production by thoroughly planning for the needs and timing of each picture and focusing on the pictures as a group, in such a fashion that each picture actually benefits the other creatively, financially, and perhaps most especially in their galvanizing effect upon global strategic partner relationships.

DOI: 10.1016/B978-0-240-81463-6.00015-2

TIME AND BUDGET ECONOMIES

Investors are not the only parties pressing the producer to be engaged in multiple pictures. Most of the producer's primary relationships—such as licensees, agents, bankers, and sales teams—are more dedicated, supportive, and reliant when the producer has several pictures in process.

Distributor Relationships

Licensees are motivated in their relationships by producers who both deliver pictures that perform strongly and provide a regular high volume of pictures. It is a combination of these two qualities that determines a producer's value to each licensee.

During a meeting with a distributor, a producer may pitch a new picture for distribution consideration, review cast ideas for another picture, and deliver marketing elements for yet another. The greater the number of significant pictures delivered by a producer, the stronger the producer's relationship is with licensees.

Agents

As presented in Chapter 10, most agencies have packaging agents, who combine internal story and performing elements with other creative elements represented outside their agencies in order to motivate the making of pictures that substantially include their clients. The best-organized production companies are those that are the most sought after by agency packagers. These agencies are pleased to meet and assist such producers on their pictures, as well as use the opportunity to approach them with agency packages. And multiple picture production necessitates regular agency meetings.

BANKS AND COMPLETION GUARANTORS

Some pictures will develop and produce in a smoother fashion and achieve higher income performance than others. Bankers and insurers tend to have a greater sense of balance and stability with those producer clients who are driving multiple pictures. Further, a slate of pictures allows the producer to offer offsetting guarantees among these pictures to banks and bonding companies. Such cross-collateralized relationships must be entered into within the bounds of the agreements set forth with the several profit participants associated with each picture. This often establishes a substantially deeper deal stability and relationship confidence with insurers and banks that is unique to multiple-picture production.

Sales Events

Producers or their representatives usually present their pictures to the six or seven major territory distributors and at international territory sales markets such as AFM and Cannes. Similar to each picture's core-territory distributor relationship, having multiple pictures strengthens international territory relationships. Additionally, multiple pictures allow the producer to amortize the significant expenses of attending these markets over several pictures.

ESTABLISHING THE PRODUCTION COMPANY BRAND PRESENCE

Production companies, especially new ones, must establish and then advance the heat of their company's global trade and consumer brand presence. As emphasized throughout this book, strategic relationships with core-territory distributors, international distributors, banks, completion guarantors, attorneys, agents, and a broad array of other major industry category participants are mandatory. The stronger these relationships, the greater the operating benefits. For key close relationships, this is best developed through consistent, confidential communiqués outside the press that are confirmed in the press. For relationships in general, a well-thought-of reputation, appropriately, is almost entirely established and sustained by the performance of the producer's pictures in the global marketplace. In fact, the *trade* brand's respect for a production company is chiefly a mirror for the global *audience's* respect for the producer's pictures.

Who we are always speaks louder than who we say we are. Likewise, a production company is substantially known by its pictures rather than its mission statement. Understanding this basic reality, producers who want to establish their production company brand with its audiences will be benefited by correlating their picture selections with their mission statements. If a producer becomes committed to produce a picture that is outside the scope of the company's brand, but wants to sustain the company's brand presence, then perhaps the producer should create another production entity for that picture.

Because each motion picture's campaign is necessarily intense and focused on that picture, typically little campaign emphasis is given to the production company. Further, it is almost unheard of for production companies to launch a campaign exclusively on themselves, or even a campaign where they are the dominant focus. This is the prevailing notion in the current culture of the motion picture industry. Like many cultures, this practice is not necessarily the most effective way to drive audiences to pictures delivered by the production company and the studio. It may be a profitable exercise for producers to consider if there may be motion picture marketing advantages associated with a production company's name becoming an icon to audiences.

There are lessons to be learned by other global consumer brands and the way in which they are marketed. Google, Nike, Microsoft, and many other brands have specific product campaigns, as well as primarily brand campaigns that, in turn, drive consumer response to their individual products. If the new product release (which every nonfranchise motion picture is) is driven by a brand name that has consumer confidence, the new product's reception and success are substantially more predictable. For their target consumers, Apple's new touch product,

BMW's new roadster, and McDonald's new kid's meal are all "must-have" purchases. Their target consumers are all substantially motivated to buy because of their perception of the brand.

From an audience perspective, Disney and its Pixar unit are currently the premiere studio/production companies with a brand reputation for delivering a specific kind of motion picture entertainment. The U.S. studios have a general reputation for delivering high-quality entertainment, but not necessarily delivering a certain style of entertainment. Associated with their style, U.S. studios are not known for skewing to any particular target audiences.

Pictures by Steven Spielberg, Adam Sandler, and George Lucas have a consumer-brand presence. They owe this position primarily to audience satisfaction with their prior pictures, but also because of their respective companies' continual and highly effective promotion and public relations output. But what of Imagine, Lakeshore, and even DreamWorks? These companies are well-known names within the trade, but they are largely without product definition to audiences.

Production companies who create a strong consumer brand presence will deliver a powerful marketing advantage for their pictures. This important marketing edge will render their pictures easier to sell and, consequently, more valuable to global licensees.

Participant Media is one of the few production companies whose pictures are consistent with its mission and are building the company's brand within the industry and with its target audiences. Their stated mission is "Participant believes that a good story well told can truly make a difference in how one sees the world. Whether it is a feature film, documentary or other form of media, Participant exists to tell compelling, entertaining stories that also create awareness of the real issues that shape our lives." And their films live up to that mission: *Fair Game, Good Night, and Good Luck, Syriana, The Cove*, and many more.

Production companies committed to becoming audience icons will refocus their companies' motion logos, include new brand marketing language in their distribution agreements, and increase their company brand strength in their pictures' advertising and promotion campaigns.

SUSTAINING BUSINESS, ARTISTIC, AND PERSONAL OBJECTIVE BALANCE

As independent producers review their responsibilities and, more pointedly, as they perform them, it becomes inescapably apparent that unless managed well, a producer's life can easily be consumed entirely with motion picture activities.

Producing well is an exceptional accomplishment and immensely satisfying. But for most of us, it is vitally important to participate in the lives of our family and friends. We need to advance our understanding of new technologies, to participate in and be nourished by the arts, to read great literature (not just screenplays), and to keep and occasionally review a personal journal. Additionally, we can balance ourselves by caring for those less able than us and perhaps even by planting and caring for a garden.

Work is the lubricant of life. When we cease to be productive, we tend to lose our purpose and place. But it should not consume us. We must plan for the seasonings in our lives, or our lives will be bland, lacking full symmetry and fulfillment. Family, contemplation, study, the arts—these are the desserts of life. Without them, we will wake up one day and find ourselves separated from our central motivators.

In the words of historian Will Durant's The Pleasures of Philosophy, "To seize the value and perspective of passing things, we want to know that the little things are little and the big things big, before it is too late. We want to see things now as they will seem forever, in the light of eternity." To strike balance in our lives between the big and small (albeit important) things, is not as impossible as it might seem. It is largely a matter of perspective, planning, and performance.

The most effective and productive leaders we know in the entertainment industry have written their short- and long-term life objectives, which they frequently revise. Doing so allows them to temper their passionate, classically well-planned filmmaking commitments. They use their written objectives to develop a detailed written plan in which they add specific appointments for their daily, weekly, monthly, and annual schedules. Yes, they actually schedule personal time with family, along with times for service, reading, study, and even (perhaps especially) play.

The power of scheduling these activities provides for balance in their lives and even gives them occasion to respond, "I'm sorry, I am booked then, but we can get together…." By keeping as faithful to their schedules as possible, these people prosper in their family relationships, thrive as teachers and learners, and experience the truly good things of life, each of which keeps them happier, more productive, and, by their admission, more creative.

In the main, producers love their work and immerse themselves in it. This is essential to achieve their finest pictures. But if this is done to the exclusion of other rich aspects of life, they may become personally weak, eventually even in motion picture production.

MANAGING LIBRARY PICTURES

As reviewed in earlier chapters, motion pictures premier in each major distribution window. Then they become library pictures, continuing their audience and earnings life primarily in global television syndication.

A wonderful phenomenon of this industry is continual audience evolution. Some television syndicators constructively measure audience evolution in seven-year cycles. Whatever the year of the picture's television premiere, in seven years, newborns will be 7 years old and are a new kid audience. Seven-year-olds grow to be 14 and become a new youth audience; 14-year-olds become 21 and thus a new young-adult audience. By the time 21-year-olds become 28 and are beginning to start families, they view entertainment from a substantially new lifestyle perspective.

Because of audience evolution, pictures should be reanalyzed by their target audiences every five years. Some pictures will warrant a more aggressive re-release strategy than others. A picture's reanalysis will assist the producer in an accurate valuation for new television syndication licenses. Other pictures may justify re-release strategies that include release through higher distribution windows, creating new advertising and public relations campaigns, negotiating campaign tie-ins with other consumer brands, and novelization re-release, among others. Motion pictures, which are the producer's inventory, should be regularly and thoroughly evaluated, kept fresh and valuable to prior audiences, and marketed to new target audiences with reasonable aggression.

Theatrical Re-release

Most motion pictures play very well on in-home media, especially as television screens enlarge, increase in clarity, and have sound advances that bring them close or beyond theater grade. But most motion pictures are produced to be experienced on a large theater screen, with pristine, powerful sound. No lights, no phones, no commercials—just pure, undiluted, audience story absorption.

Newly evolved audiences may prefer to experience re-releases of some of the highest-impact pictures in the theater. Re-releases of Disney animation classics, as well as *Star Wars*, *Gone with the Wind*, etc. all have demonstrated this tendency, especially for epic and niche pictures. It appears that there may also be new audiences and income for many other audience-proven pictures.

It should be considered, as reviewed in Chapter 2, that especially each picture's Internet campaign and media buy almost exclusively determine the success of its opening week. If the distributor is not committed to an aggressive re-release, the picture will most likely fail. Market data and original-picture release data combine to make a strong argument in favor of the likelihood that several major motion pictures will potentially perform well if re-released, either in theaters, through home entertainment, on premium cable, on network television, or on any of the newly emerging screens.

Currently, Disney is the only studio that boldly exploits its pictures in this way, and pictures that primarily exploit the kid (5 to 11) audience. And Disney does it well. A review of the theatrical grosses of these re-releases provides a clear confirmation of the power of re-released pictures with new-evolution audiences. For example, *101 Dalmatians* was re-released theatrically during the 1985 Christmas holidays, earning $31 million, and again, almost six years later in the summer of 1991, earning almost $61 million. *Snow White and the Seven*

Dwarfs was re-released in the summer of 1987, earning $46.6 million, and in the summer of 1995 this picture earned $41.6 million.

ADVANCING TEAM VITALITY AND ALLEGIANCE

The producers who analyze and direct from the perspective that the process they are engaged in is a whole and living entity best serve the production and development company team. The team is responsive to everything that affects it, thereby increasing or decreasing in its health, vitality, and productivity. Producers who understand this regularly evaluate and revitalize the team.

Much like a fruit tree, healthy teams produce appealing, good fruit, in the form of pictures and related products. And like that fruit, both products and people leave the company in their seasons, and this is a healthy sign of productivity. Some team members progress beyond the capacity of the production team; others may not be able to sustain the team's performance integrity. For either of these reasons, it is best for them to go.

Also, just as trees become burdened with unproductive growth that needs to be trimmed, so production teams may have members who are more weight than fuel. Though this process is most often uncomfortable, pruning provides for the best growth, both for these individuals and the team. Between these two extremes exists the necessity of caring for the team. This can be sufficiently accomplished only when team members are individually and regularly reviewed (twice per year is optimal).

Producers strengthen their team members when they seek for opportunities to help expand their experience, education, and responsibilities. This can be done effectively by providing team members with both the means (such as expenses for classes in screenwriting, digital special effects, and international languages) and motivation (promotion, prizes, perks, bonuses, or pay increases) for successful achievements. Providing team members with the means and the motivation results in a team that is continually expanding its performance capacities and deepening team commitment and solidarity.

Sustaining business, artistic, and personal objective balance applies to all members of the team, not just the producer. Producers can provide a broad range of benefits to their teams, which, in return, can create the greatest success attainable. These benefits begin with each team member understanding and performing in harmony with the company's mission statement, and they encompass spouse and family travel accommodations and office environment perks, including exercise rooms, nursery care, a well-stocked kitchen, and a library.

CHAPTER POSTSCRIPT

Dream expansively, plan comprehensively, work valiantly, and live completely.

CHAPTER 16
Reports, Data, and Producer's Principles

This chapter presents and analyzes industry data particularly useful to independent producers, presents information sources that enable producers to keep this data current, and brings together the cornerstone principles presented in this book that form the independent producer's most predictable foundation for success.

ENTERTAINMENT INDUSTRY STATISTICS AND REPORTS

Using regularly published entertainment data and the reports derived from this data can enable producers to more accurately perceive and forecast their pictures' target audiences, global earnings, ancillary products, optimal marketing strategies, and potential brand partners, among other highly beneficial information.

Barry Reardon retired as Warner Bros.' distribution president on March 19, 1999, after serving the studio in this position for 17 years. Reardon exercised his excellent natural audience sense and deep distribution experience in the release of scores of successful pictures. This sustained Warner Bros. for 16 years as one of the three leading studios—eight of those years in first position and five of those years in second position. In his 31-year career, he participated in and, more often, was the lead innovator in the way motion pictures were distributed.

Reardon amplified his natural marketing savvy by using a powerful studio distribution database that tracked all major releases, not just those of Warner Bros. This database was substantially developed by Reardon and continues to assist the studio in making the most predictable decisions regarding high-impact, motion picture distribution.

Every picture, regardless of its earnings, provides a lesson for its producers and distributors. The primary elements affecting a picture's earnings include the following:

- The creative heat of each picture's campaign to drive its target audiences, especially using the unique media most influencing them. As social networking continues to expand its dominance to the most senior, conservative, and slow adapters, the Internet is for some highly valuable audience segments

DOI: 10.1016/B978-0-240-81463-6.00016-4

the single most influential media. Eventually this will be true for all audiences. However, even in the most progressive markets, television commercials will continue to be a leading media and theatrical trailers, radio, print and outdoor advertising play their roles in pulling audiences; with the Internet's hybrid PR (public relations) continuing its expanded personalized influence.

- The overall target audience saturation density of the media purchased— its target audience reach and frequency, or gross rating points.
- The motion pictures that are released on the same day, as well as those within three weeks before and after.
- The theatrical release pattern (including which theaters and which screens within the multiplex are booked and how many).
- The season in which the picture is released (not only the time of year but the weather during play).
- The picture's audience satisfaction for each target group.
- Especially peer, as well as critical reviews.

All of these aspects are important tracking considerations in analyzing why pictures succeed or fail to the extent they do. These aspects should be considered during all of the phases of development, production, marketing, and distribution planning of each picture. In addition to these aspects, producers are well served when tracking other story and production-related elements that affect both grosses and profits, if they are aware of the following:

- Each picture's target audiences, their sizes, and the consumption profile in each major distribution window.
- The use of star power for their earnings effect, compared with star cost.
- The overall earnings effect of using a major director as compared with the director's cost.
- The effect, if any, of a picture's genre.
- Its MPAA rating.
- The effect of a picture's running time.

Data on several pictures, side by side, tell a story that can be used for realistic analysis instead of relying on unfounded speculation. Knowledge really is power, and to know each picture's inherent strengths and weaknesses allows both producers and distributors to mount an approach in which they can maximize each picture's target audiences for optimum success patterns.

The Most Successful Motion Pictures Ever Released in the United States

A limited profile of some important characteristics of the 35 most successful motion pictures ever released in North America is shown in Figure 16.1. To assess these pictures fairly, each picture is positioned according to its inflation-adjusted gross box office, with the number of tickets sold being estimated by dividing the inflation-adjusted gross box office by the inflation-adjusted average ticket price.

++ Includes re-releases, using ticket prices current during each release.

^ Marquee Star at the time of original release.

Position	Picture	Symbol	Est Tickets Sold In Millions	US GBO Adjust'd to 2010 Value	Prdctn Bdgts Adjst'd 2010	Prdctn Bdgt To GBO Ratio	US Studio	Producer	Director	Star Power^
1	GONE WITH THE WIND	++	202.04	$1,537.56	$58.91	26	MGM	David Selznick	Victor Fleming	Clark Gable, Vivian Leigh
2	STAR WARS	++	178.12	$1,355.49	$37.73	36	FOX	George Lucas	George Lucas	Julie Andrews, Christopher Plummer
3	THE SOUND OF MUSIC	++	142.42	$1,083.78	$53.59	20	FOX	Robert Wise	Robert Wise	
4	E. T.	++	141.85	$1,079.51	$21.82	49	U	Stvn Speilberg	Stvn Speilberg	
5	THE 10 COMMAND-MENTS		131.00	$996.91	$104.20	10	PARA	Cecil B. DeMille	Cecil B. DeMille	Charlton Heston, Yul Brynner
6	TITANIC		128.35	$976.71	$264.12	4	FOX/PARA	James Cameron	James Cameron	
7	JAWS	++	128.08	$974.68	$46.06	21	U	Richard Zanuck	Stvn Speilberg	Roy Scheider, Richard Dreyfuss
8	DOCTOR ZHIVAGO		124.14	$944.67	$73.68	13	MGM	Carlo Ponti	David Lean	Julie Christie
9	THE EXORCIST	++	110.57	$841.43	$55.33	15	WB	Wlm Ptr Blatty	Wllam Friedkin	Ellen Burstyn, Max von Sydow
10	SNOW WHITE	++	109.00	$829.49	$22.02	38	BV/RKO	Walt Disney	David Hand	Animated
11	101 DALMATIANS (Original)	++	99.92	$760.37	$29.44	26	BV	Walt Disney	Geronimi / Luske	Animated
12	THE EMPIRE STRIKES BACK	++	98.18	$747.15	$44.44	17	FOX	George Lucas	Irvin Kershner	Mark Hamill, Harrison Ford, C. Fisher
13	BEN-HUR	++	98.00	$745.78	$108.68	7	MGM	Sam Zibalist	William Wyler	Charlton Heston
14	RETURN OF THE JEDI	++	94.06	$715.79	$68.34	10	FOX	George Lucas	Richard Marquand	M Hamill, H Ford, C Fisher
15	THE STING		89.14	$678.38	$24.82	27	U	Tony Bill, &	George Roy Hill	Paul Newman, Robert Redford
16	RAIDERS OF THE LOST ARK	++	88.14	$670.76	$45.32	15	PAR	George Lucas, &	Steven Speilberg	Harrison Ford
17	AVATAR		87.73	$667.61	$280.50	2	FOX	James Cameron, Jon Landau	James Cameron	Sigourney Weaver, Zoe Saldana

FIGURE 16.1
The most successful U.S. motion picture releases of all time.

(Continued)

Position	Picture	Symbol	Est Tickets Sold In Millions	US GBO Adjust'd to 2010 Value	Prdctn Bdgts Adjst'd 2010	Prdctn Bdgt To GBO Ratio	US Studio	Producer	Director	Star Power^
18	JURASSIC PARK		86.21	$656.03	$92.04	7	U	Stvn Spielberg, & Mike Nichols	Stvn Spielberg Mike Nichols	Anne Bancroft, Dustin Hoffman
19	THE GRADUATE	++	85.57	$651.20	n/a	n/a	AVCO	Lucas, Rick McCallum	George Lucas	Neeson, McGregor, Portman
20	STAR WARS: PHAN-TOM MENACE		84.83	$645.52	$146.23	4	FOX	Lucas, Rick McCallum	George Lucas	Animated
21	FANTASIA	++	83.04	$631.96	$34.44	18	BV	Walt Disney	Algar/ Armstrong	Marlon Brando, Al Pacino
22	THE GODFATHER	++	78.92	$600.60	$30.07	20	PAR	Albert Ruddy	Francis Coppola	Tom Hanks
23	FOREST GUMP		78.55	$597.73	$75.42	8	PAR	Wndy Finerman, & Walt Disney	Robert Zemeckis	Julie Andrews, Dick Van Dyke
24	MARY POPPINS	++	78.18	$594.96	$34.14	17	BV	Walt Disney	Rbt Stevenson	Animated
25	THE LION KING	++	77.23	$587.73	$60.47	10	BV	Don Hahn	Allers, Minkoff	John Travolta, Olivia Newton John
26	GREASE	++	76.92	$585.37	$18.88	31	PAR	Aln Carr, Rbt Stigwood	Randal Kleiser	Sean Connery
27	THUNDERBALL		74.80	$569.23	$61.41	n/a	UA	Kevin McClory, Albert R. Broccoli	Terence Young	Bale, Ledger, Eckhart, Freeman
28	THE DARK KNIGHT		74.28	$565.29	$184.67	3	WB	Christopher Nolan	Christopher Nolan	Animated
29	THE JUNGLE BOOK	++	73.68	$560.70	n/a	n/a	BV	Walt Disney	Wolfgang Reitherman	Animated
30	SLEEPING BEAUTY	++	72.68	$553.06	$44.31	12	BV	Walt Disney	Clyde Geronimi	Animated
31	SHREK 2		71.05	$540.70	$170.66	3	Drm-Wrks	Lipman, Warner, Williams	Adamson, Asbury, Vernon	Bill Murray, Dan Aykroyd, Sigrny Weaver
32	GHOSTBUSTERS	++	70.73	$538.26	$62.06	9	COL	Ivan Reitman	Ivan Reitman	Paul Newman, Robert Redford
33	BUTCH CASSIDY & THE SUNDANCE KID		70.56	$536.95	$35.14	15	FOX	John Foreman	George Roy Hill	Maguire, Dafoe, Dunst
34	LOVE STORY		70.00	$532.69	n/a	n/a	PARA	Howard G. Minsky	Arthur Hiller	
35	SPIDER-MAN		69.48	$528.78	$166.06	3	COL	Ian Bryce, Laura Ziskin	Sam Raimi	

(Continued)

Kids: 5-11

Youth: 12-17

Position	Picture	Target Audiences	Genre	US Rating	Opened US Theatrical	Running Time In Hours	Tagline
1	GONE WITH THE WIND	Women, men	Romantic drama	G	12/14/1935	3.7	The most magnificent picture ever!
2	STAR WARS	Youth,kids,men,wmn	Ac Adv, Sci Fi	PG	5/24/1973	2.0	A long time ago in a galaxy far, far away ...
3	THE SOUND OF MUSIC	Women,men,families	Mscl Rmntc drma	G	3/1/1961	2.9	The happiest sound in all the world!
4	E. T.	Kids; youth,men,wmn	Adv, Drama, SciFi	PG	6/10/1978	1.9	He is afraid. He is alone. He is 3 million light years from home.
5	THE 10 COMMANDMENTS	Women, men, families	Drama	Not Rated	11/8/1952	3.7	The greatest event in motion picture history.
6	TITANIC	Youth, women, men	Rmntc drma, Ac	PG-13	12/18/1993	3.2	Collide with destiny.
7	JAWS	Men, youth, kids	Ac, Thrllr, Horror	PG	6/19/1971	2.1	She was the first.
8	DOCTOR ZHIVAGO	Women, men, youth	Romantic drama	PG-13	12/21/1961	3.3	A love caught in the fire of the revolution.
9	THE EXORCIST	Men, youth	Horror	R	12/25/1969	2.0	That man is The Exorcist.
10	SNOW WHITE	Kids, families	Ani Chldrns Fntsy	G	12/20/1933	1.4	Walt Disney's first full length feature production.
11	101 DALMATIANS (Original)	Kids, families	Anim Chldrns Adv	G	1/24/1957	1.3	It's 'arf comedy...'arf mystery...and it's howlarious!
12	THE EMPIRE STRIKES BACK	Youth,kids,men,wmn	Ac Adv, Sci Fi	PG	5/20/1976	2.1	The adventure continues...
13	BEN-HUR	Men, youth, women	Ac Adv Drama	G	11/18/1955	3.5	The world's most honored motion picture.
14	RETURN OF THE JEDI	Youth,kids,men,wmn	Ac Adv, Sci Fi	PG	5/24/1979	2.2	The Empire falls....
15	THE STING	Men, youth, women	Crime Drma Cmdy	PG	12/24/1969	2.2	All it takes is a little confidence!
16	RAIDERS OF THE LOST ARK	Youth,men,kids,wmn	Action Adventure	PG	6/11/1977	1.9	Indiana Jones-the new hero from the creators of Jaws and Star Wars.
17	AVATAR	Youth,kids,men,wmn	Ac Adv, Sci Fi	PG-13	12/17/2005	2.7	Enter the World.
18	JURASSIC PARK	Youth,men,kids,wmn	Ac,Ad,SciFi, Thrlr	PG-13	6/10/1989	2.1	An adventure 65 million years in the making.

FIGURE 16.1—CONT'D

(Continued)

Position	Picture	Target Audiences	Genre	US Rating	US Theatrical	Time In Hours	Tagline
19	THE GRADUATE	Women, men	Romantic Drama	R	12/20/1963	1.8	This is Benjamin. He's a little worried about his future.
20	STAR WARS: PHANTOM MENACE	Youth,kids,men	Ac Adv, Sci Fi	PG	5/22/1995	2.3	Every generation has a legend. Every journey has a first step. Every saga has a beginning.
21	FANTASIA	Kids, families, youth	Anmtd Mscl Fntsy	G	11/12/1936	2.0	Walt Disney's Technicolor FEATURE triumph.
22	THE GODFATHER	Men	Crime Drama	R	3/14/1968	2.9	An offer you can't refuse.
23	FOREST GUMP	Men, women, youth	Drama,Rmnc,Adv	PG-13	7/5/1990	2.4	The world will never be the same once you've seen it through the eyes of Forrest Gump.
24	MARY POPPINS	Kids, families	Chldrns Mscl Cmdy	G	8/28/1960	2.3	It's supercalifragilisticexpialidocious!
25	THE LION KING	Kids, families, youth	Anim Mscl Fntsy	G	6/14/1990	1.5	Life's greatest adventure is finding your place in the Circle of Life.
26	GREASE	Youth,wmn,kids,men	Mscl Cmdy Rmnc	PG	7/6/1974	1.8	Grease is the word.
27	THUNDERBALL	Men, wmn, youth	Ac Adv, Thrllr	PG	12/28/1961	2.2	Look Out! Here Comes The Biggest Bond Of All!
28	THE DARK KNIGHT	Men, youth	Ac Adv	PG-13	7/17/2004	2.5	Why So Serious?
29	THE JUNGLE BOOK	Kids, families, youth	Anim Mscl Fntsy	G	10/17/1963	1.3	he Jungle is JUMPIN'!
30	SLEEPING BEAUTY	Kids, families, youth	Anim Mscl Fntsy	G	1/28/1955	1.3	Now the magic moment! Full-length feature fantasy - Beautiful beyond belief.
31	SHREK 2	Youth, kids, men, wmn	Animated Comedy	PG	5/22/2000	1.5	In the summer of 2004, they're back for more.
32	GHOSTBUSTERS	Youth, men, wmn	Comedy, Horror	PG	6/7/1980	1.8	They're here to save the world.
33	BUTCH CASSIDY & THE SUNDANCE KID	Men, women, youth	Ac Wstrn Cmdy	PG	10/23/1965	1.8	Not that it matters, but most of it's true.
34	LOVE STORY	Women, men	Drama, Rmnc	PG	12/18/1966	1.7	Love means never having to say you're sorry.
35	SPIDER-MAN	Youth, men, women	Ac Rom Fntsy	PG-13	5/2/1998	2.0	With great power comes great responsibility.

Authored by Gillen Group; this report's data sources are from Exhibitor Relations Company, the National Association of Theatre Owners (NATO) Encyclopedia of Exhibition, Internet Movie Data Base, Box Office Mojo, the Motion Picture Association of America (MPAA), participating studios and production companies.

FIGURE 16.1—CONT'D

Because pictures on this list range from 1937 to 2009, our evaluation should be tempered by the vast changes in the entertainment universe during this time. Although there are many more important revelations to be discovered in analyzing this document, we will consider a few that are the most beneficial to producers and distributors.

Box Office Weighted by Gross Profit Figures

This report, in keeping with the industry standard of ranking each picture by its box office dominance, places *Gone with the Wind* in the first position. For producers, this report would be misleading if it did not also show each picture's production cost, and its box-office-to-production-cost ratio, adjusting these budgets to a 2009 currency value. If this chart listed these pictures by their gross profit, *E.T., Snow White and the Seven Dwarfs, and Star Wars* would be the leading three pictures, with *Gone with the Wind* slipping to the sixth position.

Another important insight is readily evident here: A picture's earnings capacity does not increase with its production cost. *E.T.* yields stunning box office earnings that are 49 times its negative cost. *Titanic* yielded a similar gross, but it yields a comparatively sparse four times its negative cost. What we may perceive here is certainly not that *Titanic* overspent. It should be assumed that the cost of this highly successful, broad-target-audience-appealing picture was approximately correct for its story. What we can learn is that, unlike most other consumer products, motion pictures are valued by the entertainment dynamics of their stories, and that of two stories with equal entertainment power, one may be substantially less expensive to produce than the other. Respecting this phenomenon has motivated the strongest independent producers to analyze each picture's production-cost-to-earnings ratios and some of them to establish minimum thresholds for their pictures to pass their internal greenlight.

The Studios

All the major studios are represented in the report, plus DreamWorks and Avco. Fox has more pictures represented than any other studio, with eight (including its shared credit with Paramount for *Titanic*), followed closely by Buena Vista (Disney) and Paramount with seven.

It should be remembered that throughout this period, the studios, as a group, released 200 to 500 pictures each year. These 35 are a small sampling and do not represent the dominance in studio earnings. For instance, as referenced earlier, Warner Bros. has sustained a leading earnings position among the studios during this period, although it has just two pictures represented on the list.

Producers and Directors

This is one of the most telling aspects of the report. The producers and directors responsible for these pictures are the powerhouse icons of their time. Walt Disney (the amazing talent, not the company he founded) produced six of the seven Buena Vista pictures listed, George Lucas produced four pictures and directed one, and Steven Spielberg produced two pictures and directed four. Most of these producers and directors, even if listed only once, are unquestionably industry legends.

A great lesson here is to see the close correlation between the greatest pictures ever made and the most skilled producers and directors in the industry. This is clearly the single most consistent element among the successful pictures.

Star Power

There is a strong argument for looking at a star-caliber cast when examining such pictures as *Gone with the Wind*, *The Ten Commandments*, *Ben Hur*, and *The Sting*. On the other hand, 10 of the 35 pictures, including *Star Wars*, *E.T.*, and *Titanic*, use no "star" actors. Clearly, many leading producers and directors use talent that lend themselves to the picture, rather than primarily attaching star power for the sake of the marquee.

Target Audiences

Understanding each picture's target audiences and their entertainment consumption characteristics in each major territory is essential to understanding the earnings potential of each picture.

Studying the picture's target audiences reveals some compelling and valuable characteristics. By number of target audiences, 27 of the pictures have three or more individual target audience segments. Producers discovering pictures with three or more primary target audiences should be encouraged with these pictures' higher earnings potential, simply because the audience universe being drawn upon is substantially greater.

Number of target audiences	Number of pictures
1	1
2	8
3	16
4	10

The pictures are closely divided between their most significant target audiences, with kids, youth, and men dominating 10 pictures each.

Most significant target audience	Number of pictures
Kids	8
Youth	12
Men	9
Women	6

The primary target audience is youth, then men and kids, with women again standing out as an underserved though a high entertainment-consuming audience. The most prominent target audience overall in these films is men, with women and youth close behind and kids and family last.

One of the target audiences	Number of pictures
Men	28
Women	23
Youth	26
Kids	17
Families	9

Genre

"Sci-fi is in and dramas are out." Commentary on this and every other combination of genres continues to be bantered about as if genre is a crucial picture-selection criterion for audiences. These pictures support the position that great stories well produced is the common success formula and genre has little effect on either success or failure. For these pictures, *action* is the most dominant genre category and *drama* is the next most prominent genre category. A solid story driven with action is the dominant genre mix of these most successful pictures.

Genre	Number for which it is lead genre	Number for which it is the one genre used
Action	13	14
Drama	3	12
Adventure	1	12
Romance	4	8
Animation	6	7
Comedy	2	6
Children	3	5
Science fiction	0	7
Musical	2	7
Fantasy	0	6
Crime	2	2
Horror	1	3
Thriller	0	3
War	0	0

MPAA Rating

We can clearly see from the large television-audience shares of motion pictures that have a restricted-audience rating during their theatrical release that they appeal to audiences who are restricted from viewing them at theaters and for youth, streaming, buying, or renting them during their home entertainment release window. Nevertheless, because of this restriction, all the kids, most of the youth, and most of the family audience earnings are lost during the theatrical release and significantly from home entertainment. This reduces profits as evidenced by the sparse four restricted-audience pictures on this list. The 10 general-audience pictures are primarily pictures for kids or kids and family. PG is the rating champ, with more than PG-13 and R combined.

MPAA rating	Number of pictures
G	10
PG	14
PG-13	7
R	3
Not rated	1

Theatrical Release Date

So do these pictures evidence a particular film industry golden age? On the contrary, the industry has been graced with great filmmakers throughout its brief history. Of the 35 most successful pictures, two pictures were released in the 1930s, one in the 1940s, three in the 1950s, seven in the 1960s, seven in the 1970s, five in the 1980s, five in the 1990s, and four in 2000s first decade.

And what about releasing pictures in off-season? For these pictures, as with most others, there is never a bad time to release a great picture. Some of these pictures were released in the traditionally off-season months of January, February, March, August, and September.

Running Time

The average running length for these pictures is 2 hours and 12 minutes. This includes five pictures running over 3 hours and four under 11/2 hours. Though longer pictures tend to have a higher production cost, there is no correlation between a picture's running time and its grossing capacity. Consider the stronger-earning *E.T.* at a sprightly 1 hour, 55 minutes, compared with *Titanic* at 3 hours, 17 minutes, or *The Ten Commandments* at 3 hours, 40 minutes.

Running-time category	Number of pictures
3 hours or more	5
2:30–2:59	4
2:00–2:29	13
1:30–1:59	9
1:00–1:29	4

Tag Line

The tag lines often capture a sense of the theatrical release campaign used by the studios. Reviewing these tag lines can be useful in developing a sales strategy for pictures with similar audiences and stories.

INFORMATION SOURCES

As business owners and creators, producers ought to keep current on creative, business, technology, and related information. This information allows them to keep up to date with the changing industry landscape, taking advantage of opportunities and handling the new challenges that will continue to appear with ever-speedier regularity. Fortunately, data have never been more available and convenient to access. Most sources are available on the Web or via email.

The following sections list some of the most respected and constructive sources used by entertainment executives.

Exhibitor Relations Company, Inc. (www.ercboxoffice.com)

This is one of the oldest and most used sources in the industry, providing historical and weekly box office information, trade screening reports, development and production reports, and many special statistical and narrative reports, including the following:

- Weekly box office/trade screenings/issuance of MPAA ratings/special report updates
- Bimonthly motion picture release schedules for all major and minor studios by picture, showing primary cast, director, and release date (a weekly email version includes release patterns)
- Reports on motion pictures in development, including their relative detail
- Reports on pictures in production, with creative and distribution detail
- Reports on pictures in production without distribution
- Special research on demand

NATO Encyclopedia of Exhibition (www.natoonline.org)

The NATO Encyclopedia is published annually and contains several extremely helpful reports. These are not always in the ultimate final form for analysis by producers and are for the pictures released a year prior to the one just ended, but the data are accurate and, in the main, complete. The report includes the number of theater tickets sold, total box office take, average ticket prices, average major motion picture production costs, average studio theatrical release print and advertising costs, and a report on each studio's theatrical grosses by picture, among several other excellent reports.

Motion Picture Association of America (www.mpaa.org)

The Motion Picture Association of America offers a free yearly Theatrical Market Statistics report that is a convenient snapshot of important box office and movie attendance trends.

Hollywood Creative Directory (www.hcdonline.com)

This is one of the best sources for information on studio and network executives and production companies. Though available in published form, this is most useful as an online service.

The Baseline StudioSystem (http://studiosystem.com)

This fee-based service is an industry standard providing extensive search and retrieval contact information for entertainment executives and professionals at the studios, production companies, talent agencies, and PR firms, as well as motion picture and television talent, agents, projects in development, company client rosters, literary sales, special reports, and research. The Baseline Research team provides a wide array of research services including a la carte data sales, projections, analysis, and custom report generation. This is a highly recommended source for securing hard-to-find numbers such as DVD and TV revenue and budget costs.

Nielsen Media Research (www.nielsen.com)

This is perhaps the most complete and accurate source for television-viewing information, in a broad array of published reports and custom-designed research.

Daily and Weekly Variety (www.variety.com) and The Hollywood Reporter (www.hollywoodreporter.com)

These provide daily news and maintain archives on everything regarding entertainment in the industry. They each also have research capacities.

Screen International (www.screendaily.com)

Screen International is the leading weekly magazine covering the international film markets. It provides a whole-industry perspective from some of the most knowledgeable writers and data analysts in the business. Every issue delivers analysis, opinion, and commentary on the issues, people, and products shaping the worldwide film industry.

National Cable Television Association (www.ncta.com)

This is the best initial source for understanding the 300-plus cable television network landscape. The *Cable Television Developments* book lists all the networks, their primary executives, contact information, programming and audience focuses, and subscribers.

SNL Kagan (www.snl.com)

This one of the most respected and reliable entertainment industry research firms. It publishes reports and performs sophisticated research and analysis.

Internet Movie Database (www.imdb.com)

The Internet Movie Database is one of the largest accumulations of data about films, television programs, direct-to-video products, and even video games. This is a powerful, user-friendly, free and fee-based Internet service. Utilizing the fee-based services you can also secure lists of films and the revenue they generated in all the ancillary markets with the prints and advertising (P&A) spend and budget.

Box Office Mojo (www.boxofficemojo.com)

This is an online movie publication and box office reporting service that offers free data feeds for daily, weekend, weekly, and many other box office charts.

Showbiz Data (www.showbizdata.com)

This data resource has an especially useful, free Internet news update that reports opening box office figures, tracks the top U.S. pictures for the year, updates the 10 U.S. studios by their grosses, and summarizes some of the week's top stories. The site also offers an excellent fee-based service for U.S. and international box office data and other industry information.

Lee's Movie Info Adjuster (www.leesmovieinfo.net/Adjuster.php)

This site is an amazingly effective and easy-to-use U.S. GBO (gross box office) inflation adjuster.

The Numbers (www.the-numbers.com)

This site is packed with uniquely usable data for finding picture comparables and forecasting, amazing U.S. DVD sales info—no rental or streaming numbers, but good sales—and solid U.S. and international gross box office as well.

All-Time TOP Movies (http://mrob.com/pub/film-video/topadj.html)

This site is chockfull of usable information, stats, charts, and more.

The Independent Film & Television Alliance (IFTA, or the Alliance; www.ifta-online.org)

This is the resource for international motion picture and television sales information, forms, procedures, referrals to member companies, research, and instruction. The alliance conducts the American Film Market (AFM), the premier annual sales event. It also operates what may be the entertainment industry's finest arbitration tribunal.

Film Specific (www.filmspecific.com)

This site is focused exclusively on educating indie filmmakers to the world of independent film distribution offering tools and resources to compete in a tough marketplace.

PRODUCER SUCCESS PRINCIPLES

These principles are especially for motion picture producers, but they are also profitably applied by producers of new media, television narrative and documentary programming, commercials, and even student film productions:

1. *Story.* Discovering, developing, and producing quality stories is the core focus. Story is the single most essential, important, and powerful asset upon which creative and financial success rests. This is where investments of time, study, review, hyper-polishing, and money will return the greatest overall benefits.

2. *Target audiences.* Every story appeals to specific target audiences more than to others. Producers should know who these audiences are, where they are, how many there are, what their entertainment consumption profile is, and what drives their motion picture passions. With the majority of audiences and income sourced outside the United States, this audience understanding should also be present for, at least, the eight leading international territories. Where appropriate, cover shots should be produced to deliver seamless pictures to territories outside the core-release territory. Knowing each picture's target audience universe is the most fundamental information for determining its earnings potential. This question is typically one of the first asked by distributors. The audience is the most important participant in the industry. Cater to them.

3. *Balance.* Sustaining a balance between each picture's story, targeted audiences, and potential producer's share of profits is the most predictable approach to ensure each picture's successful development, production, and global distribution—and, consequently, the producer/production entity's success.

4. *Talent.* The strongest evolution of producer and talent relationships begins with meetings that allow each to test the other's creative affinity for the story, and then continues with deal-making meetings involving the talent's agent, manager, or attorney. The producer's research, planning and preparation all help render talent attachment a predictable and even pleasant experience.

5. *Global distribution.* Producers should exclusively develop and produce motion pictures for which they have first engaged development-level collaborative relationships with a distributor in its core-release territory and at least four of the eight major international territories. Distributors do what producers cannot do. They make each unknown picture a household name to its target audiences. They set up and manage each picture's release within their marketplace. They do the impossible. Though they occasionally underperform, they are the independent producer's inseparable partners.

6. *Development.* Producers should plan and finance each picture's development in a fashion as well defined and complete as the manner in which they plan and finance each picture's production. This planning, risk-mitigated approach, and compelling deal construct will appeal to private investors, who, if the production entity needs it, should be the initial primary, if not exclusive, provider of development capital.

7. *Financing.* If development investors are used, they should substantially, if not completely, recoup their investment when production commences and should participate in the long-term income of the picture(s). Producers should use banks as their cornerstone production financing and aggregation source. Accordingly, producers should understand entertainment banking sufficiently to submit funding packages that they know will be accepted.

8. *Entertainment law.* The development, production, and sales of motion pictures consistently engage the producer in the process of representation,

negotiations, and documentations. Contract language does not always correlate with contemporary language interpretation. In negotiations, producers should be decisive, but they should *always* agree on basic terms only subject to their attorney's review.

9. *Production company team.* A producer's sustained solidarity is largely assured by the production company team. These members must be skilled, dedicated, and largely self-managed. Consequently, they must be carefully selected, refined, empowered, advanced, and allowed to monetarily participate in the team's successes.

10. *Living a full life.* In addition to skilled imagineering, producing, and releasing successful motion pictures, producers need the full symmetry of participation with their family and friends, use of contemplation and study, and participation in the arts. If these are kept in mind as producers plan and schedule their time, they will enrich and fulfill their lives.

CHAPTER POSTSCRIPT

Analyzing industry data particularly useful to independent producers, is the cornerstone principle presented in this book that forms the independent producer's most predictable foundation for success. Using regularly published entertainment data and the reports derived from this data can enable producers to more accurately perceive and forecast their pictures' target audiences, global earnings, ancillary products, and optimal marketing success.

Glossary of Terms

Above-the-Line When referring to a picture's budget, it is the budgeted cost for acquisition of rights, writers, producer, director, and principal cast.

Accredited Investor Investors (1) who are experienced in investments similar in amount and risk of the one being offered and (2) that have a minimum net worth demonstrating their ability to financially withstand the investment's failure and further evidences their financial sophistication. In the United States, "accredited investor" and "sophisticated investor" are language used by state and federal security and exchange commissions to describe investors according to parameters 1 and 2 in the preceding sentence.

ADR Alternative dispute resolution.

AFM American Film Market.

Ancillary Windows The successive earnings areas for each motion picture that are not its theatrical window of distribution. The primary ancillary windows are home entertainment, premium cable, network television, and cable/syndicated television.

Antecedents See Comparables.

Balanced Producer Gives equal weight to the creative, audience, and investment/profits of each project.

Below-the-Line All motion picture costs in the budget, excluding above-the-line costs.

Big Boxes Home entertainment retail stores, such as Target and WalMart.

Campaign Signature Refers to the analysis and quantification of ad campaigns, especially television commercials. Specific audience emotional beat categories (including comedy, romance, action/adventure, drama, science fiction, horror, and so on) are quantified each time they elicit their unique emotional responses from audience members. These responses are totaled for each emotional category. Then each emotional total is divided by the total emotional beats. The profiles of these emotional category percentages are each commercial's campaign signature.

Cash Flow Analysis A motion picture's forecast of all its income, expenses and month to month, year to year flow of cash, from all sources..

Collateral This is all of the license agreements, international sales estimates, production incentives or equity, brand tie-in agreements, talent or vendor offset agreements, private equity, and any other instruments associated with providing direct investments in the project.

Collection Account Manager A third-party company or individual who monitors and receives in an escrow account all revenue earned by a motion picture, and supervises the allocation and payment of that revenue. Two companies that we recommend are Freeway Entertainment and Fintage House.

Comparables These are previously released pictures that are comparable to the subject-picture in target audiences, genre, budget, talent, and sales/marketing abilities.

Completion Bond Issued by an insurance company, a guarantee that the picture will be delivered by the contracted delivery date, within budget, and with the specified creative elements intact.

Consumption Dynamics The manner in which specific target audiences will consume a motion picture in its various distribution windows.

Cover Shot Additional produced material that will be uniquely required in one or more territories outside the core territory for which the picture was produced. Examples include altering story elements that are too culturally specific, ensuring that there is less violence in screenings for Europe, limiting profanity for network television and in-flight screenings, and so forth.

CRI Color reverse internegative, created to make release prints.

CMP A hybrid of a Chief Marketing Officer and Producer. The duties of a CMP are to develop a strategic marketing plan, locate the target audience, create and manage a team for audience outreach and package social networking, contests, games, videos, PR, key art, website, email lists, sponsors, and promotional partners.

DOI: 10.1016/B978-0-240-81463-6.00021-8

Crowd or Tribe Funding An alternative financing model that does not include investments and only includes the donations, memberships, or preordering of products, giving none of the funders future profits in the film.

DDE Direct distribution expenses—the expenses incurred by the distributor in the process of distributing a picture, which are recoupable by the distributor from the picture's gross receipts remaining after deduction of distribution fees. Also referred to as P&A (print and advertising).

Distributor An intermediary between the content owner and the audience, responsible for marketing, distribution, collections, and distribution accounting and reporting.

EFM European film market.

Exhibitor A single theater owner or theater circuit or chain.

Film Rental The share of the gross box office due to the distributor.

Film Rental Agreement The document setting forth the terms between the exhibitor and the distributor.

Gap Financing/Funding The financing/funding typically provided by a bank, usually calculated on sales estimates received from a qualified/bankable international sales agent, on the value of the each unsold international territory. Typically discounted by the bank up to 50 percent of the territory's aggregate value.

Global Sales Analysis A global gross and net earnings forecast of the proposed picture for all major windows and ancillary earnings.

Greenlight See Internal Greenlight Analysis.

Gross Receipts Box office receipts collected from theater attendees for a particular picture.

GTV Gross-take-value.

Holding Fee A small percentage of talent's negotiated fee used to secure the director or lead cast often used to close financing.

House-nut The exhibitor's attributed amount covering the cost to provide and operate each screen.

IFTA Independent Film and Television Alliance.

Impressions The total number of advertising viewings of a particular audience during a set time.

Income-to-Cost Ratio An analysis done to estimate the producer's gross income compared with the picture's projected production costs. At least a 1:1 ratio is most often sought.

Internal Greenlight Analysis A feasibility study starting with comparable pictures and ending with cash flow projections to evaluate the potential loss/profits before undertaking extensive development costs.

Interparty Agreement An agreement that spells out the payment priority among the lending bank, the producer, presale distributors, production incentive and all other collateral, discount and deferral participants, plus the completion guarantor.

LC Letter of credit.

LIBOR London Interbank Offered Rate.

Library Releases Pictures for which one owns the copyright and governs the continuing distribution.

License Fee Escalator Clause This clause calls for the license fee to increase if the picture's gross box office earnings or other benchmark exceed a certain minimum.

License Income Earnings that come to the licensor from all sources: typically from advance/minimum guarantee or profit participation or overages.

Licensing Agreement An agreement that fully addresses all the terms and conditions relative to the license relationship.

Literary Release Letter A legal letter/document generated by the producer or production company when accepting manuscripts directly from writers and before accepting their script(s).

LLC Limited liability company.

Major Completion Guarantors Insurers and the major bonding companies owned by large insurance carriers. International Film Guarantors has the largest bonding capacity, bonding pictures with budgets in excess of $100 million. Its guaranee is backed by Fireman's Fund insurance carrier. Another of the oldest and most well-know insurers is Film Finance, which is owned by Lloyd's of London.

Mash-Ups Re-edits, typically of pre-produced elements made available to the general public.

Minimum Guarantee Flat fee amount to acquire certain rights in a picture. The guarantee amount is usually paid in installments as indicated on the deal memo and is most often 10 percent to 20 percent of the total paid upon execution of the deal memo. The balance of the payment is triggered by delivery of the picture or by access to specific elements of the picture by the licensee.

NATO National Association of Theatre Owners.

Negative Cost The actual total costs of creating the picture, which include above-the-line and below-the-line costs, delivery items, the completion bond fee, and a contingency that is usually 10 percent of the above-the-line and below-the-line costs, but excluding financing costs.

Negative Pick-up A distributor agrees to acquire certain rights, typically at least all rights in a given territory, for a fixed amount payable upon delivery to them of the picture.

One-Sheet A theater-frame size movie poster.

P&A Prints and advertising—the cost of film prints and advertising.

Participations Contingent payments to talent based on a percentage of earnings from a motion picture.

Pay or Play A contractual provision providing that if the talent is not used in a motion picture for any reason, he or she will be paid a fixed percentage, up to 100 percent, of their production performance compensation (other than the participation payment).

Points Investor and talent's profit participation in the film.

PPM Private placement memorandum or offering.

Preproduction The preparation activities that go on before the commencement of principal photography.

Presale A sale concluded before commencement of principal photography for motion picture right(s) for a fixed payment due upon delivery, plus overages.

Private Equity Cash, CDs, treasury bills, securities, and the like from private sources for financing a picture.

Producer's Gross Typically, the distributor's net less the production financing expense and the picture's negative cost.

Producer's Share The profits remaining for the producer after all production, distribution, and financing expenses have been deducted and talent has received their profits.

Production The physical creation of the motion picture, usually comprising its preproduction, principal photography, and postproduction

Promotional Tie-in A relationship in which an existing brand with similar target audiences engages a relationship with a picture to unilaterally exploit its products/services during the picture's release, using the picture's title and some of its footage/pictures in its campaign.

Royalties Contingent profit payments owed to investors, producers and talent.

SAG Screen Actors Guild.

SEC Securities and Exchange Commission.

Step Deal A deal structure, usually with the screenplay writer such that the writing process is compartmentalized into progressive steps. Each step has a fixed fee value and provides for evaluation and complete pre-agreed-upon exit remedies that allow the producer to terminate the relationship following the review of each initial step.

Street Date Release date of a motion picture into theaters or on DVD.

Studio Share The amount of the producer's net in which the studio participates for its share as a partner of the producer in making the production and distribution of the picture a reality.

Talent Current Quote What the talent was last paid for either a studio-level picture or an independent picture.

Talent Participation Contingent payments in the film's profits that are due to the key talent participants, typically the director and one or more key cast members.

Target Audience The audience that will be more interested in a picture than any other defined audience segment.

The Alliance Independent Film and Television Alliance.

Theatrical Distribution Fee The fee earned by the distributor and calculated as a percentage of the film rental. The percentage for studios is typically 25 percent to 35 percent of the film rental.

Theatrical Exhibitors Theater chains such as AMC Entertainment, Regal Entertainment Group, Cinemark USA, and Carmike Cinemas.

Trailers Movie previews of upcoming releases.

TVQ Television quotient. Most talent and many entities have a television quotient. This has to do with popularity, and the person or entity may have no relation to TV.

UPM Unit production manager.

Waterfall Financial projections of the global revenue and expenses for a making and releasing a film.

WGA Writers Guild of America.

Index

Note: Page number followed by *f* indicate figures; *t* indicate tables.

251